Part of the Community

Part of the Community

Strategies for Including Everyone

edited by

Jan Nisbet, Ph.D.

and

David Hagner, Ph.D.

Institute on Disability
University of New Hampshire
Durham

·P·A·U·L·H·
BROOKES
PUBLISHING CO

Baltimore • London • Toronto • Sydney

Paul H. Brookes Publishing Co.
Post Office Box 10624
Baltimore, Maryland 21285-0624

www.brookespublishing.com

Typeset by Pro-Image Corp., Techna-Type Division, York, Pennsylvania.
Manufactured in the United States of America by Bang Printing, Brainerd, Minnesota.

The case studies in this book are based on the authors' actual experiences. In some instances, names and identifying details have been changed to protect confidentiality. The case studies that use real names are presented herein only with the individuals' written consent.

Library of Congress Cataloging-in-Publication Data
Part of the community : strategies for including everyone / edited by Jan Nisbet and David Hagner.
    p.   cm.
    Includes bibliographical references and index.
    ISBN 1-55766-456-0
    1. Handicapped—Services for—United States.   2. Handicapped—United States—Social conditions.   3. Social participation—United States.   4. Inclusive education—United States.   I. Nisbet, Jan.   II. Hagner, David.

HV1553 .P39   2000
362.4'0973—dc21

                                    00-021848

British Library Cataloguing in Publication data are available from the British Library.

Contents

About the Editors

Jan Nisbet, Ph.D., Director, Institute on Disability, University of New Hampshire, 7 Leavitt Lane, Suite 101, Durham, New Hampshire 03824-3522, is also a tenured associate professor in the Department of Education at the University of New Hampshire. She received her doctorate from the University of Wisconsin in 1982. She has been conducting research and writing for the past 20 years on school restructuring and reform, transition from school to adult life, supported employment, self-determination, inclusive adult living, and aging. Dr. Nisbet is also former President of the Executive Board of Directors of The Association for Persons with Severe Handicaps (TASH), a national organization focused on improving the lives of individuals with severe disabilities and their families through research, training, and advocacy. She has published extensively in the field of severe disabilities, serves on numerous editorial advisory boards, and presents nationally and internationally. She is Principal Investigator on numerous state and nationally funded projects related to the community integration of children and adults with severe disabilities.

David Hagner, Ph.D., Rehabilitation Projects Coordinator, Institute on Disability, University of New Hampshire, 7 Leavitt Lane, Suite 101, Durham, New Hampshire 03824-3522, is also Co-director of the New England Regional Continuing Education Program for Community Rehabilitation Personnel. Dr. Hagner is a certified rehabilitation counselor with more than 20 years' experience in teaching, directing research and demonstration projects, and publishing in the field of vocational rehabilitation. He is currently involved in research projects on career advancement for individuals with severe disabilities and employment strategies for individuals with long-term mental illness. Dr. Hagner co-authored *Working Together: Workplace Culture, Supported Employment and Persons with Disabilities* (with Dale DiLeo; Brookline Books, 1993) and has written more than 30 monographs, book chapters, and journal articles related to employment and rehabilitation. He is a frequent speaker at conferences in the United States and has also presented papers at rehabilitation conferences in Australia, New Zealand, and most recently in Scotland, where he has also consulted with the newly formed government regarding disability and employment policy. He also serves as Consulting Editor for the journal *Mental Retardation*.

Contributors

Patty Cotton, M.Ed.
Project Coordinator
Institute on Disability
University of New Hampshire
7 Leavitt Lane, Suite 101
Durham, New Hampshire 03824

Ann Donoghue Dillon, M.Ed., OTR
Project Director
Institute on Disability
University of New Hampshire
7 Leavitt Lane, Suite 101
Durham, New Hampshire 03824

Beth Dixon
Leadership Coordinator
Institute on Disability
University of New Hampshire
The Concord Center
10 Ferry Street, Unit 14
Concord, New Hampshire 03301

Leslie Dwyer
Employment Facilitator
Diversity Concepts
525 Clinton Street
Bow, New Hampshire 03304

Cheryl M. Jorgensen, Ph.D.
Project Director and Assistant
  Research Professor
Institute on Disability
University of New Hampshire
7 Leavitt Lane, Suite 101
Durham, New Hampshire 03824

Jay Klein, M.S.W.
Director
National Home of Your Own
  Alliance
Institute on Disability
848 Shire Court
Fort Collins, Colorado 80526

Kris Kouwenhoven
Employment Facilitator
Diversity Concepts
525 Clinton Street
Bow, New Hampshire 03304

Herb Lovett, Ph.D. (deceased)
Clinical Psychologist
Boston, Massachusetts

Kim Milliken
Employment Facilitator
Diversity Concepts
525 Clinton Street
Bow, New Hampshire 03304

Debra Nelson, M.S.
Project Director
Institute on Disability
University of New Hampshire
7 Leavitt Lane, Suite 101
Durham, New Hampshire 03824

Grace Jeffrey Nelson, M.Ed.
Public Education and School
  Support Coordinator
National Education Association of
  New Hampshire
103 N. State Street
Concord, New Hampshire 03301

Thomas M. Reischl, Ph.D.
Research Associate Professor
Institute on Disability
University of New Hampshire
7 Leavitt Lane, Suite 101
Durham, New Hampshire 03824

Mary Schuh, M.S.Ed.
Project Coordinator
Institute on Disability
University of New Hampshire
The Concord Center
10 Ferry Street, Unit 14
Concord, New Hampshire 03301

Frank Sgambati, M.S.
Project Director
Institute on Disability
University of New Hampshire
The Concord Center
10 Ferry Street, Unit 14
Concord, New Hampshire 03301

Susan Shapiro-Barnard, M.Ed.
Research Associate
Institute on Disability
University of New Hampshire
The Concord Center
10 Ferry Street, Unit 14
Concord, New Hampshire 03301

Shawna Sousa
Service Coordinator
Region 10 Community Support
   Services
8 Commerce Drive
Atkinson, New Hampshire 03811

Jo-Ann Sowers, Ph.D.
Adjunct Associate Professor
Oregon Health Sciences University
3608 S.E. Powell Street
Portland, Oregon 97202

Carol Tashie, M.Ed.
Project Coordinator
Institute on Disability
University of New Hampshire
The Concord Center
10 Ferry Street, Unit 14
Concord, New Hampshire 03301

Barbara Boyd Wilson, M.A.
Marketing Director
Browne Center
University of New Hampshire
340 Dame Road
Durham, New Hampshire 03824

Leigh R. Zoellick, M.Ed.
Educational Consultant
Institute on Disability
University of New Hampshire
7 Leavitt Lane, Suite 101
Durham, New Hampshire 03824

Foreword

The Institute on Disability (IOD) professes inclusion as the right starting point—morally, legally, and economically—for practice and policy. As evidenced by the suite of social change projects described in this book, the authors understand inclusion as a horizon for goal setting and problem solving. Disability poses no barrier to meaningful and rewarding participation in every aspect of community life. Individual gifts and interests differ, but with creative accommodation and competent assistance, no sphere of life need be closed because of disability. Young children with disabilities should experience the same child care and preschool as their brothers and sisters do. Students with disabilities should have the same choice of learning opportunities, relationships, and activities as any other student. People with disabilities should work alongside the others employed in their community. People with disabilities who choose to should experience the benefits and hassles of home-ownership.

The interaction of particular people with disabilities in particular environments can pose complex problems, and many people with disabilities require careful planning and continuing assistance in order to participate fully. Supporting those involved to creatively address those problems and ensuring adequate accommodation and assistance are legitimate reasons for disability services to exist.

I read this book as a richly interwoven set of stories about what happens when courageous, creative people focus their talents on changing their state. Their unifying purpose is to make inclusion the context for communities' efforts to support families, educate children and adults, and provide opportunities for making a living and making a life. A long-term commitment to place—New Hampshire—shapes these efforts. Individual projects have time limits, but concern about bettering the communities and public structures of New Hampshire animates more than a decade of well-planned and continuing action.

The bold simplicity of these authors' conviction that inclusion is right impels practical work. Professing inclusion attracts interest and rapidly brings to light a mesh of problems that require action across many boundaries and levels. For Lucy, whom we meet in Chapter 3, to continue to develop her friendships and abilities when the time comes for her to go to preschool calls for teamwork across multiple boundaries. Her family, the staff of the Rainbow Child Care Center, the school district's preschool coordinator, and the family support team all have to reconsider their understanding of what makes sense for Lucy and other young children and decide what to do to make inclusion possible. To learn from Lucy's experience and make changes in her community, a local team has to work hard to find and build on common ground among people with different beliefs and different habits of work. For Ken, whom we meet in Chapter 7, to realize his aspiration to own a home is equally complex. It calls for changes in the mortgage market, changes in the policies of the state housing authority, changes in the way he receives personal assistance and the way the service system accounts for and spends money, changes in the ways his friends and allies see and support him, and changes in the way Ken sees himself and works for the future he wants.

It is simple to state the meaning of inclusion but difficult to set and hold it in place as a context for goal setting and problem solving. Because inclusion happens when communities shift their boundaries and practices to make room for and support people with disabilities, its advocates have more to do than simply change the practice of special educators or human services providers. Their work involves IOD staff in unfamiliar forums with new conversation partners on new topics. School restructuring provides opportunities to influence and to learn from discussions at community, state, and federal levels. The work of inclusion advocates also sets the stage for social invention. For example, a third-grade teacher may discover a gift for supporting a child with a disability, and her learning may help to shape new patterns of instruction in her school. Desire for better return on investments of public dollars shapes the ways that people and families choose their own services. Recognition that employers and co-workers are largely untapped resources opens the opportunity to create the new role of employment consultant. Inclusion advocates' work also calls people to a deeper understanding of what it means for everyone to be human with each other. Children whose emotions and behaviors puzzle and scare their classmates and their teachers call for responses based on a new appreciation of our inner lives. Parents and people with disabilities themselves gather the strength from mutual support and shared information to accept responsibility for contributing to community life and acting to make their dreams real.

Though it can be stated clearly and appealingly, inclusion runs into trouble because it calls for redistribution of power under conditions of uncertainty. Professionals can no longer be the sole experts on what is best for people with disabilities. Staff can no longer control people with disabilities by taking full charge of closed environments and schedules. Kids become key resources in realizing inclusion. Co-workers become essential to job success. People with disabilities and their family members become responsible for shaping their lives as contributing members of their communities. People have to find ways to collaborate on their journey toward inclusion without a detailed and up-to-date road map that guarantees a quick, smooth ride to a specific destination.

Advocating inclusion can be a risky task because so many people settle for so much less and justify compromise and the escape from necessary problem solving with assumptions about what is good for people with disabilities and what is possible for community environments. Withdrawal into blaming others for their lack of commitment or competence forms an appealing defense against the disappointment of failure to make or sustain efforts toward inclusion. However, as this book's stories of change show, learning better ways to engage people makes for a more adaptive strategy.

Simplistic tales of systems change abound among inclusion advocates. To hear them leaves the impression that shifting paradigmatic structures for understanding and responding to disability is no different from marketing a new style of sneakers: A clever way of telling teachers or service workers to behave differently will do the trick. You will not find such simplistic tales in this book. IOD staff ground themselves through direct engagement with people struggling to make better lives, better schools, more effective workplaces, and stronger communities. They join in inventing and testing solutions to difficult problems in everyday life, in the design of schools and assistance systems, and in policy. They look back and reflect on the effects of their efforts over time with a clarity that allows them to keep sketching better and better incomplete maps of how change toward inclusion happens.

John O'Brien
Responsive Systems Associates

Preface

This book evolved as a result of our sustained engagement in systems change over many years and our feeling that many of the details of systems change—the difficulties and tragedies, the successes, the vast scope of strategies and tactics required, the subtle decisions made on a daily basis, and the human side of change for both the change agents and those affected by change—were not being adequately addressed in most of the literature in our field. We felt that because "knowledge is power," the more we were able to understand stories of change efforts and the process of change from an insider perspective, the more effective we would be. On the basis of the work of the University of New Hampshire's Institute on Disability (IOD) to promote full inclusion of individuals with disabilities in New Hampshire, we have collected a series of accounts and perspectives on change that reflect a range of issues, ages, and life activities.

In Chapters 1 and 2, we present an overview of these efforts and some ways of thinking about systems change. In Chapter 3, Debra Nelson, Leigh R. Zoellick, and Ann Donoghue Dillon describe their efforts in creating a more inclusive system of early education for young children. Susan Shapiro-Barnard, Frank Sgambati, Beth Dixon, and Grace Jeffrey Nelson, in Chapter 4, and Herb Lovett, in Chapter 5, describe the process of working with elementary and middle schools for inclusion of individuals with severe disabilities and those individuals labeled as having an "emotional disturbance." Change efforts that involve high schools are documented by Cheryl M. Jorgensen and Carol Tashie in Chapter 6. Chapter 7 describes the process that Jay Klein, Barbara Boyd Wilson, Debra Nelson and the staff of the National Home of Your Own Alliance have been using with the human services system and with other community resources to allow adults with significant disabilities greater access to homeownership. In Chapter 8, Jo-Ann Sowers, Kim Milliken, Patty Cotton, Shawna Sousa, Leslie Dwyer, and Kris Kouwenhoven discuss their efforts to change employment services to reflect the principles and practices of natural supports. Chapter 9, by Mary Schuh and Beth Dixon, describes the process of leadership training for individuals with disabilities and their families, which has proved to be one of the most powerful and fundamental tools for generating change in education, housing, and employment. Finally, Thomas M. Reischl provides his unique view of change from the perspective of community psychology, and he comments on all of the other chapters in this book.

This book is a collaborative effort among numerous people. We are especially appreciative of the efforts of the chapter authors and of the contributions of IOD staff to the projects described in the chapters. We would also like to thank the many individuals with disabilities, their families, and the organizational staff who have been so instrumental in envisioning ways that communities can include everyone, and we would like to thank the state agencies that support individuals with disabilities in these efforts. While we were developing the overall plan of the book, Steve Murphy and Wayne Sailor contributed many valuable ideas. Finally, we owe a debt of gratitude to John O'Brien for his assistance in helping us reflect on our work and deepen our commitment to inclusion.

Jan Nisbet and David Hagner

Acknowledgments

The most important systems change lessons that we at the Institute on Disability have learned over the past 10 years include these: be more attentive to the landscape, constantly seek information and conduct research, have better timing, understand the power of being proactive, collaborate, train new leaders, organize communities and constituencies, and know when to have the good fight. Our work continues to be inspired by our colleagues, children and adults with disabilities and their families, state and local leaders, and our friends and families. We firmly believe that everyone belongs and that everyone has the right to respect and decency. We are so far from this reality, however, that we must keep trying to change the systems and supports available to people. We are fortunate to have many great people who work with us and who have supported us. In particular we would like to thank Don Shumway, who remains a leader with a vision of community.

To Dick Lepore and Herb Lovett, who both died while this book was a work in progress. We miss them. More than most, they appreciated the value of trying to change what is, the hard work involved, and the importance of reflection.

1

Systemic Reform

One Organizational Perspective

Jan Nisbet

"I fall down, I get up, and all the while I am dancing."
—*Native American saying*

In 1988, I was hired to direct the new Institute on Disability (IOD) at the University of New Hampshire. Its purpose was to foster the inclusion and productivity of citizens with disabilities and their families through model demonstration, technical assistance, research, evaluation, interdisciplinary personnel preparation, and dissemination of research related to people with disabilities and their families. New Hampshire was in the process of closing its only publicly funded state residential facility for people with disabilities. State and university officials recognized the importance of establishing a link between the University of New Hampshire and what appeared to be a rapidly evolving educational and community support system.

We (I use this term to mean the people with whom I work at the IOD and elsewhere) have all learned enormous lessons about people with disabilities and their families, systems change, universities, and ourselves. There have been successes and failures along the way. We have subjected ourselves to rigorous external evaluation to ensure that we have remained vigilant, on course, successful, and adaptive. In this chapter I draw from our experiences; my own insights; the evaluations conducted; and the literature on leadership, systemic reform, and community organizing to elucidate the many mistakes made, achievements won, and lessons learned.

People in the field of disabilities have been engaged in systems change on the behalf of and with people with disabilities and their families since before the 1950s. The most notable changes have been related to deinstitutionalization, community and family supports, inclusive education, and self-determination. Although much progress has been made, much more is required to reach a time when people with disabilities are regarded as fully participating members of society.

Engaging in systems change requires an everchanging vision. Without this vision, systems change can become a series of activities targeted at changes that barely affect people with disabilities and their families. Thus, individuals who are successful systems change agents must maintain a vision based on human values and possibilities and develop strategies that are effective in reaching that vision. One cannot exist without the other. Unfortunately, tension always exists between supporting a vision and supporting individuals as they struggle with the current system.

We at the IOD have recognized, with the assistance of outside evaluators (O'Brien, Strully, & Krippenstappel, 1995), that vigorously defending inclusion can alienate those who find themselves in systems in which inclusion appears to be more mythology than reality. The decision to place a child with a disability in a residential facility is perceived as a failure by some and a solution by others. Finding a way to support a parent who is forced to make a difficult decision and continuing to strive for full inclusion is sometimes like walking a tightrope. Other efforts, such as developing financing and support strategies to help individuals with disabilities and/or their families to buy their own homes, have been met with excitement and reticence. This reticence is a fundamental barrier to systems change. Somewhere in the collective consciousness is the notion that allowing an individual with a disability to own a home may place too much financial strain on the system—why use $20,000 of public funds to support one person in his or her own home when that money could support three people? Waiting lists and growing numbers of those in need of services can, if untethered, result in segregation rather than integration. It is exactly these traditional per-person cost analyses that must change. Investments in new structures that have the potential for generating economic and social capital (resources available through human efforts and involvement) are more likely to serve the greater good than segregation for the sake of efficiency. The development of strategies to invest in community structures that benefit people with disabilities and their families rather than strategies to invest in human services structures (McKnight & Kretzmann, 1995) will be the substance of future systems change efforts. That is not to say that services and supports are not needed; it is simply to acknowledge that entitlements can be a source of future systems change efforts in housing, employment, and other necessities associated with community participation.

How does an organization and its many partners engage in systemic reform activities that result in fundamental innovation? Both establishing the direction of change and developing a methodology for achieving that change are necessary. I have frequently found the former easier to accomplish than the latter. Although there is a substantial body of literature on systemic reform (see Schorr, 1997) and community organizing (see Biklen, 1983) that often goes unnoticed, sometimes the mistakes that we have made along the way reinforce what we should have known all along.

LESSONS

There is no bravery in admitting mistakes, only in attempting not to repeat them. The mistakes that we have made were lessons, pointers, and clarifiers; the ones that taught us the most are described in the sections that follow.

Celebrate Achievements, but Recognize Failures

New Hampshire continues to have one of the highest rates in America of out-of-state placements for students with disabilities (T.B. Parrish, personal communication, 1998). Conversely, the state has one of the highest rates of inclusion in general education. How can that be? For 10 years, the IOD has been funded to make systemic reform in the area of education of students with disabilities. Our initial strategy was to increase awareness regarding inclusive education and its benefits; to work with families; to provide technical assistance; and, ultimately, to help schools embrace a philosophy of inclusion, diversity, and community. Increasing by 50% the inclusion of students with disabilities in general education is indeed an achievement. However, we have begun to see a drift back to segregation, a slowness among high schools to include students with disabilities in general education classes, and a certain hostility toward children who have behavior problems. One could analyze these trends in a way that points the finger at a particular political climate, and certainly there is some merit in doing so, but if one studies these trends objectively, one must admit that they could have been predicted.

Making superficial change in social structures is easy and is often referred to as *Level I systems change* (Fullan & Miles, 1992). Providing technical assistance and training to a school to support inclusive education is different from entering a school to support systemic reform that includes inclusion. Between 1992 and 1997 we supported inclusion but did not focus on underlying structures, such as accessible curricula, school funding formulas, teacher preparation, the attitudes of school boards, and the media. When committed principals and teachers left, so went programs. Parents were left to make sure that programs continued despite the absence of the fundamental reforms that would ensure inclusive educational opportunities. Since 1995, we have focused on education reform in general but had to beg to be part of the discussion because we were considered special educators. By becoming part of the school restructuring and reform discussions, we were able to integrate issues of inclusive education into state policy and practice. We were expanding our focus, but we wondered whether we were diluting our efforts. The child with unusual behaviors still needed help, but we had policy meetings to go to—is it possible to do both? How does one achieve a balance? What if an individual student needs help but the school is not committed to long-term change? How can you do one without the other? In the end, what is the best investment of time and energy? These are the questions we constantly asked ourselves.

Developing a formal process for assessing decision making and taking seriously the failure of certain reforms to take hold are absolute requirements if systems change is the goal. Conversations about first- and second-order changes (Watzlawick, Weakland, & Fisch, 1974) can help people move from common-sense solutions to deeper understandings of systems.

Balance Systemic Reform with Individual Support

There is something to be said for addressing immediate problems that are indicators of systemic problems. Individual technical assistance to teachers and schools, however, cannot be the sole response to issues facing students in the classroom. Time intensive and often minimally effective, interventions targeted at students rather than at schools and systems can monopolize all of one's time. For years we targeted our efforts at individual students, believing that if we could show a school that a student with a significant disability could be supported in general education, then that lesson would flow to other students, classrooms, and schools. Sometimes that happened, to a certain degree, but more typically, the intervention affected only one or two students and required another effort the following year in another classroom with another teacher.

We soon realized that we would have to tie child-specific technical assistance with school-level and district-level change strategies. When a district called about a specific child, we would respond only if district members agreed to implement more intensive school-level training and technical assistance. Despite our commitment to this tactic, we sometimes would respond to a particularly troubling call, believing that maybe we could prevent an out-of-district or segregated placement. This mindfulness of balance between the individual and the system has kept us grounded in the everyday issues facing students and their families and has served as a reminder of the scope and intensity of work before us.

Avoid Advocating at the Expense of Systems Change

When a child or an adult with disabilities is not being supported or included, our immediate instincts are to move in and directly advocate, sometimes in the form of litigation. In the early 1990s, we were asked to testify on behalf of a young man who was receiving his education in a segregated classroom. We moved in quickly, spent a great deal of time finding facts, conducting interviews and observations, and meeting with parents. It was the right thing to do. The case, however, was lost. We did not anticipate that our involvement in the litigation would affect our ability to work with this district and surrounding districts for the next 10 years. School districts did not want to see us as part of the solution. In fact, they viewed us suspiciously. So, we did the right thing for this young man and his family but the wrong thing for the several hundred other students receiving separate services. This was one of the hardest lessons to learn. The immediate desire to help and to support inclusion must be fully assessed in terms of the positive and negative impacts of involvement. After we testified for the young man, we had to strive to be viewed as individuals who could provide technical assistance, not as the opposition.

Having learned from this mistake, we have several policies that ensure that people with disabilities and their families have advocates at the same time that we maintain our effectiveness in systemic reform. First, if we are asked to serve as an expert or evaluator on a specific case in New Hampshire, we work with the attorney or the family to find an equally qualified advocate or expert from a neighboring state. Second, if our input and perspective is absolutely imperative, we will respond to a subpoena. Third, if a family or person with a disability calls and needs technical assistance with a school or program, we request that the family or individual call the organization and ask that we be invited to assist all parties involved. This creates the potential for a positive partnership among the school, family, and consultant/technical assistant.

Stay Close to People

There is a constant temptation to focus on policy development, leadership training, systems analyses, and interagency coordination when attempting to invoke systems change. In 1998 after meeting with a large group of families about their experiences in the public schools, I realized that much of our progress is embedded in models rather than in real life. The power of positive thinking can lead to a certain lack of reality. These families' stories involved expulsion; use of aversive, poorly implemented individualized education programs (IEPs); segregation; and poor instruction. Staying connected to families and people with disabilities, not just those who are fighters and agents of change but also those who struggle to survive every day, is essential. Learning to make this connection should be part of everyone's professional development and experience and should serve as the essential marker of the reality of systemic reform.

Have a Big Picture with a Clear Focus

Initially, all of our efforts were concentrated on children and adults with severe disabilities. As we worked in schools, with businesses and public agencies, the need to see a bigger picture emerged. New efforts in school reform were excluding students with disabilities. Welfare reform initiatives were exempting adults with severe disabilities. Child protective services had no way to determine incidence of abuse and neglect of children with disabilities. Service agencies for older adults supported nursing homes at a time when deinstitutionalization was a forgone conclusion for individuals with disabilities in New Hampshire. Logically, we realized that we must engage with all of these systems and efforts to ensure the inclusion of children and adults with disabilities. That, however, is not an easy task. Moreover, each system is different, built on different assumptions and on the behalf of different groups of people. Each system has its own agencies, its own professional standards, and its own evaluation criteria. Moving to influence these systems, which is necessary, demands that other efforts are decreased, minimized, or dismissed altogether. There is no formula for deciding how to act or which efforts to support—it is partially a combination of opportunity plus expertise. However, one must ask oneself every week, when new systemic reform efforts are developed, "How are people with significant disabilities positively affected by my efforts this week?" "Is this a good investment of time?" and "What is the end goal?" A cheap camera will see everything, and all is blurred. A more carefully crafted one will see everything, and the image will be vivid.

Invest in Leadership, but Don't Rely on Leaders

Working in New Hampshire has been easy compared with working in other states. It is small and manageable. I was amazed when I was able to call state directors on their direct telephone lines. New Hampshire has a national reputation in the areas of developmental and mental health services (Braddock, Hemp, Parrish, & Westrich, 1998). Much of this success can be attributed to the vision of a relatively small group of leaders who were and are trustworthy, kind, and decent people. So why not trust one's leaders, support them, and appreciate their vision? One should, but one should also recognize that leaders leave, become ill, and/or die. Leadership can be fleeting, and there must be constant attention to development of a constituency who can step in at any time to continue the quest for full inclusion. In the late 1990s, several leaders on whom we relied left their positions for various reasons. We were surprised at how other individuals could step in and quickly change so much if given the authority to do so. We asked ourselves several times, "How could this movement toward alternative schools happen in our state?" The answer was obvious. For too long we had relied on the abilities of a couple of leaders to support the mission of inclusion of children with disabilities without affecting the necessary politicians and formal policies and without supporting a new and evolving group of leaders. The lesson from all of this is to ask, "What if this leader were to leave tomorrow? What would happen to children and adults with disabilities in this state?" If the answer is that nothing bad would happen or that things would continue in a positive direction, then systemic reform has been partly achieved.

Commit to Reforming Personnel Preparation at All Levels

Universities provide an arena for faculty and students to come together to study, learn, and develop new ideas. The IOD has been least effective in changing the personnel preparation programs in the state. We have worked to effect change in professional standards by writing personnel preparation grants, working with other institutions of higher education, and examining certification standards and making recommendations to the state. There has been some progress, but in the scheme of things, we have failed miserably to have the desired impact. Our goal, which has not yet been realized, is to bring about closely aligned general and special education teacher training programs. Teachers trained in the 1990s, for the most part, have not been taught the necessary skills to design and adapt curricula for students with diverse learning needs. Had we focused on doing the kind of work, however undesirable, that was necessary to design new curriculum methods classes and to support inclusive education internship experiences, we might now have a more positive picture of education of students with disabilities in New Hampshire. We should have started long ago to seriously work with higher education programs. Now we have to play "catch up" and refocus our efforts to support a new generation of teachers and related service professionals.

Remember that Systems Are Made Up of People

To be an effective systems change agent, one must freely and strategically nurture people. It is an unending task. Both novices and leaders need nurturing. Where do systems end and people begin? What is on paper as policy, and how is that policy translated into practice? In efforts to support systemic reform, both skills in policy analysis and human relations are essential. The absence of either can result in good policy with no constituency or bad policy with resounding support. Some people are more effective communicators and strategic partners. Others are less apt to be comfortable in situations naturally filled with conflict or differing opinions and approaches. Self-analysis is crucial in determining one's capacity to be an effective systems change agent.

Some of the best researchers may feel ill equipped to negotiate policy changes. Some of the best policy analysts may be inept teachers.

Encourage Support-Committed Champions

Systems change requires people who share a common vision but have different skills and abilities; Peters (1987) called such people *support-committed champions*. There are many roles for systems change agents. On reflection, everyone can describe individuals who have made a difference. I would like to describe briefly some kinds of people whom I have known and know. They are the brilliant strategist knowledgeable about financing and legislation and committed to long-term change; the thoughtful sage willing to exchange ideas to move the system forward; the eccentric, fast-moving truth teller more interested in the marketing of ideas than in the mechanics of change; the trouper who's in it for the long haul; the energetic and radical consumer capable of translating personal experience into a social and political platform for change; and the committed friend acting on behalf of and with people with disabilities and their families. There are others and numerous permutations of each. All have important roles in creating inclusive communities, and each must be supported and recognized for his or her contribution.

No temptation is greater than the desire to control individuals, to judge their actions as well as their thoughts, to attempt to manage them in one's own image, and to push the most difficult employees out. Certainly, some adherence to sensible policies and practices is required, yet often the most creative, the most challenging, or the most annoying people are not allowed to fully express their desire for change or their thoughts on how things could be better. We need to have a deep respect for innovators and thoughtful individuals and give them the space and support they require to make changes in systems. It is a balancing act because along the way, the most creative people may be the ones who are causing the system the most problems. Providing support, negotiating agreements, and supplying important feedback are important roles for leaders. For example, one of the most dedicated, productive, innovative staff members I have known was essentially disliked by the majority of agency directors in the state. Over time that changed, but in the beginning, I spent hours on the telephone attempting to explain certain actions and to provide backup to this person. Frankly, it would have been easier to have the person leave, arguing that relationships were being negatively affected. But in the end, the system embraced this individual. Peters said it first in *Thriving on Chaos:*

> Only the sort of person who is passionately committed to stand up to all this static and ridicule is likely to succeed. Such a person is almost a sure bet to be egotistical, impatient, and disruptive. And those traits in turn further enhance the odds of stiff rebuffs from any establishment's managers. (1987, p. 299)

Watch Out for Beavers

John Callahan (1992), the cartoonist, depicted a decimated Noah's Ark with Noah saying, "I told you not to bring the beavers." Our belief in inclusion and support, in fostering personal change, and in developing leaders is, for the most part, the appropriate strategy. In contrast, paranoia, doubt, and covert strategy only foster distrust. Erring on the side of optimism sometimes leads us to support and promote individuals who may not appear to fully embrace the philosophy of inclusion at first but who in the process learn their own personal power and strength to create change. Often these people become our professional colleagues and friends. Some of them, gradually or unexpectedly, begin to support an agenda contrary to inclusive education and community. When that happens, there is a sense of betrayal. As my friend Marsha Forest said, "Betrayal only comes from close people—that's the nature of it" (personal communication, 1999).

There is no way to predict who will change their agendas. In the end it is better to be open than closed and suspicious. The possibility of an individual's changing his or her vision from one of inclusion to one of exclusion or moderate acceptance of segregation must be recognized. In the end, strategic initiatives must never focus on the strengths of just one individual. If leaders are canonized and then change their positions, followers will follow, sometimes to unwanted places.

Retreat When Necessary to Regroup the Troops

In 1990, I had the opportunity to spend some time with Douglas Biklen in Europe, and I experienced firsthand the new communication methodology referred to as *facilitated communication* (FC). On my return to New Hampshire, I assembled three colleagues and sent them to the FC Institute at Syracuse University. Quickly, we began providing FC training and support to individuals with autism and other disabilities, and we experienced success. Within 1 year, numerous individuals were using the method. Within 2 years, there were several allegations of sexual abuse, a lawsuit, accusations questioning individuals' professional competence, an extremely negative *Frontline* public television show, additional negative media attention, and an onslaught of quantitative research that was unable to prove independent communication. In private, someone whom I respected deeply told me to stop. There were going to be serious consequences if we continued to provide training and support without the appropriate research and protocols. I decided, as Director of the IOD, to cease training and support for FC in the state of New Hampshire, which was the most painful decision I ever had to make as Director. The decision caused great personal turmoil and created chaos among families in the state and among colleagues within the IOD. I had numerous personal accounts and qualitative studies about FC but felt that we needed to have a broader group interested and supportive of the method. That is, once again, we learned that proceeding rapidly with any new methodology without the constituency of families and people with disabilities only serves to create a target for people with contrary interests and beliefs. Today, the FC effort in the state is being spearheaded by families and people with autism. People using FC, their families, and professionals have met several times to determine how FC should be presented and how to ensure that people who want to learn FC are given all of the information available. Deciding to use FC should be the choice of people with disabilities and/or their families, not the choice of professionals. Maybe the development of FC policy is easier because we have more research and practice, but more likely it is because the people driving the effort to expand the use of FC are people with disabilities and their families in partnership with interested professionals rather than the other way around.

Look Nationally, but Retain Local Ties

One tool in systemic change is garnering state and national resources to support an agenda of inclusive schools and communities. Bringing federal resources to the state requires a commitment to share information, data, research, and manuscripts with others. As this happens, there is a proclivity to travel elsewhere, to give workshops and speeches, and to provide technical assistance to others attempting to accomplish similar goals. Soon, a successful effort at the state level can become a federally funded project of national significance that provides opportunities to field test methods and strategies elsewhere. This kind of work provides additional information, refines methods, and generates energy and enthusiasm. For example, a housing project supported by the state of New Hampshire quickly became a national technical assistance project that succeeded in more than 36 states. Unfortunately, although others learned New Hampshire's lessons, the state did not have sufficient infrastructure to support such rapid development. By the time our focus shifted from the state to the national level, some of the energy in New Hampshire behind consumer-owned and controlled housing had waned. Better strategic thinking and more emphasis on state infrastructure and development would have ensured continued development. As a result of this experience, we have built better infrastructures in the national technical assistance sites, many of which are stronger than the one that generated the model initially.

Create an Environment in Which New
Ideas Are Required as a Matter of Practice

Microsoft uses a strategy that requires time-limited new ideas. This means that employees are required to present new ideas for products and services on a regular basis. Doing so is an integral part of their job rather than an optional task. People in all professions often see their work myopically without the necessary constant reexamination required to ensure constant innovation. Our partnering with families and people with disabilities has created a new context for ideas because new perspectives were presented. This partnering is essential but insufficient. Opportunities for new ideas must be created along with collegial and community assessment of these new ideas. We encourage everyone within the IOD as well as our colleagues to bring forth a new way of looking at an old issue or a new project or method that would address a complicated issue, such as school inclusion or employment, and we reinforce all open assessment of failure. In the beginning people felt that this policy was unnatural. Personnel initially were forced to sign up for a new idea. Now, however, there is growing excitement about methods that are applicable but untested in our field. Already approaches linked to experiential education, community psychology, and consumer-run organizations have been added to our array of tools available for systemic reform. We must mandate that people think, reflect, and generate new ideas if we are going to continually evaluate new approaches and strategies to improve inclusion, support, and productivity of children and adults with disabilities.

Analyze Your Actions

Figure 1.1 is a tool that any individual or organization involved in systems change can use. It captures the lessons we have learned and provides a framework for thinking and acting.

NEW DIRECTIONS

We have all arrived at a similar place in our thinking. We have learned that we must look beyond what we know and to people with whom we are unfamiliar. McKnight and Kretzmann (1995) described an agenda that required new relationships with public-sector bodies so that resources and real authority are transferred to the target—in this case the neighborhood. This agenda includes 1) shifting public funds away from traditional transfer and maintenance functions toward investment approaches, 2) developing strategies to direct public resources to development groups, and 3) developing different forms of governance that carry significant local authority. Nerney and Shumway (1996) have rearticulated these ideas in their efforts to provide states with information on self-determination for people with developmental disabilities and their families. Today, new developments in credit unions (Gerry, 1998), microenterprise (T. Davies, personal communication, 1999), resource consulting (Cotton & Sowers, 1998), and individual budgets (Nerney & Shumway, 1996) provide a foundation for reviewing the relationships among consumers, service providers, and government agencies. These new tools are largely untested in the community of consumers and professionals and provide fertile ground for

Systems change goal: _____

_____

_____

Strategies	Proposed impacts	Outcomes
Leadership development	Describe short- and long-term impact on individuals.	Constituency development
Research and dissemination	Describe short- and long-term impact on families.	New laws, rules, and regulations
Technical assistance	Describe short- and long-term impact on systems.	Changes in individual outcomes
Preservice personnel preparation	Describe short- and long-term impact on nondisability public sector.	Changes in family outcomes
In-service preparation	Describe short- and long-term impact on nondisability private sector.	Changes in service delivery and organization
Community organizing		Changes in private sector involvement
Legal advocacy		Changes in media presentation
Model demonstration		Development of new partnerships
Cooperative planning		

New directions: _____

_____

_____

Figure 1.1.   Systems change goals and directions planning sheet.

engaging the larger community in systemic reform. Change is slower than I had hoped. It is not predictable and requires a large view of the world and the ability to constantly assess the opportunities and the problems. More important, change is an organizing tool for research, action, teaching, and learning. Once, I was asked, "How can you be objective if you have an agenda so clearly focused on change and school and community inclusion?" I answered that I do not know how to do it any other way.

REFERENCES

Biklen, D. (1983). *Community organizing: Theory and practice.* Upper Saddle River, NJ: Prentice-Hall.

Braddock, D., Hemp, R., Parrish, S., & Westrich, J. (1998). *The state of the states in developmental disabilities* (5th ed.). Washington, DC: American Association on Mental Retardation.

Callahan, J. (1992). *Do what he says! He's crazy!!!* Boston: Quill Press.

Cotton, P., & Sowers, J. (1998). *Choice through knowledge: Knowledge = power.* Durham: University of New Hampshire, Institute on Disability.

Fullan, M., & Miles, M. (1992). Getting reform right: What works and what doesn't. *Phi Delta Kappan, 73*(10), 744–752.

Gerry, M. (1998). *Using credit unions to support self-determination for persons with disabilities.* Unpublished manuscript.

McKnight, J., & Kretzmann, J. (1995). Community organizing in the eighties: Toward a post-Alilnsky agenda. In J. McKnight (Ed.), *The careless society* (pp. 153–161). New York: Basic Books.

Nerney, T., & Shumway, D. (1996). *Beyond managed care: Self-determination for people with disabilities.* Durham: University of New Hampshire, Institute on Disability, Robert Wood Johnson National Program Office on Self-Determination for Persons with Developmental Disabilities.

O'Brien, J., Strully, J., & Krippenstappel, J. (1995). *Living up to your strengths: Evaluation of the Institute on Disability.* Unpublished manuscript.

Peters, T. (1987). *Thriving on chaos: Handbook for a management revolution.* New York: HarperCollins.

Schorr, L.B. (1997). *Common purpose.* New York: Anchor Books.

Watzlawick, P., Weakland, J.H., & Fisch, R. (1974). *Change: Principles of problem formation and problem resolution.* New York: W.W. Norton.

2

Supporting People
as Part of the Community

Possibilities and Prospects for Change

David Hagner

The way a society views and responds to disability and people with disabilities says as much about the society as it does about disability. American society has changed in some fundamental and dramatic ways since the 1950s and so have notions of what is acceptable, what is valued, and who belongs.

It was a big step when my daughter began to ride the school bus to kindergarten, one of a long series of steps that mark the transitions regarded as significant in the life of a community member. My daughter occasionally brought home stories of events on the school bus. One story concerned a boy with autism who rode the same bus. "Michael yelled today, and we had to tell him to be quiet. He yells because he gets mad but can't talk." It was easy for the bus riders to see how someone unable to "use words," as kindergarten children are reminded, would occasionally yell when angry. The children on the bus had an effective strategy for dealing with the situation.

In school, on the bus, and in apartment buildings, stores, restaurants and workplaces of every description, individuals who might have until the mid-1990s been hidden away in an institution are participating as members of communities. This participation has almost come to be expected, so that if one walks down the street, goes shopping, or attends a concert or sports event and individuals with disabilities are absent, something seems not right, out of place. Their absence is conspicuous.

When I went to school, I don't remember anybody there who had autism. None of my classmates used a wheelchair. Some families in my neighborhood must have had children with disabilities, but I didn't know them. If some had mental retardation, they may have lived in the institution in a nearby town. I knew a little about that place. Each year in Cub Scouts we made craft projects and brought them to the residents as holiday gifts. Some of those residents yelled instead of using words, and we were frightened by them.

Years later I worked in such an institution. I got to know some of the people who lived there and their families. Once I accompanied a gentleman about my own age, Tom, to visit his parents. Tom's father, about my father's age, told me that when he was a boy he used to walk past that institution on his way to school. Residents of the institution would stand by the fence, looking out, trying to engage passersby in conversation, and asking them for cigarettes. Tom's grandfather would tell Tom's father to walk on the other side of the street and not to go near the fence. Tom's father was telling me this story because now he had to come to terms with the fact that his son Tom lived there.

The institution Tom lived in is scheduled to shut down in a couple of years as part of that state's plan to close all of its residential institutions. People with labels such as Tom's will live in regular homes in the community. Tom himself left the institution a few years ago. He shares an apartment downtown with a friend.

Bradley and Knoll (1995) and Leake, James, and Stodden (1995) have argued that these changes in the disability field in the 1980s and 1990s are part of a large-scale conceptual change process called a *paradigm shift*. This chapter discusses these changes from a paradigm shift perspective and elaborates on the impact those shifts are having on everyone's lives.

SHIFTING PARADIGMS AND DISABILITY

Most change is incremental and evolutionary. Beliefs, theories, and practices are continually but gradually being revised, one or two at a time, within an overall framework or context which itself has a high degree of stability. *Paradigm* is a term borrowed from the philosophy of science to refer to this relatively stable conceptual framework around which change occurs.

It is easiest to understand paradigms by reference to once-dominant but now defunct paradigms. It is very difficult for one to think of one's own dominant paradigm as a paradigm. That is part of its strength. Understanding it is like being a fish in a fish tank trying to grasp the idea of being in a small tank. From inside, the tank (the paradigm) is experienced as simply the way things are. From outside, though, it is easy to see the paradigm.

The Ptolemaic solar system and phlogiston-based chemistry are two classic paradigms in the history of science. The Ptolemaic solar system placed the earth at the center of the universe, with the sun, moon, planets, stars, and other heavenly bodies traveling around the earth in perfect circles as unblemished spheres. This ancient picture of the universe, given its most complete description by Claudius Ptolemy in the 1st century A.D., stood unquestioned until the 17th century. During the 16th and 17th centuries, phlogiston-based chemistry gave a central place to the so-called element phlogiston, which supposedly combined with other materials during burning (Thagard, 1992). Investigations by Kuhn (1970) and Feyerabend (1978), respectively, of the ways in which these major conceptual systems came to be overthrown gave rise to the notion of conceptual paradigms.

Ptolemaic astronomy and phlogiston-based chemistry consisted of more than the few beliefs summarized here; each was made up of an extensive system of interdependent theories and propositions. Moreover, the concepts, the "things" that the theories were about, were themselves part of the paradigm. The terms *heavenly body* and *phlogiston* are good examples. Ptolemaic astronomy provided an explanation for the movement of heavenly bodies. The Ptolemaic system was replaced eventually by the Copernican system, but this new system did not have a new, better theory about heavenly bodies. The term *heavenly body* was retired by Copernican astronomy because it was viewed as referring to something that does not exist. The same is true of phlogiston. Modern chemistry recognizes no such substance. A new paradigm will develop its own set of new concepts. Some older terms might be retained by a new paradigm but with a change in their meanings.

Not only do theories and concepts exist within a paradigm, but the practices people engage in relative to those theories and concepts, including the types of data collection practices that make sense, also exist within the paradigm. For example, a scientific paradigm dictates what research questions arise in connection with the subject matter and what counts as evidence. Evidence is always dependent on the paradigm, not the other way around. For example, Galileo viewed several planets through a telescope and reported that he saw that they were not unblemished spheres. Advocates of the Ptolemaic system, however, disagreed with Galileo about whether the telescope was in focus (Feyerabend, 1978). To them, a lens setting in which the planet looked like what one would call fuzzy was in proper focus because it showed an unblemished sphere. To them, a telescope that appeared to show a planet with blemishes was obviously out of focus. Now people only think differently because they "know" prior to looking into the telescope how the planet should look, and they use that knowledge to focus the telescope.

In the dramatic restructuring of a conceptual system that is a paradigm shift (Feyerabend, 1978; Kuhn, 1970), a set of theories or beliefs is not the only thing that changes. An entire system of concepts and practices is replaced

by a whole new system (Thagard, 1992). The terms used to frame the older
beliefs are replaced by different, incommensurable terms, and the practices for
the validation of beliefs change with them. Paradigms cannot shift by being
directly refuted or invalidated.

Because of the seriousness and depth of upheaval involved, change from
one paradigm to another is a relatively rare event. When a new paradigm is proposed, usually a fairly long period of time passes during which some people
adopt the new paradigm and other people stick with the old one. Adherents of
either paradigm, using different concepts and counting different things as evidence for their theories, largely talk past one another, and both paradigms co-
exist. For example, Ptolemaic astronomers developed the idea of epicycles—
small circular paths around the overall circular path that a planet was supposed
to be travelling around the earth—to account for the apparent retrograde
motion of planets and other problems they had with getting their theory to
match observations. The Copernican astronomer Kepler, freed from thinking of
orbits as perfect circles, posited an elliptical motion and estimated accurate
orbits more easily without epicycles. For many decades one could use either
approach to predict planetary motion.

Eventually, in a paradigm shift, the explanations given by the older paradigm become more and more cumbersome. Ptolemaic astronomy eventually
required lots of smaller epicycles on top of the epicycles. The system became
unwieldy and was eventually abandoned.

Thus, new paradigms sometimes drive out older paradigms because they
explain phenomena more simply or more accurately. They may also be able to
incorporate new phenomena not explained at all by the old paradigm. In the
18th century, Lavoisier's newer oxygen theory and the older phlogiston theory
both provided decent explanations of combustion, but the oxygen theory also
explained phenomena related to respiration and rusting that the phlogiston theory did not explain. So after decades of resistance, the modern notion of chem-
ical elements, including oxygen, eventually won out. (Vestiges of old paradigms, however, can remain for a very long time. The term *combustion*, which
once meant *combining* with phlogiston, is still used even though combustion
is now considered to be the *removal* of oxygen. Also, people still use the
Ptolemaic expression "the sun will come out.")

A paradigm shift is to some extent a nonrational process. Gradually, proponents of a new paradigm gain influence. At first the new ideas are attacked
as false or ridiculous, or proponents of the older paradigm try to show that
they are not really new and can be incorporated into the older paradigm. Over
time, more and more people in leadership positions are persuaded of the new
paradigm's value. The old paradigm is eventually supported by only a handful of people very resistant to change and then is abandoned entirely. The
period in which the two paradigms remain parallel explanatory possibilities,
however, can cover several decades, and not all newer paradigms win. Marxist

economics is an example of a largely unsuccessful challenger to classical free market economics.

The First Shift: From Facilities to Programs

Bradley and Knoll (1995) said that they believed that not one but two major paradigm shifts have occurred in the disability field since the late 1960s. The first of these was from the facilities paradigm to what one might call the *programs paradigm*. The earlier facilities paradigm saw the needs of individuals with disabilities being met in special environments, or facilities, in which people with disabilities could be protected from "overly high expectations" and unaccepting people, could be helped to socialize "with their own kind," and could be cared for by personnel knowledgeable about these individuals' needs. Facilities included such places as residential institutions, special schools, and sheltered workshops. The facilities paradigm is typified by a comment made years ago by a receptionist at a manufacturing firm. She asked me and an individual with a disability whom I was accompanying for an informational employment interview, "Don't they have places for these people?"

This receptionist was being confronted with a phenomenon that, in her conceptual system, ought not to occur: a blemish on a heavenly sphere. Perhaps since the mid-19th century, advocates and researchers believed that individuals with disabilities such as long-term mental illness, mental retardation, autism, and epilepsy ought to be placed in facilities especially designed to ensure their care, safety, self-esteem, and development. The facilities paradigm filtered down to society as a whole, becoming the generally accepted perspective of Tom's father and other people in the community.

The facilities paradigm did not consist of only a few isolated beliefs but was instead a way of looking at the world. The language used within the paradigm (e.g., "educable," "halfway house," "sheltered workshop") reflected reality as filtered through the paradigm. In vocational services, for example, if one was asked, "Is competitive or sheltered employment more appropriate for Mr. Jones?" the answer could only be one of these two because no other options were conceivable and no other terms were allowable. People could either enter what was viewed as the world of competition for scarce jobs, where only those who met certain "readiness" criteria stood a chance, or they could work in special facilities such as sheltered workshops. The very terms "competitive" and "sheltered" carried, so to speak, the baggage of the paradigm.

As with other paradigms, there is no way to directly refute the facilities paradigm because one is either inside of it or outside of it. From the inside, phenomena are observed through the paradigm's filter. Reports of horrible conditions in institutions have been taken by adherents of the facilities paradigm as evidence that institutions need careful monitoring and quality assurance (Crissey & Rosen, 1986). Attempted escapes from a facility have been labeled as problem behaviors and used as evidence that the placement decision was correct. Compliant adaptation to the facility has been also taken as evidence that the placement decision was correct. In vocational services, people who left a sheltered workshop and succeeded at a community job "proved" that the sheltered workshop was a good preparation experience. People who left and failed at their community jobs "proved" that those individuals were not yet ready and needed more time in the workshop. Proponents of a different paradigm, however, think about disability in an entirely different way.

One can see this clearly by looking at the disability research of an earlier era from the vantage point of a different paradigm. For example, Franks and Franks (1962) reported a study of the work behavior of individuals with mental retardation that was typical of the facilities paradigm. Researchers used classical conditioning procedures to condition sheltered workshop employees to blink their eyes at the sound of a tone, then investigated whether differences in the conditioning process correlated with differences in work performance in the workshop. Such a study seems ridiculous, if not abhorrent, to people in the disabilities field today. It is not that they have a problem with the particulars of the method. In a fundamental way, though, they no longer care which people work better in a sheltered workshop nor do they see how responses to classical conditioning procedures could have anything to do with helping people with their careers. It is distasteful to professionals in the field to think of people with disabilities as being experimented on in ways so utterly different from the ways in which the vocational behavior of individuals without disabilities are studied. A person listening to this critique from within the facilities paradigm, however, would not understand why people would be so upset about a research approach that makes perfect sense to him or her.

The newer programs paradigm views the needs of individuals with disabilities not in terms of facilities but in terms of programs. According to this paradigm, children with disabilities do not need special educational facilities; they need special programming within general education environments. Adults with disabilities do not need to live in an institution; they need a residential program in the community. For work they need a vocational program, for recreation they need a recreation program, and so forth.

The shift from the facilities paradigm to the programs paradigm took place over many years, with both paradigms thriving together and adherents of each view disputing various issues and largely talking past one another. Supported employment became established as a facility-free programs paradigm alternative to sheltered employment. Advocates of supported employment gradually abandoned facility-oriented terminology, such as "nonsheltered settings," "transfer of training," and "job ready." Rather than discuss whether the expression "Everyone is job ready" or the expression "We assist people to find jobs regardless of whether they are job ready" is more accurate, proponents of supported employment simply retired the concept "job ready" as referring to something that does not exist. New concepts were developed, and the topics and methods of research in vocational services shifted as well. Parallel developments took place with respect to educational services and residential services.

Today the facilities paradigm has few proponents, although practice lags behind ideology in many communities, and the process of filtering down a different message to ordinary citizens is not complete. Yet, it is valuable to consider how big an achievement this paradigm shift has been and how far society has come in welcoming people with disabilities as part of the community. By comparison, the second paradigm shift has been more difficult to implement.

The Second Shift: From Programs to Supports

No sooner had the shift from the facilities paradigm to the programs paradigm taken hold when a second paradigm shift began, this time from the programs paradigm to what has been termed the *supports paradigm* (Leake et al., 1995; Smull & Bellamy, 1991). This paradigm does not give primary importance to programs but rather sees individuals with disabilities as citizens who need what everyone else in society needs and, consequently, views special programs with a degree of suspicion. Elements of the supports paradigm include the following:

- Individualized participation by people with disabilities in desired community environments is the starting point and context, not the goal. Every member of a community is presumed to belong. Inclusion is a central concept.
- Provision of supports takes into account expectations that adults will exercise the degree of autonomy and choice that is typical within their society.
- A combination of supports is used that includes some specialized disability supports but also such options as natural community supports and unpaid supports. Design of supports takes into account concerns about the negative social consequences of clienthood and overreliance on one type of support.
- There is a clear distinction between life goals, tied to the individual, and service goals, tied to a particular service provider. Key life decisions and plans are made independent of available services, and then services are brought into the picture as needed to implement plans made.
- Tangible social connections to and relationships with other people are seen as an indispensable element of community membership.

The following example of two individuals' lives might help illustrate the difference between the programs paradigm and the supports paradigm.

Newt and Trent

After many years living in an out-of-state institution, where he had been placed as an adolescent because of a history of aggressive behavior, Newt returned to his home town at age 27 and was placed in a community residence: a single-family home in a quiet residential neighborhood with two live-in staff members. For reasons not entirely known, Newt reacted poorly to his move to this residence, becoming very angry on many occasions. He punched and kicked holes in the wall of the house; hit his head and face, thus hurting himself severely; and injured several staff members.

Over a period of about 5 months, there were several turnovers of live-in staff, and the frequency of problems was increasing. At this point the agency providing services to Newt decided that the situation was unsafe and that his behavior was more difficult than could be handled in that residence. Newt was moved to a six-person group home designed as a residence for people considered to have difficult behavior. At this residence, stringent behavior programming was initiated. Newt was restrained for each incident of injury or destruction according to a specific protocol taught to the staff, and he earned "points" for specific periods in which no incidents were observed and for completing household chores as requested by the staff. Newt could then exchange his points for various activities that he enjoyed. Over a period of months Newt's aggressive incidents decreased, and he became much more compliant. He was offered the opportunity to attend a weekly counseling program at the agency offices (driven in the group-home van with another staff member in addition to the driver), but he refused to attend.

Trent is a 20-year-old who, similar to Newt, had become angry on many occasions as a child and had been placed out of his family home into a special group home for young people labeled "difficult to manage." Trent attended segregated high school classes in a special program for individuals with severe emotional disabilities and after high school graduation became ineligible to live at the group home.

Trent's teachers referred him to a new federally funded transition demonstration project in town. Project staff explained the project to Trent, and he decided to participate. Trent was assisted to formulate, as much as he was able, his own plan for his future beyond school through a process called personal futures planning (O'Brien, 1987). One of Trent's goals was to learn to use a computer. Other goals included getting his own apartment and a job. Eventually, he wanted to pursue getting his driver's license.

Project staff assisted Trent to begin working toward each of these goals. He was introduced to Randy, a staff member at the local commu-

nity college who knew a lot about computers, and Randy agreed to spend some time each week as Trent's mentor, teaching him about computers in return for a small monthly stipend. Staff also assisted Trent in receiving a Section 8 rental subsidy from the local Department of Housing and Urban Development office.

Trent felt that he would need some assistance with the daily routines and responsibilities of having his own apartment, so he asked a friend he knew from school, John, if he would consider being his roommate. John would be able to take advantage of the lower rent and in return provide some support to Trent.

As soon as the Section 8 subsidy process was complete, Trent and John, with assistance from project staff, looked through the daily newspaper and called about apartments for rent that looked interesting and were in their price range. Trent made the initial call, and if the person on the other end of the telephone asked a question that Trent was unsure how to answer, he would turn to John, and John would suggest what he could say. They scheduled appointments to visit apartments where the landlord accepted Section 8 vouchers, and eventually they settled on a two-bedroom, first-floor apartment in a fairly new building close to downtown.

When they moved in, project staff suggested a combination housewarming celebration and circle of support meeting. Trent, John, Randy, and several project staff sat on the carpet (they still had not moved in any furniture!) and ate take-out food while they discussed what was needed to make this situation work for them. Everyone went around the room saying what they thought the obstacles or problems might be, and the group brainstormed an approach to each problem.

When it was Trent's turn, he said, "I am a little worried that I might become angry over something while I am living here and do something like maybe punch a hole in one of these walls or something. Then I would lose my apartment." The group talked about some ways to handle this, and Trent thought that one valuable idea would be to arrange for some personal counseling so he could talk about ways to handle or possibly even reduce his anger. With assistance, he called and made an appointment.

Trent and Newt are very different people, but a few similarities are evident in their stories. Both live in the same community. Both are young men with a history of unacceptable aggressive behavior. Both have families that felt unable to have them live at home as they entered adolescence because of this problem. Both have labels of mental illness and developmental disability. Both individuals can be said to be living in the community as adults and receiving community-based services. There is an enormous difference, however, in the type and quality of community-based services being provided to Newt and Trent, and there is a vast difference in the sense in which each can be said to be in the community.

Trent realized on his own that he did not want to lose *his* apartment. When he wanted counseling, the same range of generic counseling services available to anyone else in the community were available to him. Newt was *placed* in a group home. Trent receives assistance to implement *his* goals. All of Newt's significant life decisions, such as where and with whom he will live, are made by others. Staff supporting Newt are continually faced with the problem of how to motivate, cajole, or force him to do what they have decided he should do. His only true choice is to submit to or to refuse staff demands. Assistance to Newt is in accordance with the programs paradigm, whereas Trent's assistance follows the supports paradigm.

Although the shift to a supports paradigm is in its infancy, evidence of it can be seen in many areas. In vocational services, the supports paradigm is reflected in trends toward a more consumer-centered approach and toward greater use of natural workplace supports. A consumer-centered approach places choice and control of the employment and employment supports in the hands of the consumer, or "customer" (Brooke, Wehman, Inge, & Parent, 1995). This includes personally chosen career and career change options and control over the type and source of employment support that will be provided. Use of natural supports, such as families, friends, co-workers, and employers, implies a shift in the professionals' roles from being primarily providers of support to being more facilitators of support from a wide variety of sources (Butterworth, Hagner, Kiernan, & Schalock, 1996; Trach & Mayhall, 1997). Leake et al. (1995) explained that this focus on natural supports is the central defining feature of the supports paradigm.

In educational services, the supports paradigm is reflected in the general education initiative (Jenkins, Pious, & Jewell, 1990) and in the emphasis on school inclusion and restructuring as a unified process (Berres, Ferguson, Knoblock, & Woods, 1997; Villa & Thousand, 2000). In residential services, the "home of your own" initiative (Klein & Black, 1995) is an expression of the supports paradigm.

From within the supports paradigm, it is easy to see some limitations of the programs paradigm. In the programs paradigm, people receive services by going through "intake" (often after a period of time on a waiting list) and being accepted by one or more programs. Program staff provide support to remedy "deficiencies" or care for "special needs," under the assumption that these supports require more specialized training or take more time than ordinary people in the community could or would agree to provide. Service "clients" (a programs paradigm term taken from the Latin word *cliens*— people in ancient Rome with no rights who received protection from paternalistic *patrones*) do not receive funds directly or control who receives how much funding. Most direct assistance is provided by staff with little special-ized education and training: teaching assistants, residential staff, job coaches, and so forth. These individuals are at the bottom of a pyramid-style hierarchy of personnel, with various professional and managerial staff occupying the higher positions. The emphasis of the service is on "placing" people into an appropriate school class, home or apartment, jobsite, and so forth. Objective assessment data analyzed by professionals are the basis for program and placement decisions. Failure to do well within one's placement is interpreted within the programs paradigm as a matter of inadequate skill acquisition, indi-cating a need for more programming or more sophisticated programming or possibly indicating a lack of a personal attribute called "motivation" on the part of the client, which is seen as a deficit that might eventually result in the client's discharge from the program.

This description of the programs paradigm is only intended as a broad generalization and necessarily leaves out a great deal of variation across pro-grams. As with any paradigm, anomalies crop up from time to time. One example of an anomaly within the programs paradigm is the Social Security Administration's Plans for Achieving Self Support (PASS) provisions, devel-oped in 1972, which give the recipient full control over the development of the plan and of management of plan finances. It is interesting to note that because PASS is an anomaly in a climate dominated by programs approaches, PASS provisions have been notoriously underutilized.

The supports paradigm represents a fundamentally different way of look-ing at disability from the programs paradigm. The shift to this paradigm appears to be more difficult to bring about than the shift to the programs par-adigm, although paradoxically it seems to be an easier shift for people in the community to make, such as the riders on my daughter's school bus, than for disability experts. At the present time, most services are more similar to Newt's than to Trent's.

PARADIGM SHIFTS AND SYSTEMS CHANGE

Although the shift away from facilities to programs is by now well established, the services to date that reflect a supports paradigm emphasis are small and sporadic. For example, Trent receives services from a small, time-limited, fed-erally funded demonstration grant, whereas Newt receives services from the provider organization serving most other individuals with developmental dis-abilities in his community. Similarly, most stories of fully inclusive education can be traced to a few schools with sustained university connections and grant funding (Berres et al., 1997), even though some of that funding has been for the ostensible purpose of systems change.

All change begins slowly, and many service innovations occur in the con-text of grant funding or partnerships with higher education simply because resources for innovation are scarce at the level of service implementation. But

in the specific case of change that embodies the paradigm shift from programs
to supports, broad systems change has been particularly difficult to achieve. It
is not that support-related practices are difficult or obscure. Personal futures
planning, one approach closely associated with the supports paradigm and one
that played a central role for Trent, was introduced to the field at least as early
as 1987 (O'Brien, 1987), and training in the approach has been readily available. Yet the approach was completely unknown 10 years later to Newt's service providers. Something other than a simple lack of information or skill must
be preventing change from occurring.

Several writers have noted what appears to be an increasingly large gap
between what are considered "best" or recommended practices and the most
frequent practices in the disability field. Klein and Black (1995) have noted
that although demonstration of homeownership and control have been impres-
sive, well more than 90% of adults with severe disabilities still have little or
no control over their own housing. McGauhey, Kiernan, McNally, Gilmore,
and Keith (1995) noted that in vocational services, during the time when
customer-centered and natural supports approaches were being increasingly
advocated, the number of individuals with severe disabilities working in segregated environments also increased. In education, the National Center on
Educational Restructuring and Inclusion reported in 1994 that the percentage
of students with educational disabilities included in general education
environments had remained essentially unchanged—about 34%—since the
original passage of the Education for All Handicapped Children Act of 1975
(PL 94-142) almost 2 decades earlier (Lipsky, 1994).

A paradigm shift is a difficult and demanding experience. Old ways of
thinking die hard, and in the disabilities field this difficulty is compounded by
two successive paradigm shifts that occurred in a relatively short amount of
time. The supports paradigm represents a fundamentally different way of
viewing and responding to disability. It makes an additional shift beyond the
shift away from facilities—a shift from controlling, caring for, and "treating"
people to supporting people with disabilities in reaching goals and building
connections to the community.

A great deal of time and effort has been expended in making the shift
from facilities to programs. Now, with this task not yet completed, the goal
post has been moved, so to speak, and a new paradigm shift to supports is
required. As mentioned previously, paradigm shifts are relatively rare events,
and paradigms, once established, have a high degree of stability. This is as true
of the programs paradigm as it is with any other.

When contrasted with the facilities paradigm, the programs paradigm
continues to have a great deal of explanatory power and useful practical application. Supported employment programs and community-based residential
programs, for example, have achieved outcomes superior to their facility-
based counterparts, and advocates of a supports paradigm tend to talk past

those who have a programs paradigm orientation when pointing out some of the shortcomings of disability programs. The new ideas and language of the supports paradigm can also be incorporated into the perspective of the programs paradigm without much difficulty. Choice, empowerment, personal futures planning, self-determination, natural supports, a home of one's own, the general education initiative, and so forth all can be talked about in a reasonable way from within the programs paradigm. For example, some people understand self-determination to be a new type of skills training program in which people with disabilities are trained in making choices, and so things such as self-determination curricula have been developed within the programs paradigm. Similarly, one can conduct person-centered planning as though it were another type of program (Hagner, Helm, & Butterworth, 1996).

The differing interpretations of the term *natural supports* by the programs paradigm and the supports paradigm is an interesting case of the use of the same language by different paradigms. The Rehabilitation Act Amendments of 1992 (PL 102-569) added natural supports as a new type of extended employment service. This programs paradigm interpretation caused a great deal of confusion (Test & Wood, 1996). To proponents of a supports paradigm, it did not make sense for something that occurs as a natural part of the working of community groups and environments to be a funded service. To adherents of the programs paradigm, the term *natural supports* meant one of two things: 1) a form of "dumping" people without program support or 2) a new type of program. PL 102-569 opted for the second meaning. Eventually the way terms such as *natural supports* are dealt with by the programs paradigm will become so complicated as to be unusable, but in the short run one can expect both paradigms to co-exist and talk past one another using similar language but different interpretations.

Advocates of a programs paradigm not only have a different set of ideas and theories but also see things in a different way and "see" different things. For example, the findings of a study by Greenspan and Schoultz (1981), showing that people with disabilities who lose their jobs often lose them because of social problems, had a great deal of influence on the development of supported employment programs. The study is frequently cited as supporting the notion that supported employment programs must pay careful attention to teaching social skills to supported employees. Social skills training, however, was only one of two recommendations made by Greenspan and Schoultz. The other recommendation was to assist job seekers who will need a great deal of assistance with complex social behaviors to find especially supportive work environments. Why was one recommendation widely recognized and attended to whereas the other went unnoticed? The reason is that the first recommendation fit in easily with the programs paradigm, whereas the second recommendation did not make sense within it. The programs paradigm can only accommodate the relative supportiveness of different work environments in an indirect, convoluted way, using the vocational counterpart of Ptolemaic epicycles. Karan and Knight (1986) tried to address the need of some employees with severe disabilities for supportive work environments in a chapter titled "Developing Support Networks for Individuals Who Fail to Achieve Competitive Employment." This title in itself is revealing, for within the programs paradigm—new and unchallenged in 1986—a need for high levels of natural support was interpreted as a species of failure.

The first reason that the shift has been difficult is that scientific research cannot directly help in the shift from one paradigm to another. Different research questions and different validation procedures make sense in different paradigms, so that validation or invalidation across paradigms is next to impossible. Research is conducted within a paradigm, and thus, almost every individual fact that a proponent of the supports paradigm could mention can be explained differently by the programs paradigm. A paradigm acts as a sort of lens one wears in observing and interpreting the facts.

A study by Silliker (1993) showed that the most frequent source of job leads is a job seeker's network of social contacts. This fact was taken by Hagner, Butterworth, and Keith (1995) as evidence for the recommendation to assist job seekers with disabilities to explore job lead possibilities using their network of social contacts. Test and Wood (1996) objected, countering that natural supports strategies have not been validated and that this type of recommendation should be viewed with suspicion because a proper validation study must specify such variables as the type and degree of disability of the participants. To them, Silliker's study is not relevant to supported employment practices. A proponent of the supports paradigm would disagree. Silliker studied successfully employed citizens, and his results should apply to citizens with and without disabilities, just as they apply to citizens with and without brown hair. The reason that networking is a good way to get a job has nothing to do with disability or hair color. But a fundamental assumption of the programs paradigm is that people with disabilities are different from other people in substantial enough ways to justify the need for specialized services and disability programs. Each paradigm has a different way of structuring and naming the social world (Stockholder, 1994); each has a different view of what constitutes evidence.

But the paradigm shift away from programs and toward individual supports has been difficult for a second reason. The very system that is being asked to change to this new paradigm was designed specifically to run programs. Program assumptions are embedded in such a deep and compelling way in the structure of human services organizations, in the funding systems for services, and in the roles and preparation of service professionals that the existing service system is virtually incompatible with the supports paradigm. This is the core problem in systems change in the disabilities field.

Human Services Organizational Structure

Educational, vocational, residential, and other services are supplied to people with disabilities primarily through what is called the *service delivery system*—a set of interrelated human services organizations. Human services organizations are designed to perform some operation or produce some service in a reliable way. Any organization has some basic set of standard operating procedures that give it stability. Some procedures are formalized within the organization, such as the chain of command from the top executive down, job descriptions, written procedures, forms for generating paperwork, and so forth. Other procedures are informal, developed from the bottom up rather than from the top down. These procedures form the culture of the organization.

Workplace cultures develop as a way of streamlining communication, ensuring stability and predictability, and improving morale and job satisfaction. As is true of any culture, members of the workplace culture—the employees—may not even be consciously aware of all aspects of their culture. They may not even recognize features of the culture when these are pointed out. One organizational consultant who was brought into a business organization to look at ways of enhancing productivity spent the first 2 weeks observing and making sense of the current culture. He then met with the company managers and reported that one source of difficulty might be that the company seeks most ideas from within, seldom reaching out or placing much value on outside ideas. The company CEO, outraged at this suggestion, responded, "How dare you come in here with your fancy theories, poke around for a few days, and then tell us that we don't value the opinions of outsiders!" (Deal & Kennedy, 1982).

Some features of the workplace culture—the same features that give a workplace much of its value as an environment for social inclusion and serve as the focus for many supported employment strategies—also produce a degree of resistance to change. Thus, resistance should not be summarily dismissed as unfortunate or problematic. This is only one side of the story. If there were no force for stability and thus there was force against change, service would be unreliable and the organization would be in chaos.

By and large, contemporary human services organizations were founded and originally flourished under either the facilities paradigm or the programs paradigm. Many have been or are going through a difficult process of change from one paradigm to another and are now exhausted or complacent or both. A residential services organization may have gone through a reorganization from being modeled after a group home to providing an array of more individualized supported living options. The last thing that people in that organization want to hear may be that they now ought to change once again and provide consumers with true control over their own housing choices. A vocational services organization may have gone through a long and wrenching process of organizational change to close its sheltered workshop and establish a series of group and individual supported employment options using such service models as enclaves and job coaching. That people in that organization ought to now look at a truly person-centered career assistance approach that emphasizes natural supports in the workplace may come as unwelcome news.

Understanding the degree to which human services organizational cultures are wedded to the programs paradigm is important. Even in using the term *human services organization,* one is to some extent buying into the programs paradigm. When one thinks of representative human services organizations, organizations such as the hairdresser shop downtown, local restaurants, home decorating centers, and banks probably do not immediately come to mind. Within the programs paradigm these are termed *generic services,* but that term only makes sense within that particular paradigm. In the community at large, they are simply *services.* It is understood that those served are humans. But within the programs paradigm, *human services* is a term reserved for specialized disability services.

Most disability services organizations *are* programs; that is, at their core they are nothing but a collection of one or more service programs—a residential program, a day habilitation program, a recreation program for older adults, a respite program, and so forth—housed within an organizational shell. Without the program(s), the shell is empty. Or, one might say the shell ceases to exist or ceases to have any meaning. Thus, the programs paradigm is deeply embedded in the fabric of most contemporary disability services organizations. The structure of job positions, the agenda for meetings, the physical layout of office space, and every other aspect of the organization expresses the programs paradigm. The idea of supporting people *outside* of programs quite literally makes no sense to the employees and managers of these organizations.

For example, Newt's advocate asked the service provider organization staff to provide criteria for Newt to leave his group home, and the organization provided a list of the criteria for entrance into its individual supported living program. The advocate responded that this was not what was asked for because it was a list of organization-centered program criteria, not a list of things that make sense for Newt, as an individual, to learn or to achieve. The staff were bewildered by this statement and accused the advocate of self-contradiction: "You said you wanted the criteria for movement to the individualized level, and we gave it to you; now you say that's not what you want." This situation is a clear example of adherents of two different paradigms talking past one another.

New staff of any organization are selected based on their fit with the organization and its culture and are rewarded and promoted based in part on their ongoing ability to uphold the organization's values. Applicants who think and act according to a different conceptual paradigm seldom are hired, and any staff members who slip through the recruitment and hiring process but are at odds with the dominant thinking or who come to think differently as a result of staff development, continuing education, or their experiences with consumers seldom remain with the organization. In this way, workplace cultures are passed on and remain remarkably stable over time.

An organization whose culture is embedded in the programs paradigm will resist change to a supports paradigm. Resistance will manifest itself in many different forms. At one extreme is outright hostility: "Self-determination? That's just some people from the university keeping themselves funded with some new grant. Everybody knows that people with severe disabilities aren't able to do things such as assess program quality or understand complex funding streams." (These activities seem important when everything is viewed in "programs" terms.) At the other extreme is the attempt to relabel business as usual to fit with the new trend—co-opting, so to speak, the language of the new paradigm: "Facilitating natural supports? We've been doing that for years; we just didn't call it that." There are numerous other possible responses between those extremes.

Despite resistance, organizations do change all of the time, quickly or slowly, for better or for worse. This is because the force of resistance is not the only force acting on the organization. At any given point in time, forces promoting change are at work, often from many different directions. Human services organizations feel a certain amount of pressure to keep up with new ideas and research findings or risk being perceived as backwards and stagnant. Staff bring new ideas from their professional preparation or continuing education experiences and want to try them out. Those providing funding want change in the direction of economizing and quality improvement. These are just a few of the forces for change that may act on an organization.

Kettner, Daley, and Nichols (1985) conceptualized any organizational change as operating within a field of forces that includes both *driving forces,* forces that promote or support change, and *restraining forces,* forces that oppose change and support the status quo. Each of these driving or restraining forces can be analyzed in terms of its amenability, or susceptibility, to being modified; its potency, or degree of impact; and its consistency, or stability, over time. If the driving forces are greater, change will occur; if the restraining forces are greater, things will stay the same. Although change is common, most change occurs within the context of an existing paradigm. In the case of a paradigm shift, the driving forces for organizational change must be strong enough to overwhelm the restraining force of the existing paradigm. Few forces are that strong.

Organizational theorists such as Gundry, Kickul, and Prather (1993) and Schein (1993) have noted that some workplace cultures are more conducive to change than others. Those that can be categorized as "creative organizations" (Gundry et al., 1993) or as "learning organizations" (Schein, 1993) tend to have certain characteristics in common. The cultures of such organizations tend to be characterized by a sense of freedom and open communication; an air of playfulness; a concern for people; and an appreciation for a certain amount of conflict, debate, and risk taking. One can speculate that an organization with these characteristics would have a better chance of changing to a new paradigm than one without those characteristics.

Service Funding and Regulation

Today's human services organizations exist within the wider context of governmental funding and regulation. Even private organizations depend on public funds, and each organization must function in such a way as to capture its share of those funds. Governmental funding and regulation of services for individuals with disabilities has never wavered from the impulse that initiated this funding in the 19th century—the impulse to provide care and treatment for dependent and sick people (Munford, 1994; Radford, 1994). Thus, funding and regulations are linked to models of care in which people with disabilities are seen as recipients of care that is specifically interpreted as medical or quasi-medical. In the United States, the largest single source of government funding for disability-related supports is Medicaid, administered by the Health Care Financing Administration. In 1996 expenditures for its two primary programs, Intermediate Care Facilities for the Mentally Retarded and Medicaid Home and Community-Based Services, totaled almost $14.5 billion (Anderson, Lakin, & Prouty, 1997). State funding has been oriented toward a similar care model, and the trend toward managed-care approaches to state funding of disability services continues and strengthens this orientation.

Any mechanism that dispenses funds independent of consumer plans reinforces the programs paradigm and is inherently disempowering (Hagner & Marrone, 1995). When an organization, for example, receives an annual contract for a dollar amount to provide certain types of services for a specified number of consumers, the consumers are seen as filling slots in the organization's programs. People-processing procedures channel the unique aspirations of individuals into the existing slots and enforce program compliance (Hasenfeld, 1983). If consumers are given any choice at all, the choice is among preestablished services presented in the form of a bundle that must be accepted or rejected altogether (The Roeher Institute, 1994). Some services in the bundle may be wanted, and others may be unwanted. For example, if a program maintains a speech-language therapist on staff, some part of each consumer's funds goes to pay for the salary, benefits, and office of the speech-language therapist, whether any particular consumer wants speech-language therapy or chooses the speech-language therapist employed by the organization.

Government regulations tend to be program oriented as well. For a time I served on the board of directors of an organization based on the idea of life-sharing in which a group of people, some with and some without disabilities, would share a home as equals. Each year, in the name of quality assurance, the program-oriented state developmental disabilities regulatory body required the organization to create further separation between those with disabilities (the clients) and those without disabilities (the staff) so that eventually the original ideal of life-sharing was impossible to sustain. The only alternatives were to abandon this ideal or allow individuals with disabilities to go without desperately needed funds. Numerous stories of program-oriented state regulations and their effects on the lives of individuals with disabilities can be found in Condeluci (1991) and Schwartz (1992), two key books reflecting a supports paradigm orientation.

Not all legislation is program oriented. As mentioned before, the PASS program is supports oriented. The Americans with Disabilities Act (ADA) of 1990 (PL 101-336) is also clearly supports oriented in its assertion that individuals with disabilities represent a discriminated-against minority and that reasonable accommodation is needed to ensure these people's civil rights to participate in the same environments and activities as other Americans. The ADA, however, provides no funds, nor does it directly regulate any services.

Professional Development and Roles

Some support needs of individuals with disabilities are complex and specialized. These needs must be met by or in collaboration with professionals with the requisite knowledge and skill. Each profession brings to the table its own point of view and its own history and values, and each has its particular bit of turf to defend. Most professionals today are steeped in the programs paradigm and the training and development of those professionals perpetuates that paradigm.

Speech-language therapists find language pathology in people who pronounce words in atypical ways, occupational therapists look at people from the perspective of the physical functioning they know how to treat, and so forth. Each profession looks through its own lens and the needs of people the professionals come into contact with are defined in the terms familiar to the profession.

One professional spoke up at a meeting to disagree with a proposal, saying, "I am very concerned about the impact of this on the EI population." This sort of concern is a double-edged sword. What is an "EI population"? Why not say, "I am concerned about the impact of this on young children?" The difference is slight but the cumulative effect of such differences is enormous. The *early intervention (EI) population* is a concept created by federal law that refers to people who became the targets of intervention, that is, participants in disability programs, as young children. The group includes both people with disabilities and others considered at risk. To some well-trained professionals, an artificially created population such as this attains a special ontological status: the EI population is more real to them than are actual young children.

All professions define reality from a particular viewpoint, and their definitions are accorded a certain social status and influence. The professions with the highest status within society exert the greatest influence. For example, in an employment demonstration project for individuals with mental illness, employment specialists begin their discussions of how various individuals are doing in their jobs or job searches similar to this: "Mr. So-and-so is a Caucasian male in his late 30s. He presents as a slow, withdrawn individual." These employment specialists are emulating the case presentation format popular in the field of medicine—specifically, psychiatry. Psychiatrists have the highest status and are the highest paid individuals in the field of mental illness, so their language, concepts, and values are the most widely emulated in services to people with psychiatric disabilities. Ordinarily, people don't speak of a person as "presenting," but within the medical culture, the term is widely used.

New recruits into professions such as psychiatry, social work, special education, physical therapy, and rehabilitation counseling are systematically and deliberately socialized into the norms, language, history, and values of their profession through a series of professional development experiences. A central experience is the field placement or internship. Student internship field sites by and large consist of programs. Interns are rewarded for learning to function within the programs paradigm as they become more and more socialized into their particular profession. The power of this socialization process in replicating staff members who share the same basic viewpoint, that is, the same conceptual paradigm, as their teachers and mentors cannot be overstated.

IMPLICATIONS FOR SYSTEMS CHANGE

In a relatively short span of time, the disability field has witnessed two dramatic changes, first from a facilities orientation to a programs orientation, and then from a programs to a supports orientation. Conceptual change, however, has not always filtered down to the level of service provision, and much more must be done before the expansive vision of community inclusion and self-determination embodied in the supports paradigm can be achieved. On the basis of this chapter's analysis of paradigms and paradigm shifts, some implications can be drawn for the process of changing the services that affect the daily lives of individuals with disabilities.

Approaching Change as a Largely Nonrational Process

If the field of forces analysis of organizational change (Kettner et al., 1985) is on the right track, one can expect that any proposal for change within an organization will meet some degree of resistance. Some of this resistance will have little to do with the content of the change being advocated. Variables such as staff members' fears about the future of their jobs and the inertia of established organizational cultures will offer resistance no matter what change is in question. Also, if, as has been argued, the notion of a paradigm shift is applicable to the field of disability policy, one can expect that those advocating change and those resisting change will be approaching the situation from vastly different conceptual paradigms, using different terms, looking at the world differently, and largely arguing past one another.

This has two implications. First, change can only succeed if it is at least in part driven from within the organization by internal change agents or champions of a new idea or new practice. Change efforts in which external change agents act as allies of, consultants to, and critical friends of internal change agents have the best chance of success. Thus, it is common to hear consultants say, "We can make a good organization into a better one, but we can't make a bad organization into a good one." Some impetus for change and potential for doing things differently within the organization must link to outside assistance for that assistance to have any impact.

Second, change is unlikely to be a simple matter of convincing those with certain ideas of the superiority of some new idea so that those individuals then start acting differently. One can expect that such simple situations will be the rare exception. Yet, a great deal of activity called *systems change* in the disability field assumes this simplistic model of change. That is, the change effort consists of content-oriented training and technical assistance focusing on imparting knowledge and skills to disability services providers and program managers in the hope that change will come about as these staff members begin to apply their new knowledge and use their new skills.

Such content-focused interventions will always fall short because paradigm change is not a rational process. The problem is not one of missing information or skills, but one of approaching a situation in an entirely different way. Despite its name, most effective technical assistance is not very technical. Hagner and Murphy (1989) interviewed staff who had played a central role in the change of several organizations from sheltered workshops (following the facilities paradigm) to supported employment (following the programs paradigm). These staff members often reported that outside consultation was an important element in shaping change but that its value rarely lay in the provision of specific technical know-how or information. Rather, an outside perspective had value as a source of emotional support to change agents as a way of reconnecting them to the ideals and values that motivated their work and as a source of legitimacy from an expert source, to bolster the change agents' case. One might call these outside people *paradigm shift mentors*.

As an alternative to content-focused assistance, the process consultation models developed by Edgar Schein (1988) are likely to have greater systems change impact. Process consultation focuses not on imparting any particular strategies or information—most organizations have the internal resources to seek out whatever new information or know-how might be needed once the organization has made up its mind about what it wants to accomplish—but rather focuses on development of the capacity of the organization to renew itself and adapt to changing circumstances. Gundry et al. (1993) investigated the characteristics of what they referred to as a "creative organization." As mentioned previously, the internal environment of such an organization is characterized by challenge, freedom, dynamism, trust, allowance for idea time, playfulness and humor, acceptance of healthy conflict and debate, employee support, and risk taking. Organizations with these characteristics are able to change as the circumstances surrounding the organization change.

Nevis, DiBella, and Gould (1996) isolated 10 factors that they believe facilitate organizational learning, and these factors can form the basis for process consultation strategies. These include 1) a "scanning imperative" to keep aware of the environment in which the organization functions; 2) a willingness to look honestly at gaps between targeted outcomes and actual performance; 3) a concern for accurate measurement; 4) a valuing of experimentation; 5) a climate of openness; 6) a commitment to continual staff development; 7) operational variety; 8) multiple advocates, or champions, of change ideas; 9) hands-on, involved leadership; and 10) a broad systems perspective. When technical assistance is replaced by process consultation aimed at making an organization stronger based on these 10 factors, organizations find themselves in a better position to be aware of paradigm shifts and to change along with evolving paradigms.

The Development of New Organizations

The supports paradigm is a radical challenge to the way disability organizations do business. These organizations were founded and grew successful within a different context, and they operate within a tangle of interorganizational and funding relationships that make change difficult. Thus, people seeking services that respect their individuality and truly help facilitate community connections often cannot find in a community even the beginnings of a different attitude, a questioning of current practice, or the tiniest seed of change to nurture in the organizations available to them.

In this situation, creating a new organization from scratch is often the most effective strategy. This is exactly how the pioneers of institutions, sheltered workshops, and special schools for people with disabilities went about implementing the facilities paradigm. Creation of an organization without programs baggage has been a part of many change efforts that follow a supports orientation (see Chapter 8). For the same reason, advocates of substantial educational restructuring have been drawn toward the idea of establishing new charter schools. Systems change efforts aimed at implementing the supports paradigm can be expected to include the provision of start-up assistance for new types of support organizations.

Changes in Service Funding

Third parties, not consumers themselves, generally pay for disability services. This means that individuals with disabilities are consumers in a different sense than are consumers who purchase most other goods and services. In fact, some individuals with disabilities object to the term *consumer* because it masks a lack of control in the guise of a benign and empowering term. An individual with a psychiatric disability introduced as a consumer at a meeting several years ago stood up and said, "I am not consuming anything. I am being consumed."

Existing funding practices and the regulations imposed by those providing funds are inextricably tied to the programs paradigm. A true paradigm shift must change the way services and supports are paid for. Hagner and Marrone (1995) have advocated tying all service funding to the achievement of individual goals, set independently of service provider input. One contracts with a realtor *after* deciding to sell one's home; one doesn't invite the realtor to a family meeting in which buying a bigger house or building an addition is discussed. An individual might approach service providers for information, but he or she doesn't give them a vote in his or her own life decisions. Those with whom one deals as a service provider are seldom (and only accidentally) members of a network of trusted support people. And one wisely assumes that if one brought them in on the decision, they would have an interest in steering the decision in a way that would benefit them.

One can expect effective change to include fairly significant transformation in service funding patterns and policies. For example, voucher systems have been proposed as a mechanism for allowing funds to follow individuals, not services (Bertsch, 1992). Under this approach, an individual authorizes payment to the people or organization(s) whom he or she believes can provide needed services. Specialized disability services, generic community services, and also informal or nonprofessional services alike can be selected. Another form of voucher system allocates some or all funds directly to individuals on a cash basis to achieve outcomes that have been identified.

When funding is tied to the implementation of individual plans, consumers do not fill slots in a system of prearranged services. When a good or service is not available, a request for proposals or a help-wanted ad is developed, social networks are canvassed, and the good or service is *made* available. Some service systems are experimenting with a mechanism known as *service brokerage* (The Roeher Institute, 1994) to assist individuals in selecting and contracting with service providers and maintaining accountability of funds.

Change Outside the Disability Service System

For communities to effectively include all of their members and turn diversity into an asset instead of a problem, those communities themselves have to change. Change cannot be restricted solely to that which might occur within the system of disability services. Disability services are inextricably linked with the way society as a whole views and responds to disability. Efforts must be broadened in two directions.

Gravitating Toward Universal Design   First, community environments and organizations can be assisted to think in terms of universal design. Often the same changes that benefit individuals with disabilities benefit others. People who have small children or who are carrying packages, as well as those who use wheelchairs, welcome the installation of electric door openers. People pushing strollers benefit from curb cuts. A company that learns how to meet the support needs of its employees with disabilities becomes a better place for all employees to work. A classroom organized for cooperative learning can both better include a child with an emotional disability and lead to improved school performance for all children. Assisting organizations outside of the disability world builds community competence and unity and creates allies to further the process of change.

Thus, one can expect those who take school inclusion seriously to identify with broader school restructuring efforts (Kugelmass, 1997), expect people serious about support to families of children with disabilities to unite with efforts to support all families, expect people serious about housing for individuals with disabilities to find much in common with those seeking to make housing more affordable to people in general, and so forth.

In the past, Newt's parents and Trent's parents felt that they could not safely keep these individuals in their homes. The supports to do so were simply not available. Today, some workplace cultures cannot, in fact, accommodate much diversity. This is not just bad news for people with disabilities; this is bad news for all of us. Change must ultimately include changes in the way all of us, at all levels of social organization, support families, employees, and one another.

Using Personal Relationships   One lives one's life in the context of relationships with others. In training sessions, I often ask how many individuals in the audience have an address book—a written record of names, addresses, and telephone numbers of their friends and relatives. Invariably, every hand goes up. The names recorded in this way are part of one's social network, supports, and connections to the community. (My great-aunt had no formal education and was illiterate, but she kept a list of telephone numbers important to her taped to the wall by her telephone. The list had no names, just numbers. She knew who went with each number by its position on the list.) People respond to personal appeals from those whom they trust, and systems changes can consist of a critical mass of many personal changes, each of which is the result of a trusting relationship. Thus, one can expect teachers, employers, mortgage lenders, and all other members of the community to take initial steps toward including individuals with disabilities based on a personal connection and personal appeal from someone they trust. Schwartz (1992) has called this function "going a-calling."

From within the supports paradigm, it is obvious that facilitating personal ties between individuals with disabilities and others in the community is part of any service mission and any staff member's job. In practice, though, implementation of this paradigm is a rarity. I usually ask audiences at training sessions and presentations to estimate how many of 108 participants with disabilities in a statewide natural supports demonstration project they believe would have had an address book at the start of the project. The audience is pretty sure that the number is small or I wouldn't be asking, but few people guess the correct number: zero. Trent has an address book. Newt doesn't.

To build personal connections and to enlist community members in doing a better job of inclusion, change advocates must begin with their own personal social networks. There is no real alternative. A study of examples of good co-worker support (Hagner, Cotton, Goodall, & Nisbet, 1993) found that in most cases some personal connection existed between the employee or the employment staff and someone at the jobsite. One can expect to find the same process of personal networking behind good examples of inclusion in other domains as well.

CONCLUSIONS

In analyzing some of the difficulties in shifting to a supports paradigm in the approach to disability, one should not underestimate what has been accomplished in a relatively short span of time (see Chapter 5). I do not expect to hear, "Don't they have places for these people?" again, and the combined efforts of many people over many years has brought about that fairly significant change—the physical presence of people with disabilities—in our culture. That most of these individuals are surrounded by programs speaks to the need for further change efforts. That ordinary community members seem willing to adopt a support approach rather easily, whereas service providers and administrators struggle with it, ought not to be taken as some sort of indictment. It is inevitable that people who are deliberately and systematically trained to see the world through a certain mind-set and who are constantly rewarded for doing so have a degree of unlearning to do that other people cannot imagine. Conceptual paradigms penetrate deeply into the way individuals think and act.

In paradigm shifts, outmaneuvering and outlasting resistance is part of the game. One can expect that adherents of the programs paradigm will continue to exert influence for many decades. One may be stuck with vestiges of the approach even longer. But as has been the case time and time again across many fields of endeavor, if enough people work at systems change hard enough, with a clear enough vision, and keep at it long enough, the supports paradigm will one day be "the way things are."

REFERENCES

Americans with Disabilities Act (ADA) of 1990, PL 101-336, 42 U.S.C. §§ 12101 *et seq.*

Anderson, L., Lakin, K.C., & Prouty, B. (1997). Trends and milestones: Medicaid long-term care recipients grew by 37%, costs by 25% in 3 years. *Mental Retardation, 35,* 147–148.

Berres, M., Ferguson, D., Knoblock, P., & Woods, C. (Eds.). (1997). *Creating tomorrow's schools today: Stories of inclusion, change and renewal.* New York: Teachers College Press.

Bertsch, E. (1992). A voucher system that enables persons with severe mental illness to purchase community support services. *Hospital and Community Psychiatry, 43,* 1109–1113.

Bradley, V., & Knoll, J. (1995). Shifting paradigms in services to people with disabilities. In O. Karan & S. Greenspan (Eds.), *Community rehabilitation services for people with disabilities* (pp. 5–19). Boston: Butterworth-Heinemann.

Brooke, V., Wehman, P., Inge, K., & Parent, W. (1995). Toward a customer-driven approach of supported employment. *Education and Training in Mental Retardation and Developmental Disabilities, 34,* 309–319.

Butterworth, J., Hagner, D., Kiernan, W., & Schalock, R. (1996). Natural supports in the workplace: Defining an agenda for research and practice. *Journal of the Association for Persons with Severe Handicaps, 21,* 103–113.

Condeluci, A. (1991). *Interdependence: The route to community.* Delray Beach, FL: St. Lucie Press.

Crissey, M., & Rosen, M. (1986). *Institutions for the retarded.* Austin, TX: PRO-ED.

Deal, T., & Kennedy, A. (1982). *Corporate cultures.* Reading, MA: Addison Wesley Longman.

Education for All Handicapped Children Act of 1975, PL 94-142, 20 U.S.C. §§1400 *et seq.*

Feyerabend, P. (1978) *Against method.* New York: Schocken.

Franks, V., & Franks, C. (1962). Classical conditioning procedures as an index of vocational adjustment among mental defectives. *Perceptual and Motor Skills, 14,* 214–242.

Greenspan, S.I., & Schoultz, B. (1981). Why mentally retarded adults lose their jobs: Social competence as a factor in work adjustment. *Applied Research in Mental Retardation, 2,* 23–38.

Gundry, L., Kickul, J., & Prather, C. (1993). Building the creative organization. *Organizational Dynamics, 22*(4), 22–35.

Hagner, D., Butterworth, J., & Keith, G. (1995). Strategies and barriers in facilitating natural supports for employment of adults with severe disabilities. *Journal of the Association for Persons with Severe Handicaps, 20,* 110–120.

Hagner, D.C., Cotton, P., Goodall, S., & Nisbet, J. (1993). The perspectives of supportive coworkers: Nothing special. In J. Nisbet (Ed.), *Natural supports in school, at work, and in the community for people with severe disabilities* (pp. 241–256). Baltimore: Paul H. Brookes Publishing Co.

Hagner, D., Helm, D., & Butterworth, J. (1996). "This is your meeting": A qualitative study of person-centered planning. *Mental Retardation, 34,* 159–171.

Hagner, D., & Marrone, J. (1995). Empowerment issues in services to individuals with disabilities. *Journal of Disability Policy Studies, 6,* 18–36.

Hagner, D., & Murphy, S. (1989). Closing the shop on sheltered work. *Journal of Rehabilitation, 55,* 68–74.

Hasenfeld, Y. (1983). *Human service organizations.* Upper Saddle River, NJ: Prentice-Hall.

Jenkins, J., Pious, C., & Jewell, M. (1990). Special education and the regular education initiative: Basic assumptions. *Exceptional Children, 56,* 479–491.

Karan, O.C., & Knight, C.B. (1986). Developing support networks for individuals who fail to achieve competitive employment. In F.R. Rusch (Ed.), *Competitive employment issues and strategies* (pp. 241–255). Baltimore: Paul H. Brookes Publishing Co.

Kettner, P., Daley, J., & Nichols, A. (1985). *Initiating change in organizations and communities: A macro-practice model.* Pacific Grove, CA: Brooks/Cole.

Klein, J., & Black, M. (1995). *Extending the American dream: Homeownership for people with disabilities.* Durham: University of New Hampshire, Institute on Disability.

Kugelmass, J. (1997). Reconstructing curriculum for systemic inclusion. In M. Berres, D. Ferguson, P. Knoblock, & C. Woods (Eds.), *Creating tomorrow's schools today: Stories of inclusion, change and renewal* (pp. 38–65). New York: Teachers College Press.

Kuhn, T. (1970). *The structure of scientific revolutions* (2nd ed.). Chicago: University of Chicago Press.

Leake, D., James, R., & Stodden, R. (1995). Shifting paradigms to natural supports: A practical response to a crisis. In O. Karan & S. Greenspan (Eds.), *Community rehabilitation services for people with disabilities* (pp. 20–37). Boston: Butterworth-Heinemann.

Lipsky, D. (Ed.). (1994, Spring). National survey on inclusive education [Special issue]. *National Center on Educational Restructuring and Inclusion Bulletin.*

McGauhey, M., Kiernan, W., McNally, L., Gilmore, S., & Keith, G. (1995). Beyond the workshop: Integrated and segregated day and employment services. *Journal of the Association for Persons with Severe Handicaps, 20,* 270–285.

Munford, R. (1994). The politics of care-giving. In M. Rioux & M. Bach (Eds.), *Disability is not measles: New research paradigms in disability* (pp. 265–284). North York, Ontario, Canada: The Rocher Institute.

Nevis, E., DiBella, A. & Gould, J. (1996). *Understanding organizations as learning systems.* Cambridge: Massachusetts Institute of Technology, Organizational Learning Center.

O'Brien, J. (1987). A guide to life-style planning: Using *The activities catalog* to integrate services and natural support systems. In B. Wilcox & G.T. Bellamy (Eds.), *A comprehensive guide to* The activities catalog (pp. 175–191). Baltimore: Paul H. Brookes Publishing Co.

Radford, J. (1994). Intellectual disability and the heritage of modernity. In. M. Rioux & M. Bach (Eds.), *Disability is not measles: New research paradigms in disability* (pp. 9–28). North York, Ontario, Canada: The Roeher Institute.

Rehabilitation Act Amendments of 1992, PL 102-569, 29 U.S.C. §§ 701 *et seq.*

Schein, E. (1988). *Process consultation.* Reading, MA: Addison Wesley Longman.

Schein, E. (1993). How can organizations learn faster? *Sloan Management Review, 34,* 85–92.

Schwartz, D. (1992). *Crossing the river: Creating a conceptual revolution in disability and community.* Cambridge, MA: Brookline Books.

Silliker, A. (1993). The role of social contacts in the successful job search. *Journal of Employment Counseling, 30,* 25–34.

Smull, M.W., & Bellamy, G.T. (1991). Community services for adults with disabilities: Policy changes in the emerging support paradigm. In L.H. Meyer, C.A. Peck, & L. Brown (Eds.), *Critical issues in the lives of people with severe disabilities* (pp. 527–536). Baltimore: Paul H. Brookes Publishing Co.

Stockholder, F. (1994). Naming and renaming persons with intellectual disabilities. In M. Rioux & M. Bach (Eds.), *Disability is not measles: New research paradigms in disability* (pp. 153–180). North York, Ontario, Canada: The Roeher Institute.

Test, D., & Wood, W. (1996). Natural supports: The jury is still out. *Journal of The Association for Persons with Severe Handicaps, 21,* 155–173.

Thagard, P. (1992). *Conceptual revolutions.* Princeton, NJ: Princeton University Press.

The Roeher Institute. (1994). *Service brokerage: Individual empowerment and social service accountability.* North York, Ontario, Canada: Author.

Trach, J., & Mayhall, C. (1997). Analysis of the types of natural supports utilized during job placement and development. *Journal of Rehabilitation, 63*(2), 43–47.

Villa, R.A., & Thousand, J.S. (2000). *Restructuring for caring and effective education: Piecing the puzzle together* (2nd ed.). Baltimore: Paul H. Brookes Publishing Co.

3

Catching the Wind, Changing the Rules

Enhancing Community Options for
Families of Young Children

Debra Nelson, Leigh R. Zoellick, and Ann Dillon

"Mainstreaming is trying to get children with disabilities into the game to compete. Inclusion changes the rules so all kids belong."
—*Norman Kunc (1998)*

March: Anticipation and Anxiety

The deflated party balloons hanging limply from the chandelier were a sign of a birthday come and gone. As she waited for the early intervention (EI) people to arrive, Karen Martin thought about the changes in her life since Lucy's joyous birth 2 years ago. There were so many smiles, coos, and milestones in the first year and a half. But around 18 months of age, Lucy slowly stopped talking, the smiles drifted away, and she became lost to her parents. Karen and her husband Rich began a desperate search for answers that finally ended with Lucy's being diagnosed

Community Options in Early Care and Education, discussed in this chapter, was a project of the University of New Hampshire Institute on Disability/University Affiliated Program, funded from 1994 to 1999 by the U.S. Department of Education Early Education Program for Children with Disabilities Program Grant No. H024B40014.

with pervasive developmental disorder (PDD). Today Donna, the EI speech-language therapist, and Charlene, the family support coordinator, were coming to meet Karen and her family and begin the process of helping them get the supports and services they need.

In communities throughout the country, the winds of change have been unleashed. There is an energy stirring within homes and libraries, in child care centers and community preschools, and in public swimming pools and neighborhood playgrounds. The message, once faint and unclear, is growing louder: *ALL CHILDREN BELONG!* It is a message of progressive change, a growth in spirit as well as practice, a shift from tentative trials to firm commitment.

This chapter explores the power of local communities to create quality inclusive early care and education programs and activities for all young children and their families. Through the eyes of one family and the story of a collaborative early childhood team, the chapter presents the issues, struggles, and ultimate successes in the journey to promote belonging for all young children. The chapter is based on the actual experiences of a statewide demonstration project in New Hampshire called Community Options in Early Care and Education. In addition, this chapter reflects the following guiding principles:

- All children and families belong in communities.
- Supports and services must be only as special as necessary.
- Children with disabilities and families must be supported with a family-centered approach and a "whatever it takes" attitude on the part of providers.
- Solutions to problems in a given community lie with the people who live and work in that community, and the role of outsiders is to lend support to their efforts.

The next section of this chapter describes the signs of positive change in early care and education that have resulted from a convergence of forces in the legal, social, and educational realms during the 1990s. Signs of resistance to change are also presented, such as the continued segregation of young children in special education and other programs.

Through the story of the early childhood team, the third section of this chapter illustrates a process for creating change at the local level that benefits all young children. Five common roadblocks to change are described: 1) misinterpretations or disregard of disability law requirements by those making decisions about supports and services, 2) parental requests for special programs, 3) outmoded beliefs about models of service delivery, 4) availability and quality of early childhood programs and services, and 5) concerns about costs and lack of trained staff to support children in the community (Nelson, Zoellick, Nisbet, & Tracy, 1997; Smith & Rose, 1994). The fourth section of this chapter discusses factors that promote or hinder the efforts of local teams to facilitate change in their communities. The fifth section of this chapter speculates on the characteristics of inclusive communities, the contributions and roles of various community members, and the continued need for support so that communities can become more inclusive.

Throughout the course of the chapter, the story of Lucy's family progresses across a 12-month time span. It begins with the difficult decisions faced by the Martins and culminates with Lucy's participation in a community preschool program that proves successful for her and her family.

POSITIVE CHANGE AND PASSIVE RESISTANCE: A MIXED BAG IN OUR COMMUNITIES

April: Lucy's Family Learns About Options

Donna and Charlene, the two EI specialists, arrived at the Martins' door with wide, warm smiles, quickly putting Karen and Rich at ease. Although the two women came with forms and papers, their first priority was to hear all about Lucy and to listen to the Martins talk about their lives and needs. Karen described how Lucy gradually changed from a lively and contented toddler to a withdrawn and almost silent little girl. Once Lucy had been diagnosed with PDD, Karen said that she and her husband worried about how this new diagnosis would affect Lucy, her brother Eric, and the family as a whole. A specialist had told them that Lucy needed intensive training from special therapists and had prescribed a specific program of 40 hours of intervention per week. Karen, Rich, and Lucy's pediatrician, however, were eager to explore other options and opinions before making a decision.

Rich explained that Lucy had been attending a neighborhood child care program 3 days per week since the age of 12 months. The Rainbow Child Care Center seemed like such a nurturing place for Lucy, but ever since the diagnosis had been made, the teachers had been worried about their ability to meet her needs. They wondered whether Lucy needed a special program with people who were trained to work with her to continue to grow and learn.

As they listened, Donna and Charlene learned much about this family. They understood the delicate balance between listening to parents' concerns and hopes and offering suggestions, guidance, and information that are helpful without being overwhelming. Charlene waited until Karen and Rich grew quiet. She then described the Parent-to-Parent net-

work, a national family support program that connects families to one another to share information and experiences, and told Rich and Karen about a family of a 4-year-old with PDD who lived in the next town. Charlene explained that some families had found it helpful to talk with another family with similar experiences as they began the task of choosing supports and services. The Martins accepted the family's telephone number but indicated that they'd like to think it over. Knowing that making the first call may be difficult for some parents, Charlene added, "If you decide that you'd like to talk with this family, you can either call them yourselves or we can ask them to call you, whichever you prefer."

Next, Donna addressed the family's request for more information. She offered to send them some recent articles on PDD that other families had found helpful. She told them about a parent support group meeting to be held at the library the next week and encouraged them to attend. The topic would be "Dreaming About the Future for Your Child." The meeting would provide Karen and Rich with a chance to meet other parents, hear about some community programs, and learn about some strategies that parents can use to form a long-term vision for their child's future. Donna explained how having a dream for the future can guide decisions about programs and services today. She also gently acknowledged, "Sometimes it's hard to take the next step when you don't have a direction. This group might help you determine your priorities for Lucy's future."

The remainder of this first visit was spent discussing the array of options that were available to the Martins, including those that have worked for families in similar situations. Although the information was a great amount to digest, Karen and Rich were grateful to have choices. They also appreciated that EI staff would assist them through the confusing process of making decisions when faced with numerous possibilities and conflicting information from various specialists. Given their busy schedules and long list of concerns, Karen and Rich were happy to learn that EI supports and services would be flexible and geared toward making things work for their whole family, not just Lucy.

With all of the options on the table, Donna led a discussion of choices, describing what some families had chosen to do as well as new ideas on how to customize services to meet the Martins' needs. As they talked, Rich and Karen felt that an outline of a plan was finally emerging after several months of chaos. Donna asked if she could visit the Rainbow Child Care Center with Rich or Karen to talk with the staff and to see Lucy with her friends. As the visit drew to a close and everyone had agreed on the next steps, Donna took out the paperwork to enroll the Martin family in the EI program. Karen looked at her calendar and found the best date for a visit to Rainbow.

Signs of Progress

"Let's bring services to kids, not kids to services as we do now."
—Tom Hehir (1996), professor of education at Howard
University and former U.S. Department of
Education Special Education Director

A strong climate for inclusive communities emerged in the United States during the end of the 20th century. Families, providers, local school boards, legislators, and national leaders all have joined forces with a common goal: to support young children with disabilities to participate in community life. These efforts have indeed stirred the winds of change in a number of realms:

- *Philosophy:* There has been a philosophical shift from partial participation of some children (i.e., mainstreaming) to full participation for all children (i.e., inclusion) (Early Care and Education Committee, 1993b).
- *Policy:* More local, state, and federal leaders are taking a stand for inclusion and inserting natural environments into both legislative regulations and quality indicators for programs (Hehir, 1996). With the following compelling words of advice, Marsha Forest (1997) turned the debate about inclusion upside-down. She advocated, "Do not defend inclusion. Make others justify segregation" (p. 15).
- *Legislation:* The responsibility to promote belonging once rested solely with parents and advocates. School districts and other programs now are required to demonstrate that children with disabilities cannot benefit from participating with their peers prior to removing them from typical environments (Rogers, 1993).
- *Practice:* More than one half (51.6%) of children ages 3–5 with disabilities attended typical preschool classes during the 1995–1996 school year, compared with less than one quarter (23.8%) during 1992–1993 (U.S. Department of Education, 1998).
- *Vision:* More parents are dreaming of a positive future for their children (Schuh et al., 1996), which begins with participation in community programs and activities right from the start.

The ways in which early care and education providers are educated to work in the field also are changing. Rather than have separate courses on disability, separate certifications, and separate training programs, some personnel preparation and in-service training programs are beginning to infuse information on disabilities into the general education curriculum. In New Hampshire, for example, medical students and others in disciplines related to young children and their families (e.g., education, social work, nursing, physical therapy, speech-language therapy, occupational therapy, nutrition counseling) have opportunities to engage in family support activities, such as respite care, as part of their coursework. Similarly, the New Hampshire Red Cross offers information on caring for children and adults with disabilities within the context of its caregiving courses. Finally, more specialists throughout the country are receiving training in the collaborative consultation model (Hanft & Place, 1996). In this model, a primary role of specialists is to consult and collaborate with typical providers and families to meet the needs of children. These changes reflect a shift in models of service delivery from one in which supports and services were primarily "special" to one in which they are primarily typical (Tashie et al., 1996).

Signs of Resistance

Despite these heartening indicators of progress, much work remains to be done. Too many young children with disabilities, particularly those with severe disabilities, remain segregated in special programs or are excluded from early childhood programs in their community. In a national survey on preschool inclusion, Wolery et al. (1993) found that less than half of the kindergarten programs (49.8%) and only 42.7% of Head Start programs surveyed had at least one child with disabilities enrolled during the 1989–1990 school year. Statistics for prekindergarten programs and community programs were even worse: Less than one third included at least one child with disabilities, and fewer than 15% enrolled young children with more severe disabilities, including mental retardation, visual or hearing impairments, or autism.

It is difficult to understand why young children with disabilities and their families continue to be isolated, segregated, and excluded despite powerful evidence on the many benefits of inclusion and the lack of evidence that segregated programs produce better outcomes (see, e.g., Bricker, 1995; Guralnick, 1997; Mallory, 1997; Rogers, 1993). Particularly disturbing is the fact that some professionals and leaders continue to justify the removal of young children from typical environments based either on numerous faulty rationales or on barriers that may be overcome with diligence and creativity. The next section of this chapter explores five common roadblocks to inclusive communities.

Lucy's story illustrates how an individualized family support plan (IFSP)[1] was created with the family. The IFSP team, which consisted of EI providers,

---

[1]The individualized family support plan (IFSP) is included in Part C of the Individuals with Disabilities Education Act (IDEA) Amendments of 1997 (PL 105-17), which guides supports and services to young children age birth to 3 years old who have disabilities and their families. Although the regulations use the term *individualized family service plan*, New Hampshire chooses to use the term *individualized family support plan*, which reflects the state's philosophy of family-centered supports.

child care staff, and family members, worked together to develop a plan that included supports and services at home and in the community. In creating this plan, the team had to sort through the conflicting recommendations from specialists (i.e., 40 hours per week of intensive therapy from therapists versus supports and therapy within a typical preschool) and to overcome the fears, attitudes, and concerns of several key players.

PROMOTING BELONGING FOR
YOUNG CHILDREN: WHAT'S SO DIFFICULT?

May: Creating an Individualized Family Support Plan

After the meeting with the EI staff, Karen spoke on the telephone with two families whose children had PDD. From their stories, she gained a few tips on supporting Lucy's development, working with professionals, and taking care of herself during stressful times. She found it comforting to talk with other parents about her deepest fears and to learn that other families had survived the initial trauma of coping with a disability. For Karen and Rich, hearing that other children with diagnoses similar to Lucy's were thriving in preschool and kindergarten with support was almost like peering into a crystal ball. For the first time since the diagnosis, Karen began to feel hope that their lives might resume some sense of normalcy.

Karen also visited the Rainbow Center with Donna, where they talked to the toddler room teacher and watched Lucy play. Finally, an EI assessment team came to the Martins' house to play with Lucy during a quiet time and learn all they could about her. Included on the team were Donna, a speech-language therapist; Charlene, a family support coordinator; and a physical therapist. They were able to see Lucy in a comfortable environment among her own toys and belongings and watch her interact with her brother and parents.

The EI team and family met again to determine the goals and strategies to incorporate into the IFSP. They first talked about all of Lucy's strengths, agreeing that her strongest abilities were in visual and fine motor tasks, like completing simple puzzles. Her primary needs were in communication and socialization, such as talking and playing with friends. Because Lucy spent about half of her days at the Rainbow Center, it made sense to support the staff there as well as to work with the family at home. Donna became the primary service coordinator for Lucy's family. She spent about 2 hours each week at Rainbow observing Lucy, conducting group activities, observing the assistant who worked in the room, and consulting with the teacher and center director on how to encourage Lucy's communication throughout the day. Goals for Lucy included playing next to another child for at least 5 minutes, taking turns with a friend (e.g., on the swings, at the water table, with a toy), and indicating what snack she wanted when given two choices. Donna and Lucy's parents also created a plan to enhance Lucy's communication at home. Rich added that he would like to take Lucy to the grocery store without worrying about her screaming.

After visiting preschools and talking with other families of children who have PDD, the Martins decided that it would be helpful to work with a speech-language therapy assistant trained in strategies to support children with PDD. Under Donna's supervision, this assistant spent 10 hours per week on various activities, including meeting with the family, working with Lucy and her team (including Rainbow Center staff), and discovering strategies to help Lucy become more communicative, more involved in play, and better able to accept change. The assistant's calm, quiet approach incorporated sharing toys and talking with Lucy.

An occupational therapist spent 2 hours per week on sensory integration (SI)[2] techniques first with Lucy, her family, and the speech-language therapy assistant in Lucy's home and the community, then incorporating activities at the Rainbow Center with the rest of the toddler room children and staff. In addition, an energetic social work student volunteer named Dave was available to the family for 5 hours each week. He went to the Martins' home and played with Lucy, her brother Eric, and a child who lived next door, using activities that the therapist and specialists had designed, such as pushing a weighted stroller and climbing on a barrel made of inner tubes, so that Lucy could further benefit from SI techniques at home (Williamson & Anzalone, 1997). Eric enjoyed these games and often played them with Lucy when Dave was not around. Through his time with Lucy's family, Dave gained valuable knowledge about young children, PDD, and working with families while also earning college credit in an independent study course.

The IFSP for Lucy's family included approximately 19 hours per week of supports and services from EI staff and volunteers, according to the choices and needs of the Martins. Lucy continued to go to the Rainbow Center for child care 3 days per week, which her parents paid for just as they had been doing for Lucy all along and had done previously for her brother. The staff received consultation and support from the school district's therapists.

Though most of the IFSP goals were related to Lucy's needs, the Martins chose to add one for themselves. They requested help in identi-

---

[2]Sensory integration (SI) is "the complex process of organizing sensation from the body and the environment for use" (Williamson & Anzalone, 1997, p. 29). Children with SI difficulties may exhibit various problems, such as hyperreactivity (low sensory threshold) or hyporeactivity (high sensory threshold).

fying and training someone who could take care of Lucy and her brother a few Saturday evenings each month so that they could go to the movies. Taking time for themselves was one piece of advice from other parents that they planned to follow.

With the IFSP in place and the assurance that it was a changeable plan, Karen and Rich felt more confident about helping their daughter. The plan they developed was more in sync with their values and needs than was the rigid 40-hour per week program of therapy recommended by one specialist. The team set a date to meet again in 1 month to determine how well the supports and services were working for Lucy and her family, to make adjustments as necessary, and to talk about her journey to preschool.

Even though she was only 2 years old, Lucy's parents were eager to plan early for the time when they would stop receiving EI services. Therefore, Donna suggested that they might want to meet Sally, the preschool coordinator for the district. She invited Sally to a coffee chat where she could meet the Martins and some other parents of 2-year-olds receiving EI services.

Common Roadblocks and Alternate Paths to Inclusive Communities

Even within communities where people are highly motivated to promote inclusive early care and education, five stumbling blocks repeatedly have been identified: 1) misinterpretations or disregard of legal requirements for placement in the least restrictive environment and natural environments, 2) parental requests for special programs, 3) outmoded beliefs about models of service delivery, 4) availability and quality of early childhood programs and activities, and 5) concerns about costs and lack of trained staff (Nelson et al., 1997; Smith & Rose, 1994). Creative strategies have been used to overcome each of these roadblocks.

Roadblock #1: Misinterpretations or Disregard of Legal Requirements The Individuals with Disabilities Education Act (IDEA) Amendments of 1997 (PL 105-17), the most recent reauthorization of the Education for All Handicapped Children Act of 1975 (PL 94-142), has had a profound impact on the lives of children and young adults with disabilities, their families, and their communities. According to the Office of Special Education Programs (OSEP; 1997), "Prior to [PL 94-142's] implementation in 1975, approximately 1 million children with disabilities were shut out of schools and hundreds more were denied appropriate services." These students, benefiting from the provisions of the law (described in the following sections), have far exceeded expectations and have graduated from high school, enrolled in college, and participated in the work force in unprecedented numbers (OSEP, 1997).

Least Restrictive Environment The increasing number of children with disabilities receiving supports and services in typical environment along with their peers is due in part to the "least restrictive environment" (LRE) clause of IDEA 1997, which requires that

> To the maximum extent appropriate, children with disabilities, including children in public or private institutions or other care facilities, are educated with children who are not disabled, and special classes, separate schooling, or other removal of children with disabilities from the regular educational environment occurs only when the nature or the severity of the disability of a child is such that education in regular classes with the use of supplementary aids and services cannot be achieved satisfactorily. (Sec. 612[a][5])

According to Rogers, court decisions have supported the right of children with disabilities to participate in typical classrooms:

> In recent years, the federal courts have been interpreting these rules [IDEA and Section 504 of the Rehabilitation Act of 1973 (PL 93-112)] to require that children with very severe disabilities must be included in the classroom they would attend if not disabled even when they cannot do the academic work of the class if there is a potential social benefit, if the class would stimulate the child's linguistic development, or if the other students could provide appropriate role models for the student. (1993, p. 2)

Natural Environments for Infants and Toddlers Part C of IDEA 1997 (concerning infants and toddlers with disabilities) also contains an LRE requirement that services "to the maximum extent appropriate, are provided in natural environments, including the home and community settings in which children without disabilities participate" (Sec. 632[4][g]). Furthermore, the IFSP must contain "a statement of natural environments in which EI services will be provided, including a *justification of the extent, if any, to which services will not be provided in a natural environment*" (Sec. 636[d][5], emphasis added).

EI programs, school districts, and other organizations that provide special services for families of young children with disabilities sometimes misinterpret or disregard this legislation. They place young children in self-contained programs (programs only for children with disabilities or programs with disproportionately more children with disabilities than children without disabilities) with no previous attempt to offer support in typical environments and with little or no evidence that the children could not benefit from these typical environments. This practice of "start with special environments, move to general environments" violates children's civil rights and denies young children with and without disabilities opportunities to be with and learn from their peers.

A common barrier to the participation of infants and toddlers with disabilities in typical programs, services, and activities is the misinterpretation of the concept of *natural environments* (Sec. 632[4][g] of IDEA 1997). By definition, *natural environments* mean places in the community where a child or family would go if the child did not have a disability. These environments include home, neighborhood play groups with young friends, parks and playgrounds, child care homes and centers, the local pediatrician's office, and so forth. Sometimes, however, people believe that the term *natural environment* applies only to buildings. For example, some people might consider a play group offered only to toddlers with disabilities at the EI offices on Main Street to be a "natural environment" because the building is in the community. The building houses the practices of several local pediatricians, and families of children with and without disabilities bring their young children there. The EI program office itself, however, is not a place where children without disabilities and their families would go for a play group experience, and therefore, the Main Street EI office does not meet the natural environments standard.

Related to the concept of natural environments is the concept of *natural proportions,* which means that the percent of children with disabilities in any given program or activity does not exceed the percent that typically occurs in the community. In most communities, children with developmental disabilities represent approximately 10%–12% of individuals (Janko & Porter, 1997). To remain within the natural proportions guidelines, a preschool with an enrollment of 15 children, for example, would include no more than 1 or 2 children with disabilities.

Frequently, programs and activities offered in natural environments disregard the natural proportions guideline. In these instances, children with disabilities are clustered together such that they represent 20%–50% or more of the participating children. For example, a speech-language therapist may offer a play group for preschoolers at the town library (a natural environment) but enroll five children with speech delays and one child who is typically developing (80% of the children have disabilities). Or, an EI program may invite one or two children without disabilities to join an existing play group at the home of a family (a natural environment) in which six children with disabilities participate (not natural proportions). A better alternative would be an existing play group in each family's community in which staff could offer appropriate supports so that each child with a disability could participate. Where no play group readily exists, many programs have supported families to host them in their neighborhoods or to enroll their child in a child care or other community program for a portion of the day. A speech group at a town library can be an appropriate option for families if the ratios follow natural proportion guidelines.

A Program Is Not a Place   An EI or preschool special education program is a composite of supports and services that addresses a child's development and enables him or her to benefit from educational experiences. A program is not a place. Too often, EI or preschool special education providers look for one place that will meet all of a child's developmental needs. A child's preschool program should instead consist of several options, such as attending library story hour on Monday morning, a family child care home on Tuesday and Thursday, and swimming lessons at the town pool on Saturday afternoon. EI or preschool special education providers can help support the child, family, and staff in all of these environments, thus creating a complete program. It is the responsibility of specialists to work together with families and community providers so that young children with disabilities can gain access to typical places in the community.

The Confusion of Inclusion   The term *inclusion* is surrounded by confusion and controversy in the field of education. As applied to young children and their families, the term is no less confusing or controversial. In a preliminary report published by the Early Childhood Research Institute on Inclusion, Janko and Porter remarked,

> Inclusion is at most an implicit concept in state and federal special education law, and we have no widely agreed-upon definition of inclusion that is applied in all environments in which children with disabilities and those without disabilities come together. (1997, p. 7)

They contended that it is more difficult to define the concept clearly than it is to describe the characteristics of an inclusive environment, such as the following:

- No child is rejected because of a disability.
- Children with disabilities are represented in natural proportions (about 10%–12%).
- Children with disabilities are invited to and supported as they participate in typical early childhood activities.
- Children with disabilities have the opportunity to attend child care and schools in their own neighborhoods. (p. 7)

Confusion regarding the definition of *inclusion* frequently is manifested in practice. For example, some programs defined as inclusive are in actuality "reverse mainstream" programs. In a reverse mainstream program, children with disabilities comprise 20%–99% of the enrolled children and may be treated quite differently from the other children. Such programs may have an overabundance of staff and helpers, a paucity of typical early childhood experiences, and a heavy emphasis on therapy.

Still other programs that define themselves as inclusive allow students with disabilities to participate with other students only for brief periods of time. For instance, during one library's story hour, children with disabilities are invited to hear the story but then are asked to retreat to a separate room for an alternative craft project and snack. Children in a self-contained preschool may join those in a community program only for music and playground time.

Finally, there is tremendous disagreement among professionals as to whether all children can benefit from inclusion. As long as professionals are unwilling to begin with the premise that all children belong and take the action steps necessary to make that premise a reality, there will always be young children who are segregated from their peers. Inclusion will only be successful if children, families, and early child care and education providers are truly supported. Such support may involve people, materials, financial resources, training, or increased communication between providers and specialists. It may also involve public awareness activities, such as explaining federal regulations and the benefits of inclusion to early childhood educators, school boards, and superintendents or offering literature to the local media on depicting young children with disabilities first as children.

New Hampshire's Early Care and Education Committee adopted a broad definition of inclusion that embeds within it the principles of family-centered support and respect for cultural diversity:

> Inclusion indicates full participation in community life by young children with disabilities and their families, according to a family's cultural background and choices. Families of children with disabilities enjoy the same access to community services and places that all families enjoy. For example, support is available to families such that all children can attend their neighborhood school, receive health care at the local pediatrician's office, receive child care at the home of a neighbor, play at the local playground, pray at the families' chosen place of worship, and participate in story hour at the town library. (1993b, p. ii)

Roadblock #2: Parental Requests for Special Programs A second major roadblock to supporting young children and their families in natural environments is family requests for special programs. Families might make such a request for the following reasons: 1) advice of physicians, therapists, other professionals, or other parents; 2) belief that their child's developmental, health care, or social needs can only be addressed in special programs with specially trained professionals; 3) lack of awareness about viable alternatives; and 4) concern that their child would be ridiculed or excluded by children without disabilities within community programs or activities. For example, parents of a child with extensive needs such as PDD or multisensory impairment may have been told early on by a certain physician that their child's development can be facilitated only with 40 hours of therapy per week. On the basis of this recommendation and with their child's best interests at heart, these parents may request a self-contained preschool placement for their child before any discussion has taken place with the entire individualized education program (IEP) team.

Operating self-contained programs on the basis that "parents want them" creates a classic catch-22 situation for providers who promote inclusion. The mere presence of a special program as an option subtly communicates several incorrect messages to parents: that "special is better than typical," "more services are better than fewer," "professionals must think that such a program is necessary and preferred (or they wouldn't offer it)," and "we must work now to get children ready to belong later." Therefore, no matter how carefully choices are explained to families, the existence of a specialized program will undoubtedly influence some parents to select this option. An apt description for this paradox is the "if you offer it, they will come" dilemma.

Since the early 1990s, many providers have acknowledged the importance of offering family-centered supports and services. *Family-centered* means that providers respect the family's values, trust the family, work together, are flexible, relate to the family as people, look at the whole picture (child in context of family; family in context of community), recognize parents as the decision-makers, and are creative in resolving dilemmas in ways that are helpful to families (Edelman, 1991).

Some providers believe that in the interest of being family-centered, they must always comply with family requests for specialized programs. Although it is imperative that professionals adhere to the principles of family-centered support, they also have an obligation to provide families with the resources and information they need to make informed choices. Thus, being family-centered does not mean that professionals must refrain from offering different information or options that the family may not have considered. In these instances, professionals have an opportunity to work together with the family to find a solution that will meet the families' needs while adhering to the principles of family-centered support and promoting exemplary practices.

There are at least five courses of action that an EI program or school district can take that may lead to different choices by parents:

1. *Provide families with timely and relevant resources* to ensure that they have the information and guidance they need to reconcile conflicting advice from professionals and to make educated choices. Include information on personal futures planning (Mount & Zwernik, 1988) or other tools to assist families to keep sight of their dreams and goals for their children when making choices about programs and services.

2. *Work together with parents to create whatever supports are needed* for the child to successfully participate in early childhood activities and for parents to feel safe that their children's needs (e.g., social/emotional, health, educational, safety) will be addressed. This step may involve the professional's asking the question, "What else are you concerned about?" over and over until parents have exhausted their list of worries. It also may require the creation of back-up plans for scenarios that are most uncomfortable for families (e.g., "What happens if a child has a seizure and the teacher is out of the room?").

3. *Link parents with other families* whose children have successfully participated in community programs. Perhaps arrangements could be made for

parents to observe another child with disabilities similar to their own child's in a community program.

4. *Communicate to parents that services are flexible and changeable;* that is, "nothing is written in stone." Professionals may suggest a short trial for the community placement (e.g., 2 months, less if the parents request), after which the team will reconvene to determine how it is working and to make adjustments as necessary. During this trial period, one individual may be assigned as a readily accessible contact person who checks in with the family to answer questions and address concerns. A trial period for a program about which families feel uncertain enables many parents to take a risk that they might otherwise avoid if the commitment were long term.

5. *Determine who is giving families messages* such as "special is better than typical," "more is better than less," and "your child can't possibly succeed in a community program," and hold discussions with those individuals about exemplary practices.

It is critical that providers examine their own deep-seated beliefs about who belongs in typical early childhood programs. In subtle or not so subtle ways, a professional's beliefs may be conveyed to families and influence their choices. Every effort should be made to adopt exemplary practices, which include supporting all children within natural environments. As Lucy's story continues, it illustrates how the team has implemented several strategies to create a collaborative, supportive relationship with the Martins.

June: Revisiting the Individualized
Family Support Plan and Planning for Preschool

During the first month when Lucy's IFSP was implemented, Lucy responded well to the SI techniques, the speech-language therapy modifications to the toddler classroom, and the efforts of the entire team involved in her care and education. Rainbow staff felt more confident that their center was the right place for Lucy. The specific information on supporting children with PDD shared by Donna, the frequent visits by Donna and the other therapists, and the overlapping support between the center and home contributed to their feelings of confidence. The child care staff appreciated the opportunity to participate in a monthly lunch meeting attended by local preschool teachers. This group, when led both by the EI team and by school district personnel, offered time to share ideas, support one another, and enjoy lively discussions on topics of mutual interest.

In spite of Lucy's extensive developmental needs, her parents began to feel more relaxed about the program. Though somewhat unsure at first if they had made the right decision for Lucy, they were reassured by her steady progress and happy smiles. In the beginning, the family found it difficult to get used to all of the adults who were coming and going from their home and their lives. Donna had worked with these people to create a schedule for visits that was most convenient for the family. For example, the speech-language therapist shifted to offering support at the Rainbow Center instead of at home. Karen and Rich particularly appreciated how the EI team was always willing to address their priorities, regardless of the planned agenda, and how the team members had assimilated themselves respectfully and creatively into the life of the family.

Karen and Rich had an opportunity to meet Sally, the preschool coordinator for the school district, at a gathering for parents. The meeting, co-sponsored by the EI team and Parent-to-Parent, included child care for Lucy, Eric, and other children. Sally's reputation for fairness, working together with families, and caring about the individual needs of children was reassuring. Many parents were relieved to meet someone from the school district with whom they felt comfortable.

Roadblock #3: Outmoded Beliefs About Models of Service Delivery
The notions that "special is better than typical," "more is better than less," and "we must get children ready to belong" compose the third major stumbling block to supporting young children with disabilities in typical programs. These outmoded beliefs have little or no support in the research and field experience regarding early care and education.

Special Versus Typical   When parents learn their child is to be given a label of "special," as in special education, special health care, or special needs, it is natural for them to assume that their child now needs special attention. Although specialized supports and services are often necessary, this does not mean that a child's world must become dominated by specialized activities, nor that only people with special skills can make a difference in the child's life. Every effort must be made to ensure that families have access to what are termed *natural supports,* to community activities, and to typical opportunities.

Natural supports are the people, places, or things that exist already in a child's community. Friends, siblings, neighbors, grandparents and other extended family, pharmacists, bus drivers, and others in the community are readily available and valuable sources of assistance for families of young children with disabilities. A family's home, the neighbor's house, the town library, the school playground, a city recreation center, the local preschool, the neighborhood child care home, a local pediatrician's office, and the family's place of worship are places where other families of young children are likely to be found. Similarly, the backyard sandbox and swing set, the neighbor's swimming pool, toys found on the shelves of major toy stores, and computers may be evident in the lives of many families of young children. All of these people, places, and things are rich sources of natural supports that can promote growth and development. Therefore, two important guidelines for creating support plans for young children with disabilities and their families are 1) "look to ordinary first" and 2) choose supports that are "only as special as necessary."

Finally, for inclusive early care and education to succeed, three common practices must be avoided: 1) "plucking" children from community programs where they are successfully enrolled and placing them in special programs, 2) forcing children into split placements (e.g., community preschool in the morning and special education preschool in the afternoon), and 3) placing children into community programs with inadequate support. All of these practices can frustrate children, staff, and families and interfere with children's progress.

More Therapy or Less   The notion "more is better" is typically applied to therapies, in which additional hours or units of direct therapy are presumed to produce greater gains in development for children with disabilities. An example of this thinking is if three units of speech per week are good, then five units of speech and two of occupational therapy must be better.

Since the mid-1990s, parents, community providers, and specialists have begun to notice that 3 hours in a quality community preschool with appropriate support, for example, can benefit a child's speech and language development more than five units of pull-out therapy can. As any early childhood educator knows, the animated chatter of a group of 3-year-olds during snack and while sharing toys with friends throughout the day are strong motivators for communication. Similarly, physical and occupational therapy that occur throughout the day with friends at the water table, in the sandbox, or on the swings can produce better outcomes than 30 minutes in a corner with a therapist (Bruder, 1993; Dunst, 1998). If an occupational therapist and preschool teacher engage in collaborative consultation, many opportunities for a child to work on muscle coordination can be embedded in the typical routines that are so important to his or her individual education. Therefore, the answer to the question "Is more always better?" is "No." Taking advantage of daily routines and being open to ideas and collaborating to maximize a child's potential growth and development produce better outcomes for young children than simply adding more units of direct therapy (Bruder, 1993; Dunst, 1998).

Getting Ready to Belong   The assumption that children must be "ready to belong" (i.e., master skills before inclusion) is alarmingly prevalent in society. For example, some early childhood programs may require that a 3-year-old with cerebral palsy be able to use the toilet by him- or herself before being enrolled in preschool. This assumption has prevented countless children from gaining access to typical activities and is as unrealistic and inappropriate as telling a toddler not to take a few steps until he or she is able to walk across the room.

Norman Kunc, an internationally known speaker, family therapist, and educator who was born with cerebral palsy, challenged the traditional special education paradigm that children must first acquire skills before they can learn, grow, and play alongside their peers. Not only is this paradigm *backward,* according to Kunc (2000), but it also has failed to demonstrate the anticipated progress for learners with severe disabilities. A new paradigm must be adopted based on the assumptions that belonging *precedes* skills. Kunc asserts that a child's desire to belong "provides him or her with the motivation to learn new skills, a motivation that is noticeably absent in segregated classrooms" (p. 80). He recommended that programs first ensure that all children belong; then make accommodations as needed; and finally, work on skill development.

A considerable body of research counters the notions that special is better, that more is better and that children must be prepared to belong. Children with disabilities who participate in typical early childhood programs 1) demonstrate more complex social play and more appropriate social interactions, 2) initiate interactions with their peers more frequently than children in self-contained special education preschool programs (Lamorey & Bricker, 1993), and 3) demonstrate an accelerated rate of development (Bruder, 1993). In short, "Young children learn best when they are in settings that contain children with a range of abilities, sociocultural backgrounds, ages, interests, and temperaments" (Mallory, 1995).

Children without disabilities also benefit from having children with disabilities in their programs. Children without disabilities who have had opportunities to attend inclusive early childhood programs display less prejudice and fewer stereotypes and are more helpful to others than those who did not have this experience (Peck, Carlson, & Helmstetter, 1992). Children also are enriched by the opportunity to enjoy friendships with children who have disabilities (Rogers, 1993).

Roadblock #4: Availability and Quality of Early Childhood Programs
A fourth roadblock to inclusive early care and education is the number of quality early childhood programs located in the community that are available and considered appropriate placement options for eligible infants, toddlers, preschoolers, and kindergartners with disabilities. Communities throughout the country vary widely with respect to available resources for their citizens, including early childhood options. Cosmopolitan areas and university-based communities are likely to have an abundance of choices for the care and education of young children. Far fewer options may be apparent in rural communities and in those experiencing economic hardship. Preschool special education teams, in particular, often report that the lack of quality early childhood programs in their communities is a barrier to placing children in typical options.

Availability of Early Childhood Programs and Services To address the issue of availability, three assumptions must be challenged: 1) that every preschooler who is eligible for special education services must be enrolled in a structured preschool program; 2) that children must be enrolled in preschool immediately on their third birthday; and 3) that there is a scarcity of programs.

First, not every family of a 3-year-old wishes to enroll their child in preschool. For many reasons, families choose a wide array of options to meet the needs of their children. Such options include the following: 1) keeping a young child at home as the family may have done for the child's older siblings; 2) making arrangements for the child to play with other children through regular visits with the neighbors, trips to the library, or participation in a gymnastics program at the YMCA; 3) planning for preschool when the child turns 4 years old; or 4) a combination of activities best suited to the needs of the child and family.

Professionals can discuss preschool as an option for children with disabilities but must be prepared to offer services in a variety of environments. When some families choose and receive supports and services at home and in places other than preschool, the demand for preschool spaces is lessened. It is often difficult for preschool special education coordinators and other specialists to accept such alternatives to structured preschool as viable and valid. The saying "one size fits all," however, does not apply to 3-year-olds, and the option to receive services at home and in various places in the community clearly falls under the definition of natural environments in IDEA 1997.

Second, not every child must be enrolled in preschool on his or her third birthday. When young children are determined to be eligible for preschool special education services, IEP teams might automatically seek a preschool program in which to place these preschoolers by their third birthday, regardless of the success of their current program or the timing of their birthday. If a child's birthday falls in late winter or early spring, he or she may be engaged in a routine that involves EI services, child care, or other activities. Also at this time, most typical preschool programs have full enrollments and are winding down their program year. District staff may panic at the lack of apparent options and place the child in a district-operated, center-based program to comply with the law. In contrast, rarely do families who have preschoolers without disabilities change programs midstream if their child is experiencing success, and rarely do they disrupt their schedules to enroll their children in preschool in the middle of the year. Thus, in the interest of promoting typical experiences, providers should seek alternatives that maintain continuity in the lives of children and families and respect their tolerance for change. Examples of such alternatives include contracting with EI providers to continue providing services until the start of the next preschool year (i.e., September) and offering supports within the current environment(s) while reserving a place for the upcoming year in the preschool of the family's choice.

Third, by operating from an "abundance mentality" (Covey, 1989), new options are discovered. An abundance mentality "is the paradigm that there is plenty out there and enough to spare for everybody.... It opens possibilities, options, alternatives, and creativity" (Covey, 1989, p. 220). Relative to families with young children, an often-voiced concern is the difficulty of finding quality programs for eligible children while maintaining natural proportions of children with and without disabilities. If providers adopt an abundance mentality, however, more options would present themselves. This involves 1) shifting one's view of a community's existing resources beyond traditional preschool programs; 2) conducting a broad inventory of resources in the community for young children and their families; 3) exploring options that were never considered before, such as child care provided in someone else's home that, with support, can provide many social and language opportunities for children; 4) creating "satellite" programs of local providers who receive support from a quality preschool or child care center; 5) approaching the local Montessori program; and/or 6) collaborating with Head Start.

This shift in perception of available resources is particularly useful when young children enrolled in EI programs are no longer eligible after their third birthday. In these instances, some EI programs have collaborated with other agencies and providers to implement a follow-along tracking system such as the *Ages and Stages Questionnaires* (Bricker & Squires, 1999), which is a parent-completed developmental screening tool. When concerns about child development emerge, families are referred to appropriate services or activities.

Quality of Early Childhood Programs and Services   In 1994 the Carnegie Corporation of New York reported that "more than half of all mothers return to the workforce within a year of the baby's birth; many of their infant and toddlers spend thirty-five or more hours per week in substandard child care" (p. 2). Thus, quality of early childhood programs and services continues to be a pressing concern to parents and providers alike. During the 1990s, research increasingly focused on the issue of quality and identified the characteristics that are associated with exemplary programs (see, e.g., Accreditation Council on Services for People with Disabilities, 1995; Bredekamp & Copple, 1997; Carnegie Corporation of New York, 1994; Cryer & Harms, 2000; Love, Schochet, & Meckstroth, 1996; Task Force on Recommended Practices, 1993; Whitebrook, Howes, & Phillips, 1990). Some common factors that contribute to higher quality programs include low child–adult ratios; higher level of staff education; low staff turnover; higher wages for staff; specialized training in early childhood education for teachers; administrators with prior experience; and strong, loving caregiver–child relationships (Buysse & Winton, 1997).

In particular, the lack of available, affordable, quality child care has reached a crisis in this country. According to Phillips (1997), there is ample reason to be worried:

> As millions of American children are moving into child care, most of these settings fall short of any standard that any of us...would consider optimal. Barely adequate has become the term of art to describe the typical child care arrangement in this country...The quality of the child care environment sig-

nificantly affects virtually every domain of development that we know how to measure, whether it's problem solving skills or social interactions or attention span or verbal development...it's the difference between high quality and that barely adequate care that we see all too often.

Despite this bleak picture, there is evidence that increased attention on quality child care by federal and state governments will provide opportunities to address this issue. In fact, "child care became a new priority for nearly every one of the fifty states [in 1997], with more initiatives than ever before" (*Working Mother,* 1997). With the welfare reforms of the 1990s, even greater numbers of children will require child care as their parents are required to work outside the home. Several programs, such as the federal Child Development Block Grant program, have allocated funding for child care costs for working families with low incomes.

The quality of some community programs may be less than exemplary but not so poor as to endanger the health and welfare of children. In these instances, EI or special education professionals can have a positive impact when staff are willing to improve. For example, a local preschool could be supported to adopt developmentally appropriate, family-centered practices throughout the program while special educators or therapists coordinate with staff on meeting the needs of one child. Some districts and EI programs have engaged wholeheartedly in a series of activities designed to enhance quality for all children. They have offered workshops or discussion groups for area preschool directors and teachers; provided in-house consultation or training for family child care providers and others; arranged mentorships and site visits for providers; and set up lending libraries of books, training materials, and toys for providers and families.

Beyond the issue of quality in general is the extent to which typical early childhood programs are prepared to include all young children. Many EI and school district personnel assume that community programs are inadequate to meet the "demanding needs" of children with disabilities. Some providers believe that the intervention or educational program offered by specialized environments requires a level of training far beyond the experiences of the average preschool teacher, child care provider, or children's librarian. As noted previously, this assumption is without foundation in research and practice. In fact, the significant benefit to young children with disabilities of participating in typical early childhood programs with support contradicts the notion that the average preschool teacher, child care provider, and others cannot address their needs (see Bruder, 1993).

In the past, it may have seemed easier for specialists to keep children with disabilities in self-contained programs rather than in privately run early childhood programs that did not adhere to the same quality standards. The demand for quality child care and preschool options in most of the nation's communities, however, makes it imperative that the public and private sectors work collaboratively to meet the growing needs of all young children in their community.

Roadblock #5: Concerns About Costs and Lack of Trained Staff   In 1997 OSEP reported that "over 1 million children, many of whom would have been placed in separate schools and institutions 25 years ago, are being educated in neighborhood schools, saving an average of $10,000 per child per year." The fifth and final major roadblock to inclusive communities for young children is thus a groundless concern about costs and the lack of trained staff to support young children with disabilities in typical programs and activities. Many EI programs and school districts assume that it is far more expensive to support children in community programs than in self-contained, center-based ones. This assumption is not necessarily true. For some children who require little support, the costs of a community program will be lower than a self-contained special education program. For those requiring intensive supports, the costs may be equal or greater in the community as compared with a self-contained environment.

Regardless of how costs of special programs would compare with costs of typical programs, relying on the cost factor as the foremost consideration for placement decisions would be shortsighted as well as contrary to IDEA 1997 requirements. Such a comparison fails to consider the long-term benefits of either kind of program. Although there is little evidence that overly specialized early childhood programs produce better outcomes for children with disabilities than inclusive ones, the positive short-term and long-term effects of attending a high-quality preschool program with peers have been documented substantially (*The Condition of Education,* 1995). For example, the High/Scope Perry Preschool longitudinal study (Schweinhart & Weikart, 1993), which examined the effects of preschool programs on children up to 27 years later, offered the following compelling results on the critical importance to society of quality early childhood programs:

* *For every dollar invested* in high-quality, active learning programs for young children living in poverty, *$7.16 is returned.* Savings are realized in the areas of schooling, taxes on earnings, welfare, the justice system, and crime victimization.
* Children at risk who participate in high-quality preschool programs have *a significantly higher graduation rate* than children at risk who do not.
* Children who attended a high-quality preschool program spent *less than half of the time in special education programs* than did children in the no-program group.

Although the question of cost remains an important one, many special educators have come to the conclusion that other considerations are more important. In the words of one administrator, "The issue shouldn't be cost per se but quality in relation to cost. If an integrated model will result in better child outcomes, we can't afford not to provide it" (Bruder, 1993, p. 43).

Among other considerations, supporting young children with disabilities in the community calls for staff who are willing and able to shift their roles from direct service provision only to collaborative consultation (Hanft & Place, 1996). This shift will require EI and preschool special education teams to acquire skills relevant to their new roles as well as to allocate time to address the associated logistical issues. It will also require the support of school district and EI program administrators, who can provide incentives for adopting a new model of service delivery and ensure that teams receive the necessary training and planning/coordination time.

Through creativity and collaboration, existing resources can be utilized effectively to support young children and their families in natural environments. For example, staff training, transdisciplinary teaming, and collaborative consultation can be cost-effective ways to meet the needs of young children with disabilities while benefiting all young children and families who participate in early care and education programs and activities. School districts and EI programs could also pool resources with others in the community who share a mission of quality, inclusive early care and education. Pooling resources presumes that school districts, EI programs, and other special programs are not "in it" alone and often results in better outcomes for children and families than could be accomplished by a single agency or organization.

Other strategies to maximize resources include the following: school districts could partner with service organizations for children with disabilities to set up an efficient Medicaid billing system while simultaneously working with the local parent–teacher association and school board to ensure that recouped dollars are allocated for preschool services, and school districts could establish interagency agreements with EI programs or other school districts to provide collaborative consultation services at a local child care center. The latter strategy can reduce duplication of services when different school districts place children in the same community program; reduce staff travel time when the child care center is located far closer to one district or program than another; and reduce the number of specialists who go into the child care center on a day-to-day basis and, thus, can be less intrusive.

August: Lucy's Team Meets to Discuss
Transition from Early Intervention to Preschool
Although Karen and Rich Martin had talked with their service coordinator about preschool, this was the first chance to gather the entire EI team, the community providers, and two school district representatives in one place. Planning an agenda ahead of time with Donna helped Karen and Rich to feel that it was "their" meeting. After introductions, Karen and Rich told the group about their daughter Lucy and the dreams

*they held for her future, which they had formulated after the parent
meeting at the library.*

*With obvious pride, Karen and Rich passed around a snapshot of a
smiling Lucy playing in the sand with friends at the Rainbow Center.
They vividly described their little daughter with brown curly hair—a
child who loves listening to music, rocking in her chair, and watching
Big Bird on television faithfully every night at 5 o'clock. It was important
to them that Lucy grow up surrounded by friends and participating in
typical childhood activities. They envisioned her as a teenager having
pizza parties and sleepovers, going to movies with groups of kids, and
attending the local high school. They hoped she would find a job she
liked and would be able to live in her own place someday. They wanted
Lucy to have anything that she wanted for herself, including college, if
that became one of her dreams. Karen and Rich were well aware that
Lucy would experience many challenges and obstacles. They looked to
the team for suggestions on how best to support her.*

*The Rainbow staff continued the conversation with stories about
Lucy's love of colorful picture books and her growing interest in the
classroom's pet rabbit. Lucy was a delightful addition to the small group
in the toddler room, and the staff had seen her make strides engaging
other children in social play and using more and more words to communicate. With a donated computer and support from the Rainbow
staff, Lucy had begun to use technology to make her needs known and
to create picture stories. Donna had brainstormed with the staff on how
to include Lucy in all of the activities and accommodate her needs.
With careful observation and supervision, they had learned when to
offer assistance and when to fade support for Lucy to participate
throughout the day, whether she was resting in a quiet space or actively
playing with other children. They were pleased to report that the preschool teacher at Rainbow was eager to have Lucy join her group once
Lucy turned 3.*

*When it was time for the district representatives to talk, the pre-
school special education teacher told the group about their self-
contained preschool program, housed at the local elementary school.
Lucy would be eligible to ride the district's preschool bus to and from
home or the child care center. With so many therapists on staff at the
preschool, she felt that Lucy could make wonderful progress. Other children in the district were being included in typical community
preschools, but because of Lucy's extensive needs, the preschool special
education teacher didn't think that Lucy could be successful outside of
the district's classroom.*

*Karen and Rich were reluctant to agree with her, thinking that Lucy
was already successful right where she was. It was difficult for them to*

think about sending Lucy to another school. Rich and Karen decided to visit the special education preschool to see what it was like. The meeting concluded with the team members agreeing to meet again in 2 months to discuss Lucy's progress. They would also discuss the Martins' impressions of the special education preschool as an option for Lucy.

Later, as Sally, the preschool coordinator, drove back to her office, she was troubled by the discussion about Lucy's placement. The district had been making an effort to support other children in community preschools. Why not Lucy? If Lucy was doing so well at Rainbow, did it make sense to pull her from there and put her in a separate program? The family needed flexible child care, which was provided at Rainbow. Changes were difficult for Lucy. Why make her flip-flop between home, child care, and a preschool? Sally began to wonder what it would take for Lucy to be supported in the Rainbow Center's preschool program.

Common Practices and Inertia for Change

A number of outmoded beliefs and common practices have been described that interfere with community participation for families of young children, along with suggested alternatives. All of these beliefs and practices may drain energy and resources and create an inertia for change. The next section describes the power of parents, providers, and community leaders to create sustainable change when local teams are committed to the belief that all children belong.

THE POWER OF LOCAL COMMUNITIES TO CREATE SUSTAINABLE CHANGE

> *"Service systems build on people's deficiencies; communities on their capacities."*
> —*John McKnight (1989, p. 38)*

Creating a Structure: The Synergy of Local Teams

Practitioners like Sally and families like Lucy's have been working diligently to open the doors of typical preschools, child care programs, Head Start, and other community activities to young children with disabilities and their families. Most of these efforts, however, have focused on a single aspect of community life, such as preschool education or child care. Few have attempted to combine agendas; draw on the collective strengths of parents, providers, and other citizens within a given town or city; and promote changes in various community activities and programs such that all young children and their families can participate.

The Community Options in Early Care and Education project of the Institute on Disability (IOD) at the University of New Hampshire was designed to utilize community strengths to facilitate the inclusion of young children and their families. A holistic approach adopted by the project ensured that the child's and family's life within the context of their community was the benchmark for determining where and how families were supported to participate.

Community Options began supporting communities by combining the leadership efforts of six collaborative local teams, a state-level advisory committee, and a statewide technical assistance and support network with a series of systems change and public awareness activities. Teams were selected through a request-for-proposal process, which required them to describe the changes they wished to bring about in their communities. At a minimum, each team included the following: a parent of a young child with a disability, a special educator, a general educator, a child care provider, a preschool provider, a family support coordinator, an EI provider, and a Head Start representative (if available in that community). At their discretion, teams also included other interested and helpful representatives, such as health care providers, librarians, business representatives, school board members, kindergarten teachers, principals, special education directors, directors of agencies for people with developmental disabilities, religious leaders, and recreation program staff.

Teams were charged with five primary responsibilities intended to enhance services in their communities: 1) *support families of young children to choose, gain access to, and participate in community programs;* 2) *support local providers and programs* to include young children with disabilities; 3) *promote systems-level change* in programs and practices that prevent families and young children from enjoying a full community life (e.g., close a self-contained preschool operated by the school district in favor of neighborhood preschools); 4) *heighten awareness* of inclusive early care and education within their communities; and 5) *support one another* as well as others with an interest in inclusive early care and education, via networking, information sharing, and technical assistance.

Ongoing support and technical assistance were offered to teams by project staff via site visits, weekly telephone contact, networking activities, workshops, resources, and materials. Teams received financial support of up to $10,000 per year for 2 years to carry out a series of objectives (within the parameters of the project) that were identified by the team and based on local needs. Financial support was obtained through collaboration with the New Hampshire Statewide Systems Change Project and the New Hampshire Department of Education's Bureau of Early Learning (Part 619 discretionary funds).

From 1994 to 1997, Community Options participants throughout New Hampshire demonstrated the power of local teams to create sustainable change in their communities. Collectively and individually, team members changed policy, influenced practice, and enhanced the quality of supports and services for the young children and families in their communities. Here are examples of their successes:

- *The number of young children enrolled in segregated preschool programs within project communities decreased* from 48% in the 1992–1993 school year to 21% in 1995–1996. Statewide, New Hampshire also experienced a reduction in the number of young children in segregated programs (from 39% in 1992–1993 to 34% in 1995–1996) for that same time frame, though this change was far less dramatic than for project communities.

- *More than 300 children were enrolled and supported in typical early childhood programs* with assistance from community teams. About one third of these children, whose families received support to enroll them in child care or other options, were in the birth to 3 years age range. The remainder were ages 3–6 years and were supported to enroll and participate in a variety of community programs. Of the 142 young children enrolled in community programs in 1996, 23% had been diagnosed with autism, developmental delay, hearing impairment, visual impairment, orthopedic impairment, or multiple disabilities or as "other health impaired."

- *Fifty new early childhood program options became available* to young children with disabilities. *New program option* was defined as an existing early childhood program in the community in which either no children with disabilities had previously been enrolled or no children from the team's school district or EI program had ever been placed. The majority of options were private preschool programs, child care centers, or family child care programs. Teams, however, also brought aboard library story hour programs, gymnastics programs, and playgroups.

- *Two self-contained programs* (a kindergarten program and a preschool program) for young children with disabilities *were closed* in favor of community placement options.

September: A Community Team Forms

Since Lucy's team last met to discuss transition, Sally, the preschool coordinator for the district, received eight referrals for preschoolers in 3 weeks. Frustrated by the lack of options and opportunities in the community for families of young children with disabilities, Sally decided to pull together a team of people from the community who could work jointly on this and other issues of mutual concern.

Sally invited several members of Lucy's IEP team to join other community members in forming the group. This included Donna from EI, some of the district's preschool teachers and therapists, the town librarian, a Head Start teacher, a kindergarten teacher, the special education director, the elementary school principal, a pediatric nurse from the local health clinic, the family support coordinator from the agency that serves people with developmental disabilities, Lucy's mother, and two other parents. This group, self-named the Early Childhood Team, agreed to *come together once a month to discuss issues and opportunities, to develop plans and activities to address their top priorities, and to develop recommendations for changes in policy to better promote and support inclusion for young children and their families in their community.*

The meeting started with a discussion of team members' own visions and assumptions about inclusion and quality early childhood programs. To their surprise, they discovered that there were vast differences in opinion regarding the definition of inclusion, who could benefit, and what the group should prioritize. The group recognized that a group facilitator was needed, and Sally, with the group's approval, assumed that role. Other group members took on additional roles to make the group work smoothly, including time keeper, note taker, researcher (to gather additional information), and parent link (to contact other parents).

Sally suggested that for the next meeting each team member complete a community needs assessment, a questionnaire that rated the status of various recommended early care and education practices within the community. This tool could provide a starting point for their discussion of priorities. The Head Start teacher volunteered to send each member some interesting articles on inclusive early care and education that he had collected. The group adjourned, having established regular monthly meeting times for the year and other vital logistics, including who would bring the refreshments the following month!

The story of the Early Childhood Team in Lucy's community reflects the early experiences of the teams that participated in the Community Options project. It was essential for the groups to spend the necessary time up front to engage in open, honest discussion and team-building activities, establish "ground rules" for meetings, and secure administrative support from their respective organizations (if relevant) to participate on the team before they could prioritize tasks. One of the ground rules adopted by every team in the Community Options project was that team members must feel safe to express their opinions, even when these differ from those of the other team members.

The Early Care and Education Priority Rating Scale (Early Care and Education Committee, 1993a), a community needs assessment used by the Community Options teams, provided a starting point for discussion as well as an ongoing mechanism for tracking progress over time. When members of the team were reluctant to try a new approach, they were encouraged to read good articles on quality inclusive early care and education, visit community programs that were successfully including young children with disabilities, talk with colleagues who worked in community environments, and/or discuss their concerns with the team. Thus, teams were able to agree on at least one or two priorities with everyone's approval.

Each team had a facilitator who played a critical role in focusing the group and moving through the agenda. Team facilitators served as chair of the meetings and ensured that all members received copies of minutes and materials. It was essential that the team facilitator have sanctioned time available to serve in this capacity. In instances in which the team facilitator was over-extended, progress was sometimes impeded and it became necessary for another member of the team to assume that role.

It also was important for group members to determine up front the roles they would assume and the contributions they could make given the strengths they possessed. For example, the kindergarten teachers in one community quickly realized that they could educate the local preschool providers about the skills young children are expected to have when they enter kindergarten. The kindergarten teachers were concerned about the developmentally inappropriate emphasis on academic skills within several of the local preschools. To address this issue, they arranged for round-table discussions with the preschool staff over lunch, during which they disseminated information on developmentally appropriate practices. As a result, some preschool teachers discovered that social skills such as getting along with friends and asking a friend to play were of more use in kindergarten than was the ability to complete a numbers worksheet.

Similarly, lively discussions were held in one community on thematic versus child-directed units of learning (i.e., organizing curriculum around themes versus creating curriculum around children's interests). Special education teachers, therapists, and community providers learned much about themselves and reached a higher understanding about how children learn. When one team identified funding as a major barrier, the director of the local organization serving people with disabilities arranged for a staff member to set up a Medicaid billing system within the school district, which recouped $70,000 for the school district during the first year. Thus, team members all contributed their expertise and resources, achieving far greater outcomes collectively than they could have as separate organizations or individuals.

October: The Second Early Childhood Team Meeting

As fall sent ripples of color over the town, the group resumed their discussion on inclusion for young children. Sally, the facilitator, tracked the discussion and pointed out areas of agreement. Though in consensus on many points, the team agreed to disagree on a single definition of inclusion. Some believed that all children could benefit from inclusion, whereas others did not. The struggle over definitions and philosophy of inclusion did not keep them from realizing there was still much to be done for the young children and families in the community.

They next turned their attention to the results of the community needs assessment, in which two top priorities had surfaced. One was inclusion; the other was health care services. After some discussion, they chose two goals in the area of inclusion that were attainable and impor-tant to all of them: 1) to find and support at least three more child care/ preschool programs in town interested in enrolling young children with disabilities and 2) to reduce the number of children in the district's self-contained preschool by finding appropriate alternatives for any newly referred child.

For some members of the Early Childhood Team, fear and panic began to influence the discussion. Would the teachers and therapists from the district's preschool still have jobs? How might their jobs change? Did they even want to change? Sally recognized their discom-fort and suggested that the group discuss the dynamics of change, their feelings and concerns about it, and how they could cope with the chaos that is part of the change process. By the end of the emotionally charged discussion, the preschool coordinator assured district staff that their expertise would be essential in any new arrangements or changes, and the team was prepared to move on.

Supporting Teams to Bring About Change: Factors that Contribute to Success

Several factors supported the Community Options teams to bring about sub-stantive changes in their communities. From the early team-building stage of their development to their second or third year when they were recognized in their communities as a force for positive change, teams benefited from three areas of influence: 1) state-level support, 2) team characteristics, and 3) an individualized approach to support for the team (from project staff and associ-ates) as well as for community providers and families (from team members).

November Through June: Progress and Setbacks for the Team

With the first snow of the new season falling, the team heard from the preschool special education teacher. She had visited several local early childhood programs and had talked with staff about the possibility of enrolling some children with disabilities in their programs. What sur-prised her the most was the excitement and enthusiasm on the part of the early childhood program staff who were familiar with cooperative learning, developmentally appropriate practices, and team teaching, and who saw how these concepts could be applied to teaching children with special educational needs. Teachers also recognized what a valu-able resource the special education team could be for their classrooms. Team members discussed the wide range of supports and services that might be available to private programs and became excited about moving forward with their initiative.

Over the next 7 months, the team made substantial progress on their goals. Three new programs enrolled young children with disabilities, including a child care center, private preschool, and a YMCA early childhood program. The preschool special education team met weekly to discuss ways in which they could be more efficient in applying the collaborative consultation model and delivering supports and services within local early childhood programs. When Sally received new referrals, the preschool special education team worked diligently with the families and Early Childhood Team to create individualized plans within typical early childhood programs rather than enroll additional children in the self-contained special education preschool. The team planned that within 1 year, the self-contained program would close as currently enrolled children moved on and no new children were admitted.

When faced with setbacks, the team rallied to overcome them. When the superintendent and school board questioned the new approach, the special education director called on the Early Childhood Team parents to give a brief presentation on their experiences to the school board. When the preschool special education team reported that there simply were not enough options for all of the children being referred, the team brainstormed several long- and short-term solutions. These included reserving slots in good programs well in advance, approaching additional private providers on including young children with disabilities (they had not yet spoken with the director of the Montessori preschool in town), exploring the possibility of expanding the Head Start program by using available space in the elementary school, and supporting private child care providers to obtain certification from the state. They also discussed the fact that not every family of an eligible child wants preschool and that in those instances, individualized plans could include home-based services along with other options the family might choose (such as a playgroup).

When several parents whose children were leaving EI requested that their child be placed in the self-contained preschool, the preschool special education team called on the Early Childhood Team for support. The parent members offered to talk with the concerned parents (if they agreed to) about their positive experiences with community programs, and to accompany these parents on visits to various preschools. The local Parent-to-Parent coordinator suggested that district staff ask these families about their fears and concerns regarding community programs; what aspects of the self-contained program they believed their child would not receive in the community; and whether (with an acceptable plan in place to address concerns) they would be willing to enroll their children on a short-term, trial basis. In addition, the team determined that it would be helpful to have Donna, as a representative of EI, speak with her colleagues and the local pediatrician who may have been advising parents about the transition for their children into the segregated preschool. Donna had learned that meeting with pediatricians and other professionals to talk about ways in which they could work together to support the family provided an opportunity to share information about exemplary practices. With new information on how the school district successfully supported community programs, both EI staff and medical professionals learned about the benefits of inclusion.

The team experienced several setbacks and numerous benefits, both expected and unexpected. Team members greatly enjoyed the opportunity to share ideas, brainstorm, pool resources, and receive support from one another that the meetings offered. They also appreciated their time together, the casual but productive nature of the meetings, the laughs they shared, and the delicious refreshments. As they neared the end of their first year with several successes to their credit, the team decided to continue the process. They dedicated the June meeting to a discussion of lessons they had learned, goals to be targeted for the upcoming year, and resources they would need to meet their goals.

State-Level Support

In New Hampshire, several state agencies have taken a leadership role in supporting communities to include young children with disabilities. The New Hampshire Department of Education added to its computerized information system a category for preschool placements labeled *community program*. The Department has encouraged districts to submit applications for approval to utilize a variety of early childhood programs as placement options. Districts must simply describe their philosophy and general curriculum for preschool special education and ensure that community programs will abide by the districts' standards. Thus, districts can truly individualize programs for children by offering a menu of choices that includes home-based support; support in a variety of child care, preschool, and other early childhood programs and activities; or a combination thereof. Some districts in New Hampshire have included as many as 20 options under this category. The Department has also offered preschool discretionary grants as incentives to support change in local practice.

The Early Supports and Services Program (Part C) in the New Hampshire Division of Developmental Services has provided visionary leadership in the state's EI system. This lead agency requires that all EI supports and services be delivered in natural environments with natural proportions of young children with disabilities to young children without disabilities. It also provides training and incentive grants to assist local providers in offering supports and services that are family centered, community based, and otherwise exemplary. Similarly, the state's Child Development Program has dedicated funds to the on-site training of and technical assistance for local child care providers to care for young children with disabilities. The firm commitment of several state leaders to promote belonging for all young children has set New Hampshire on a statewide course of change.

From the beginning, one of the most valued resources for the Community Options project was a state-level advisory committee dedicated to enhancing services for young children and their families. Members of this group included each of the directors or coordinators from the state programs just named as well as the following individuals: two parents of young children with disabilities (one of whom participated on the New Hampshire Interagency Coordinating Council), an educational consultant from the Statewide Systems Change Project; the director of Tri-County Head Start, the executive director of the New Hampshire Developmental Disabilities Council, a public health nurse from the state's Bureau of Special Medical Services, a director of a child care/preschool center, and a director of one district's special education program. This group was instrumental in assisting the Community Options project to identify resources and brainstorm solutions to any barriers that were impeding the progress of the teams. With assistance from this group, the project was able to research policy issues and recommend changes, maintain a statewide perspective on issues, and leverage resources (e.g., agencies co-sponsored workshops presented by nationally known professionals on topics of interest to team members, provided a second year of funding for team efforts via preschool discretionary funds, and researched policy issues).

The state-level advisory committee provided a ready mechanism for teams to air their concerns and for advisory committee members to keep apprised of issues at the local level. Having the support of the state-level advisory committee also lent credibility to the work of the teams. For example, when school board members or administrators questioned team activities, the team was able to call on the project's state-level advisors for support.

Team Characteristics and Practices

The second factor contributing to the success of Community Options teams involved team characteristics and practices, as described next.

Vision and Commitment   Teams that had at least one "visionary" among their ranks, as well as commitment from each member to work through difficult times, had the greatest success in achieving their goals. The visionary was able to keep the group focused on the long-term outcomes and excited about the process. When barriers were raised, successful teams were able to pinpoint the problem, strategize solutions, and find resources to overcome the difficulty. For example, when one team realized they had insufficient funds to run their pilot preschool and family center for a second year, team members wrote grants and approached local businesses for support. Within a short time, the team had acquired all of the needed funding, including contributions from an HMO (health maintenance organization), the New Hampshire Charitable Foundation, and local businesses.

Approval from the Beginning   When teams consisted of a majority of members who were not involved in early discussions of visions and goals, it was difficult to move forward. It is therefore important to ensure that all new members receive an orientation prior their first meeting, during which they can discuss how the team's efforts relate to their members' areas of interest. Otherwise, much time can be wasted in backtracking and discussing goals.

Skilled Facilitator   Individuals who serve as team facilitators must be skilled in this role. They must be familiar with good meeting practices (Thousand & Villa, 2000), group dynamics, and adult learning styles. One support offered by project staff was to assist newly appointed team facilitators to gain skills and confidence in this role.

Members Take Care of Themselves and Celebrate Success   During the orientation meeting with each team, the project urged them to adopt the following motto: "Work hard, eat well, laugh a lot." The project disseminated an "inclusion survival kit" to each team that contained many fun items such as tiny parasols for rainy days, miniature champagne glasses for celebrating success, and a pair of children's sunglasses for helping others to see the paradigm shift from special to typical. When teams ensured that meetings were enjoyable, were supportive of all members, and included celebrations of successes (however small), they were able to sustain their efforts over time. One team dedicated an entire meeting to the topic of stress. The team facilitator darkened the room, lit scented candles, and played soft music while members sat on floor pillows and shared strategies for coping with stress. At the end of the third project year, staff convened a statewide gathering. Teams, providers, advisors, and some family members cruised aboard the M.S. Mount Washington on one of New Hampshire's beautiful lakes to discuss outcomes, share strategies, and celebrate success.

Individualized Support for Teams, Providers, and Families

The third critical factor in supporting teams to bring about change was individualized support for teams, providers, and families.

Individualized Support for Teams   Together with project staff, each team generated an individualized technical assistance and support plan at the beginning of each year. This flexible plan described the nature and amount of support or resources that the team anticipated would be needed from project staff in order for them to achieve their goals and objectives, as well as responsible people and timelines needed. Teams requested a variety of assistance, ranging from training on collaborative consultation and assistance in developing a resource packet for families to evaluating a pilot preschool program and preparing a presentation for the school board.

Individualized Support for Community Providers Teams were encouraged to utilize the individualized technical assistance and support plan approach with the community providers with whom they collaborated to include young children with disabilities. This approach was greatly appreciated both by team members and by community providers. Team members were able to clarify the nature, amount, and scheduling of their work with providers, whereas providers enjoyed the individualized approach to meeting their needs based on their own priorities, concerns, and preferred learning styles. Information on individual children and their specific disabilities, resources, funding, and opportunities to meet with other providers were the most frequently requested types of support.

Individualized Support for Families Support for families was the purview of the service coordinator from the area agency, a member of the IEP team, or other organization chosen by the family. Although Community Options teams did not directly support families, various team members did so as part of their professional responsibilities. Thus, family issues were presented to the team either by the parent members or (anonymously) by team members whose job was to offer families support. The role of the team was to promote changes in the community such that family issues would be addressed. For example, if the local librarian felt unsure of how to include a child with Down syndrome in story hour, the team would offer him or her technical assistance, while suggesting that he or she hold one or two places (of 15 openings) for children with disabilities to participate. If the team learned that a young child with developmental delays was refused child care by a provider in the neighborhood, team members would try to work with that provider (with parental permission) to address concerns or would assist the family in finding alternatives.

March: From Individualized Family Support Plan to Individualized Education Program—An Early Childhood Program Works

As she neared her third birthday, Lucy was making great strides at the Rainbow Center. The other children loved her and played with her in and out of school! Donna now spent more of her time talking with Rainbow staff about how to support Lucy to talk with her friends than she did addressing their fears of teaching a child with a disability. The speech-language therapy assistant had lessened her direct support as Lucy's social and communication skills had grown, and the team gained confidence in their ability to implement the techniques she had suggested.

Dave continued to spend time at the Martins' home and at the Rainbow Center. He had taken Lucy and her brother to the library story hour, the store, and several events in the community. Karen and Rich became more relaxed, feeling very confident in the decisions they had made thus far and that the support they had created for Lucy was a perfect match. Lucy was talking in short sentences and visiting with friends on the weekends. Over the past few months, she had also become more playful with her brother, other family, and friends.

When the IEP team met again, they were ready to talk about placement. Preliminary IEP goals had been written by the team during a meeting in February, with the understanding that they would be adjusted when Lucy began her preschool program. Karen and Rich had visited the district program, and although the program seemed quite nice and the staff were very friendly, they thought it might be too big a change for Lucy—too many new teachers, new children, and new schedules and rules. Lucy had begun to open up to the children at the Rainbow Center. Donna wondered if moving her would put a halt to the positive changes all had seen.

The group was quite comfortable with each other at this point and was able to express themselves with few reservations. This was a critical time for the group, however, and Lucy's placement had been a difficult topic for discussion. In past meetings, the special education staff had voiced opinions that although the toddler program was fine, Lucy would require a more intensive program at preschool, one that would be difficult for the Rainbow staff to achieve. The district staff felt it was their responsibility to prepare Lucy for kindergarten and that she would have the best chance of gaining the needed skills in the special education environment. The staff at the Rainbow Center felt strongly that with continued support, Lucy could be very successful in their preschool program. Lucy's parents saw pluses and minuses to both the special education program and the Rainbow preschool. Sally wanted to try to keep Lucy at the Rainbow Center but knew that it would be a new experience for many members of her staff.

Each of them was wrapped up in his or her own thoughts as Karen began the meeting by reviewing the IEP goals, which were similar to the IFSP goals the EI team had been addressing. As team members discussed ways to support Lucy to talk with and become more comfortable around other children, the preschool special education teacher (who was reluctant about inclusion) leaned back in her chair and smiled and said, "I've been having such a hard time in my own mind figuring out what would be best for Lucy. I really thought that she would be better off in our program, but hearing all of these goals and objectives has made it much clearer. She's already begun to talk to and form relationships with chil-

dren at Rainbow, and they are the ones that she will go on to kinder-
garten and elementary school with. It just makes sense to support her
where she already is. A collaborative consultation model has already
proven successful with Lucy and the Rainbow staff. I can continue right
where Donna leaves off, and Lucy will be able to stay at Rainbow."

Karen and Rich agreed, and with that settled, it was decided that
the EI team would continue to support Lucy for the rest of the school
year and through the summer. This would ensure a smooth transition to
preschool special education and continuity for Lucy and her family. The
costs of therapy and other supports on Lucy's IEP would be picked up
by the school district from the date of her third birthday. The district's
special education teacher would continue to observe Lucy and begin
offering supports to her classroom in September when Lucy joined the
preschool group at the Rainbow Center.

There were smiles of relief on everyone's faces. They recognized
how difficult it had been for the preschool special education teacher to
change the way she provided services from direct teaching to consulta-
tion and support for early childhood programs in the community. With
all of the important decisions made, the team dug into the chocolate
birthday cake baked by Lucy and her family—to celebrate not only the
birth of a child, but the birth of a community effort!

INCLUSIVE COMMUNITIES FOR YOUNG
CHILDREN: AN IDEAL AND A CHALLENGE

In an ideal world, inclusive communities embed the most exemplary of practices into every program and service for young children and families. Children
are supported by EI staff, school districts, and other specialists at home and in
typical early childhood programs in natural proportions. The practice of plucking children from successful family-chosen child care programs or preschools
and placing them in special programs is replaced by sending supports to those
community sites. Similarly, the practice of placing children into community
programs with little or no support has been discontinued in favor of offering
collaborative consultation in the community by trained teachers and therapists.
Rather than force children into split placements (e.g., community preschool in
the morning and special education preschool in the afternoon), agencies work
collaboratively to extend the hours at one site and offer ample supports.

In an ideal world, the people who offer early care and education services
undergo personal growth and change. Providers from the fields of education,
health, recreation, and child care adhere to the principles of family-centered
support; they listen to families, welcome them as valued partners, and support
them in making well-informed decisions. These providers understand that
sound practices and quality early care and education apply to all children.
They are confident in their knowledge of child development, know where and

how to acquire support and resources, and believe that all children can participate in their programs or services.

In an ideal world, families have formed long-term visions for their young
children with disabilities and let those visions guide their decisions along the
way. They are clear in their desire for their children to enjoy typical "little kid"
experiences, including the chance to have friends in the neighborhood and to
ride to preschool in carpools rather than on the stigmatizing special school bus.
Families have become vocal, skilled, and valued partners with providers in
their communities. Some have stepped confidently into leadership roles, advocating change in policy and practice with their school boards, administrators,
agency staff, and legislators. Once, parents and caregivers felt constant pressure to become the educator, therapist, advocate, and service coordinator for
their child with a disability. Although parents must continue to promote their
child's development in the context of the families' lives, they now understand
that their most critical role is as loving caregivers for all of their children.

Finally, in an ideal world, people find creative ways for children with various disabilities and their families to participate in all aspects of community
life. From the child care providers, bus drivers, and local teens to the pharma-
cist, elementary school principal, and pediatrician, the attitude and actions of
the people throughout the community clearly convey one message: We will do
whatever it takes to support all of our children.

This chapter has presented the challenges and positive outcomes of one
state's efforts to stir the winds of change in early care and education. Through
stories of Lucy's family and a local team convened to enhance early childhood options in their community, this chapter has described how the national
ideals of exemplary practice in early care and education were filtered down to
the state and local levels. Several common reasons that promoting inclusive
early childhood programs and activities has been so difficult were considered
as well as suggested alternatives to some of the practices that interfere with
this goal.

In her book on successful social programs, Lisbeth Schorr (1997) contended that communities must be strengthened from the inside as well as from
the outside to successfully promote change. This approach, reflected in the
Community Options project, should be applied throughout the country if quality inclusive early care and education is to become a reality for all families of
young children. In doing so, teams must continue to bring people to the table,
capitalize on a community's strengths, support families in positions of leadership and in dreaming of a positive future for their young sons and daughters,
celebrate success, learn from setbacks, and publicize their efforts.

REFERENCES

Accreditation Council on Services for People with Disabilities. (1995). *Outcome measures for early childhood intervention services.* Towson, MD: Author.

Bredekamp, S., & Copple, C. (Eds.). (1997). *Developmentally appropriate practice in early childhood programs* (Rev. ed.). Washington, DC: National Association for the Education of Young Children.

Bricker, D. (1995). The challenge of inclusion. *Journal of Early Intervention, 19*(3), 179–194.

Bricker, D., & Squires, J. (1999). *Ages & stages questionnaires (ASQ): A parent-completed, child-monitoring system* (2nd ed.). Baltimore: Paul H. Brookes Publishing Co.

Bruder, M.B. (1993, Winter). Early childhood community integration: An option for preschool special education. *OSERS News in Print,* 38–43.

Buysse, V., & Winton, P. (Eds.). (1997, Spring). *Early Developments, 1*(1).

Carnegie Corporation of New York. (1994, April). *Starting points: Meeting the needs of our youngest children.* New York: Author.

The Condition of Education [On-line]. (1995, August). Available: http://www.ed.gov/pubs/CondOfEd_95/ovrvw.html

Covey S.R. (1989). *The seven habits of highly effective people.* New York: Author.

Cryer, D., & Harms, T. (2000). *Infants and toddlers in out-of-home care.* Baltimore: Paul H. Brookes Publishing Co.

Dunst, C. (1998). *Research themes: Communities.* Paper presented at the National Early Childhood Technical Assistance Systems Research to Practice Summit on Inclusion in the Early Years, Washington, DC.

Early Care and Education Committee. (1993a). *Early Care and Education Priority Rating Scale.* Durham: University of New Hampshire, Institute on Disability.

Early Care and Education Committee. (1993b). *A vision for early care and education for young children with disabilities and their families in New Hampshire.* Durham: University of New Hampshire, Institute on Disability.

Edelman, L. (1991). *Delivering family-centered, home-based services: A facilitator's guide to accompany the videotape.* Baltimore: Project Copernicus, Department for Family Support Services, Kennedy Krieger Institute.

Education for All Handicapped Children Act of 1975, PL 94-142, 20 U.S.C. §§1400 et seq.

Forest, M. (1997). *Inclusion news.* Toronto: Inclusion Press International.

Guralnick, M.J. (Ed.). (1997). *The effectiveness of early intervention.* Baltimore: Paul H. Brookes Publishing Co.

Hanft, B.E., & Place, P.A. (1996). *The consulting therapist: A guide for O.T.s and P.T.s in schools.* San Antonio, TX: Therapy Skill Builders.

Helm, T. (1996, November). *Reflections on the early childhood provisions of IDEA: Progress and future directions.* Keynote address presented at the National Early Childhood Technical Assistance System Meeting for Part H and Section 619 Programs and Early Childhood Projects of IDEA, Washington, DC.

Individuals with Disabilities Education Act Amendments of 1997, PL 105-17, 20 U.S.C. §§1400 et seq.

Janko, S., & Porter, A. (1997, March). *Portraits of inclusion through the eyes of children, families, and educators.* Seattle: University of Washington, Early Childhood Research Institute on Inclusion.

Kunc, N. (1998, November 19). *Belonging right from the start: Supporting young children in community settings.* Paper presented at Early Childhood Seminar Series: Creating Inclusive Early Care Communities—Building a Foundation for Cooperative Behavior, Lewiston, Maine.

Kunc, N. (2000). Rediscovering the right to belong. In R.A. Villa & J.S. Thousand (Eds.), *Restructuring for caring and effective education: Piecing the puzzle together* (2nd ed., pp. 77–92). Baltimore: Paul H. Brookes Publishing Co.

Lamorey, S., & Bricker, D.D. (1993). Integrated programs: Effects on young children and their parents. In C.A. Peck, S.L. Odom, & D.D. Bricker (Eds.), *Integrating young children with disabilities into community programs: Ecological perspectives on research and implementation* (pp. 249–270). Baltimore: Paul H. Brookes Publishing Co.

Love, J., Schochet, P., & Meckstroth, A. (1996). *Are they in any real danger?: What research does—and doesn't—tell us about child care quality and children's well-being.* Princeton, NJ: Mathematica Policy Research, Inc.

Mallory, B. (1995). *Final report to the Preschool Task Force and Concord Development Program.* Unpublished report. Durham: University of New Hampshire.

Mallory, B. (1997). Educating young children with developmental differences: Principles of inclusive practice. In C. Seefeldt & A. Galper (Eds.), *Continuing issues in early childhood education* (pp. 213–227). Columbus, OH: Merrill.

McKnight, J. (1989, January–February). Why "servanthood" is bad. *The Other Side,* 38–40.

Mount, B., & Zwernik, K. (1988). *It's never too early, it's never too late: A booklet about personal futures planning.* St. Paul, MN: Metropolitan Council.

Nelson, D., Zoellick, L., Nisbet, J., & Tracy, N. (1997). *Community Options in Early Care and Education: Continuation application* (CGDA.: 84.024B). Durham: University of New Hampshire, Institute on Disability.

Office of Special Education Programs (OSEP). (1997). *Overview: The Individuals with Disabilities Education Act (IDEA)* [On-line]. Available: www.ed.gov/offices/OSERS/IDEA/overview.html

Peck, C.A., Carlson, P., & Helmstetter, E. (1992). Parent and teacher perceptions of outcomes for typically developing children enrolled in integrated early childhood programs: A statewide study. *Journal of Early Intervention, 16*(1), 53–63.

Phillips. D. (1997, June). What new brain research tells us about young children. *EDInfo* [On-line]. Available E-mail: listproc@inet.ed.gov

Rogers, J. (1993, May). The inclusion revolution. *Research Bulletin,* (11), 1–6.

Schorr, L. (1997). *Common purpose.* New York: Bantam Doubleday Dell.

Schuh, M., Dixon, B., Tashie, C., Clarke, J., Dillon, A., Shapiro-Barnard, S., Hagner, D., Nelson, D., & Nisbet, J. (1996). *From vision to reality: A manual to replicate the New Hampshire Leadership Series: Working with people with disabilities and their families to create positive futures.* Durham: University of New Hampshire, Institute on Disability.

Schweinhart, L.J., & Weikart, D.P. (1993, November). Success by empowerment: The High/Scope Perry Preschool study through age 27. *Young Children,* 54–58.

Smith, B.J., & Rose, D.F. (1994). *Policy and practice in early childhood special education series. Preschool integration: Recommendations for school administrators.* Pittsburgh: Research Institute on Preschool Mainstreaming.

Tashie, C., Shapiro-Barnard, S., Schuh, M., Jorgensen, C., Donoghue-Dillon, A., Dixon, B., & Nisbet, J. (1993). *From special to regular, from ordinary to extraordinary.* Durham: University of New Hampshire, Institute on Disability.

Task Force on Recommended Practices. (1993). *DEC recommended practices: Indicators of quality in programs for infants and young children with special needs and their families.* Denver: Division for Early Childhood.

Thousand, R.S., & Villa, R.A. (2000). Collaborative teaming: A powerful tool in school restructuring. In R.A. Villa & J.S. Thousand (Eds.), *Restructuring for caring and effective education: Piecing the puzzle together* (2nd ed., pp. 254–291). Baltimore: Paul H. Brookes Publishing Co.

U.S. Department of Education. (1998). To assure the free appropriate public education of all children with disabilities: Twentieth annual report to Congress on the implementation of the Individuals with Disabilities Education Act.

Whitebrook, M., Howes, C., & Phillips, D. (1990). *Who cares?: Child care teachers and the quality of care in America. Final report of the National Child Care Staffing Study.* Oakland, CA: Child Care Employee Project.

Williamson, G.G., & Anzalone, M. (1997). Sensory integration: A key component of the evaluation and treatment of young children with severe difficulties in relating and communicating. *ZERO TO THREE Bulletin, 17,* 29–36.

Wolery, M., Holcombe, A., Venn, M.L., Brookfield, J., Huffman, K., Schroeder, C., Martin, C.G., & Fleming, L.A. (1993). Mainstreaming in early childhood programs: Current status and relevant issues. *Young Children, 49*(1), 78–84.

Working Mother [On-line]. (1997). Child care: How does your state rate? Available: http://www.womweb.com/stateint.htm

4

What Have We Learned About Creating Inclusive Elementary Schools?

Susan Shapiro-Barnard, Frank Sgambati,
Beth Dixon, and Grace Nelson

Robert Coles (1989) began his book, *The Call of Stories: Teaching and the Moral Imagination,* with a description of his work as an intern at a psychiatric hospital. He wrote about the two supervisors with whom he was assigned to meet each week to report on his patients. The first doctor asked him about his diagnosis of the patients' conditions. This doctor wanted labels, terms, numbers, and psychiatric definitions. The second doctor, Coles recalled, was strangely uninterested in such conclusions. Instead he urged Coles to gather the patients' stories—not merely the histories composed during preliminary interviews, but the true stories of his patients' lives. He suggested that Coles might learn more by respecting ambiguity rather than by denying it, by embracing the details that initially seem trivial, and by recognizing that conclusions of any kind are seldom final. When reading about how Coles followed this second doctor's wise advice and listened to the stories of his patients, one becomes unexpectedly suspicious of black-and-white charts, graphs, and summaries and surprisingly confident in the gray area that lies among them.

This chapter describes in a broad sense what we—the authors of this chapter and the people with whom we worked to support inclusion in New Hampshire—have collectively learned about creating inclusive elementary schools. Although there certainly is sufficient information to be quantified, we have chosen to share what we have learned through four personal stories, one from each of the authors of this chapter. It is our hope that, as was the case for Coles, these stories will allow for a more meaningful exchange of information than might occur were we to simply list, graph, and chart our experiences thus far. The stories are interspersed with some general commentary about where we have been, what we have learned, and what we are still trying to understand.

Our vision is that all students with disabilities can be supported to learn and grow in general education classes alongside their peers. Many aspects of our educational system, on the local and state levels, do not support that vision. Therefore, our work on the behalf of students with disabilities has needed to be of a systemic nature. It began with courageous and committed families and educators who dreamed of new possibilities for children and schools. Over the years the nature of the work has changed, but the heart of the effort remains the same. We are strongly interested in making schools welcoming places.

Four stories follow. We begin with Frank, an inclusion facilitator who, years ago, worked in an institution. His tale chronicles some of the history of education for students with disabilities in New Hampshire and reminds us of how far we have come, as well as how far we still have to go. Next, we look at inclusion through the eyes of Beth, a parent, who trusted her sense about what her son's education could and should be, even when professionals told her it was not possible. Her story illustrates the power of a vision. The third story is that of Susan, a former special education teacher, who, by having more questions than answers, realized the bottom-line difference between mainstreaming and inclusion. Her story is a reminder that belonging cannot be conditional. Grace tells the final story. She is a general education third-grade teacher who demonstrates that what students need most is a teacher who cares, works with dignity, and is courageous enough to learn as much as he or she teaches.

WE'VE COME A LONG WAY: AN INCLUSION FACILITATOR'S STORY

A Field Trip, 1969

As a college sophomore, I participated in a field trip to an institution. I was not prepared for the experience. I walked by classes of young children who ran out into the halls to greet us and passed what staff called the "behavior mod" unit, where children sat on the floor along a cinder block wall. They had rags tied around their heads. These children, I was told, were called "the head bangers" and they were in "therapy." It was explained to me that when a child did not bang his or her head or engage in some other self-abusive behavior for a predetermined number of seconds, he or she would be rewarded with a small chocolate candy. It was hard to observe and even harder to understand what was going

on in the minds of the staff members who watched a child hurt him- or
herself and then calmly intervene. None of it made sense to me.

Perhaps the first thing we have learned about creating inclusive schools
is that we can never go back. We can never return to the practices that Frank
describes—which we learned to call "educational" and to regard as being a
good idea. It is frightful to recognize that most people were doing the best that
they knew how, just as we proclaim to be doing today.

Self-Contained Special Education, 1973

A few years after college I began work as an assistant teacher in a
school located in a church basement. My class consisted of 10 students,
ranging in age from 5 to 11, who didn't meet the public school system's
criteria for entry into its special education program. It was easy to
become involved in the lives of these incredible children both in and
out of the classroom. On weekends I would make home visits, often lis-
tening to parents tell of the hopes and dreams they held for their sons
and daughters. I didn't realize then that most of the world did not share
these visions. In school we had worked on "self-help skills," "preaca-
demic skills," and "socially appropriate behaviors." These were the skills
we thought children needed to enable the parents' dreams to come true.
*   One day a group of local high school students provided me with a*
dose of reality. My students and I were out walking in the community,
and as we passed the local high school, several students began to whis-
per and make comments: "Look at that one!" "What's wrong with this
one?" I soon realized why they made these comments. The students at
the local high school had never met the students with disabilities who
lived in their town. The children in my class had been separated from
their peers without disabilities from the start. Although many shopkeep-
ers, neighbors, members of the church, and others went out of their way
to be friendly, their friendliness was born of sympathy. The children in
my class were not valued as individuals in the community. No one
looked at any of them and saw a future.

Frank's experience with the students from the local high school speaks
directly to one of the greatest limitations of segregated education. Children are
divided and hidden from one another so that adults can be more comfortable.
Clearly, we must respond by building the capacity of our schools and communities to support and value all children. This is surely a worthy goal.

Perhaps it is also a goal that has a corollary. Think for a moment about
the business world. Corporate leaders, looking to revitalize their organizations,
often strategize ways to fire employees who are perceived as no longer con-

tributing to the forward movement of the company. Increasingly, however, leaders have learned that more important than determining how to excuse the "dead wood" of the organization is determining how that dead wood came to be. What in the organization's culture created it?

What does this example have to do with inclusive education? Although countless individuals work to learn all they can about creating schools in which all students belong and although this chapter is dedicated to this effort, working to understand how segregated education came to be is equally important. Otherwise, it might happen again.

Laconia State School and Training Center, 1978

After receiving a graduate degree, I accepted a position as a teacher at Laconia State School and Training Center—at that time, New Hampshire's institution for people with intellectual disabilities. For the first two years I taught in the Toll Complex, which was the institution's school. My involvement, however, went far beyond the classroom. Laconia wasn't just a school for individuals with severe disabilities, it was their home. Each child had his or her own story of abandonment, love, abuse, or hope.

I remember Ross, one of my students. On a few occasions, I would awaken on a Saturday morning to a pounding on my door. Even though I lived several miles from the institution, I knew that the knock belonged to Ross. After visiting my house once on a field trip, he began to see my home as a possible escape. A call to let the school know where Ross was, a conversation, and some breakfast were inevitably followed by the trip back, complete with my halfhearted admonishment for Ross not to run away again. We both knew I really didn't mean it.

Several years after I began working at Laconia, the deinstitutionalization exodus began. The process was difficult and at times just as devaluing as the past had been. Well-intentioned professionals "shopped" for the individuals with pretty faces and quiet mannerisms; these people would be the first to leave. The rationale at the time was that these individuals could be integrated into the community more easily, as the public would be more accepting. The selection process was difficult to watch—as though you were seeing your own child being the last to be chosen for a team, over and over again.

I left Laconia in 1987. Before doing so, I had the opportunity to visit a number of former residents who now were living in the community. Though the closing of the institution was a victory, some individuals' situations were only slightly better than what they had left behind. Isolation and loneliness were a way of life for some. The closing of the institution's doors—doors that absolutely needed to be closed—did not

guarantee that other doors would open for the former residents. There
was much work to be done.

We have learned and are still learning that systems change is more than
the mere cessation of one system; it's the simultaneous creation of something
new. We learned this when we closed institution doors, and we learn this today
when we place students with disabilities in general education classes but do
not adequately address their support needs. It is common knowledge that
meaningful experiences for children do not just happen, that they must be
grown and developed by adults. So when we fail to do this work of cultivation
in schools, students with disabilities are at risk of living on an island in the sea
of their inclusive classroom. This is true regardless of how beautiful the class
photograph might be.

New Hampshire Department of Education, 1988
I was hired by the New Hampshire Department of Education as the one
and only state consultant for students labeled as having "severe" and
"profound" disabilities. These students were now being educated in
public schools, and school personnel needed guidance. I provided assis-
tance to classroom teachers and special education teams throughout the
state regarding inclusion and least restrictive environments. I was
responsible for overseeing two demonstration projects supporting stu-
dents with severe disabilities in general education classrooms. In addi-
tion, I acted as the liaison between the Department of Education and the
New Hampshire Statewide Systems Change Project.
A great deal of planning and discussion in those days centered on
bringing students who attended separate schools and out-of-state resi-
dential facilities back into their home communities. The battles were
often emotional, and the decisions—to come back home or remain in
an institution—were often made by lawyers and judges who barely
knew the child.
In other instances, my involvement with school districts originated
with parents who were frustrated that their sons or daughters were being
educated in a segregated rather than a general education classroom.
And finally, some parents, whose children already had been placed in
general education classrooms, requested assistance with integrating their
children's related services into the general education curriculum.

Belonging is something that we have needed to learn a lot about. We have
often tied belonging and placement together. Doing so really is not hard to justify at first, but on closer inspection may make one presume a stronger connection between the two than actually exists. Having a child move from an

institution to the local school may have appeared to be an invitation to the child to belong, but the segregated classroom in that school where he or she ended up spending the day solidly reconstructed past segregation. Welcoming students with disabilities into general education classrooms is a closer approximation of belonging but often still is incomplete. Frequently, when push comes to shove, and a class meeting occurs at the same time that a student with disabilities is scheduled to receive physical therapy, the meeting may continue without him or her and without anyone's even acknowledging that this exclusion is happening. What was hoped to be belonging proves only to be situational membership. Here's another scenario: A student with disabilities is a full-time member of a general education classroom, supports are provided, and related services are integrated. She has a desk just like her classmates, uses a gym locker, and is a member of a Brownie troop—she even gets in trouble during class sometimes. But she does not belong. How do we know? Because she shows us—with her eyes, as she watches her peers giggling and holding hands as they run by her, and with a cringe on her face as she hears her teacher apologize, once again, for forgetting to include her in the class project. It does not yet seem that we know how to respond.

Inclusion Facilitator, 1991[1]

After almost 4 years at the New Hampshire Department of Education, I accepted a position as inclusion facilitator in the Kearsarge Regional School District. I was excited because I wanted an opportunity to reaffirm for myself that all kids could really and truly be fully included in every aspect of the school environment. My job was to work with classroom teachers to support students with disabilities in general education classes.

In September I walked into Simonds Elementary School, in Warner, New Hampshire, and was greeted by a teacher at the door with her arms folded telling me that she was a wreck and hadn't slept for days in anticipation of the first day of school when Abby would arrive in her classroom. She went on to tell me she never saw Abby's individualized education program (IEP), hadn't met the classroom assistant, didn't know how or what to teach this student, and so forth. Listening to this frantic

---

[1]An inclusion facilitator's job is to support classroom teachers to educate students with disabilities in general education classrooms. The inclusion facilitator usually retains the responsibilities of service coordination, or case management, for a student, but provides little or no direct instruction. Instead, this person meets with the classroom teacher and the assistant (if one is assigned) to plan modifications to classroom lessons and activities that can enable the student to participate fully and learn. The role of the inclusion facilitator is vital to the success of inclusive education, yet we have wondered whether this role, over time, might perpetuate the separateness of two educational systems. In New Hampshire, educators in this role are supported with training, technical assistance, and, most recently, a graduate specialization program at the University of New Hampshire.

teacher, I vowed to myself that this would never happen again. In the future, all teachers who had a student with severe disabilities assigned to their class would have the opportunity to observe the student in his or her current classroom, participate in the writing of the IEP, attend workshops and training sessions, and visit other inclusive schools and classrooms prior to the start of the school year. These teachers would also be guaranteed planning time with me (the inclusion facilitator) and with other support staff. If a paraprofessional was assigned, time would be allotted for the teacher to meet with this person as well. Arranging all of this was not an easy task, but we did it—and it worked. It worked very well.

In this instance, Frank was able to recognize the teacher's feelings as justifiable anxiety at the onset of what would be, for her, a new experience. Professionals, however, have sometimes regarded colleagues who are fearful and angry about students with disabilities entering general education classrooms as uncaring, rude, or even unfit for the profession. In some schools there has been an unspoken expectation that a "good teacher" will welcome every student without a moment's hesitation.

In retrospect, we have realized that our colleagues who asked, "Why is it that you want this student to be in my class? What will the student get out of it? What am I supposed to teach her?" were not necessarily trying to keep students with disabilities out. Instead, their personal philosophy strongly held that all students in their classes must learn, and they took this seriously. The introduction of a student whom the teacher perceived that he or she could not teach, made the teacher feel fear—not necessarily fear of the student—but rather a fear of his or her own professional failure. This deepened understanding has enabled us to offer supports that are more meaningful, positive, and relevant than the supports that we may have offered in the past.

A clear shared vision, administrative involvement, and a strong team that values the parents as full members all were significant factors in success at Kearsarge. Flexibility—the attitude that it's okay if something doesn't work because we can just try something else—was another key element. As a team, we believed that no one person had all of the answers but that collectively our knowledge, skill, and creativity would enable us to be successful. Perhaps most essential to the inclusive community we established was the shared responsibility that every educator felt for every student.

The role of an inclusion facilitator as a change agent is complex. It is important to support classroom teachers as much as possible and to listen carefully to a variety of ideas and perspectives. At the same time, the inclusion facilitator must remain absolutely clear about the goal of full inclusion—regardless of his or her colleagues' views—and must have a range of strategies for reaching that goal.

Children have moved out from behind locked metal doors to school playgrounds and general education classrooms, their rightful place. Our challenge is to make sure that this place works for them and for all children. It has been argued that true school reform is not possible until all students are included in the school community. Therefore, it is essential that advocates of inclusion and educators who are passionate about school restructuring work collaboratively to create a singular vision for school communities that encompasses both equity and excellence.

THE JOURNEY HOME: A PARENT'S STORY[2]

Our family has shared many adventures. Our youngest child, Andrew, has led us through one of our more significant journeys. Andrew was born a beautiful blonde with blue eyes, weighing 8 pounds and 7 ounces. My husband, Will, and I and our three other children welcomed Andrew with the greatest of joy. Our children looked at him in awe and anticipated the fun they would have watching him grow, smile, walk, and talk. As a family, we talked about all of the cute things that babies say and do, and I recalled for my children stories about each of them as babies.

When Andrew was 7 months of age, we were thrown into a strange and unfamiliar world of disbelief, a world in which we felt incompetent and powerless. Andrew had been diagnosed as having cerebral palsy, and our voyage took its first detour. He started in an early intervention program and was provided with physical, occupational, and speech-language therapy. We waited and hoped that he would somehow be "fixed" and become once again the child we all felt we had lost. We waited.

During the course of the next 2 years, I realized that we hadn't lost anyone. Andrew was the same beautiful child I had brought home from the hospital. He had the same needs that all children have—to be fed, taken to the park, played with, read to, and loved and cared for by his family and close friends. He didn't need to be "fixed"; we accepted Andrew as a complete person.

---

[2]Part of this story is adapted with permission of Singular Publishing Group, Inc. From Calculator, S., & Jorgensen, C. (1994). *Including students with severe disabilities in school: Fostering communication, interaction and participation.* San Diego: Singular Publishing Group.

Perhaps this family's lesson is one that our educational system needs to learn as well if we are to ever achieve true systems change: that a disability is just one part of a person. Although most people nod in agreement with this statement, educational practices and policies often do not reflect it. Educational plans for students with disabilities are, in many instances, centered on a student's label or diagnosis. Never mind that a child is an avid fan of dinosaurs. If he or she has mental retardation, there is a strong precedent that, for this child, functional life skills curricular goals are far more important than studying dinosaurs. When planning curriculum, it should never be denied that the child has a disability, nor, however, should it ever be denied that he or she likes dinosaurs. We must be vigilant in our attention to this matter.

Early Intervention and Kindergarten

School at age 3? My other children had played with their friends in the neighborhood at that age and in so doing had learned to communicate, play, and interact. I listened to the experts explain how Andrew was not "ready" to be with children his own age. Instead, he would spend 2 hours every day on a little yellow bus to attend a 2½-hour readiness program. There he would receive intensive one-to-one instruction from teachers, assistants, and therapists in a cubicle or behind a partition.

Just before he turned 4, Andrew began walking independently. He had us all running as he moved to touch all of the things he had previously been unable to reach. He had a sparkle in his eyes as he explored his world. We thought that this was usual until his teachers began describing him as a child with no attention span and no concept of danger.

Parents know their children best, yet it is still difficult for some professionals to understand this simple truth. Unfortunately, the aura of professional expertise is often strong enough to convince even the most confident of families that what they want for their son or daughter is not as appropriate as what the professionals feel that the child needs. For this reason, we need to be mindful about the composition of a child's educational team. Although it is customary to bring together a group of adults who know the most about children, disabilities, and schools, it is equally if not more important to bring together the people in the child's life who care the most. Though we seldom consider caring to be a prerequisite for team membership, the advice and contributions of these people will ensure that the hopes, dreams, fears, and nightmares of the student and his or her family are recognized and respected.

Our team requested a consultation from a communication specialist to discuss augmentative and alternative communication for Andrew. He was not speaking yet, and our team felt that it was time to bring in another "expert." I couldn't sleep the night before the assessment. I tried to figure out a way that I could prevent this professional from hearing all of the things that Andrew couldn't, shouldn't, wouldn't, won't, or cannot do before even beginning his evaluation. I found the communication specialist in the hallway and, because I was nervous, could only think to say, "Please keep an open mind."

The communication specialist looked at Andrew and smiled. Andrew was crazy about him right away. Together, they tried a basic form of signs and functional gestures, and Andrew responded. I am pleased to say that my fears were unfounded because this man looked at my child and saw the same Andrew I saw. It was the first time that an expert offered positive observations about my son before launching into a slew of recommendations.

From Special to Typical

Over time I began to question the wisdom of programs that separated children according to their levels of ability. Andrew's special education teachers were telling me that he lacked imitation skills, but when I thought about all of the time he spent working in a cubicle, my mind screamed, "Who is he supposed to imitate?!" I knew that children learn from each other, so I asked the team to enroll Andrew in a typical pre-school. My suggestion was met with stares of disbelief and knowing looks that meant that I was clearly a parent "in denial."

The next big hurdle was kindergarten, which meant another big meeting for Will and me. We worked out our game plan ahead of time—Will would play the "tough guy" as we tried to secure a typical kindergarten experience for Andrew. We quickly learned that the team wasn't ready for such a bold move, so we compromised. Andrew would attend a special education program 4 hours each day and would then visit the kindergarten at that school (not our neighborhood school) for a short time. The plan was to gradually extend the amount of time he spent in the kindergarten as he demonstrated success in this setting.

One day I visited the kindergarten to see how Andrew was doing. He arrived a few minutes after me, accompanied by his entire special education class. I kept watching. The kindergarten teacher greeted the group by announcing to her students, "Here come our special friends." The kindergarten children slouched in their chairs. No one interacted with Andrew except the adult who was seated beside him.

We requested a team meeting the following day. We expressed our concerns that Andrew's time in the kindergarten was more like a field trip than the beginning of his membership in the class. Six weeks later, Andrew was fully included in kindergarten. Soon after, his teachers remarked that he often looked to his peers for support rather than to

*adults for help as he had always done before and that the other kids
were truly enjoying being with him.*

There are school districts that have spent years preparing for one student
to be fully included in general education. Other school districts have decided
to close all special education doors and include every student in a matter of
minutes. There is not one pace for change that guarantees sustainability or that
ensures success. A given school system's unique history and experiences with
initiating and sustaining other change initiatives seem to be the best indicators
of how that district might most effectively proceed with inclusion. But we
must remember that children are waiting.

Just a Kid in the Neighborhood

*One day while Andrew and I were walking around the annual local fair
in our town, a young girl about Andrew's age approached us and asked
if Andrew would like to go on one of the amusement rides with her. He
was 5 years old, and it was the first time that he had been asked to play
with a friend—unlike my other children, who had gone to dozens of
places with their friends by the same age. It was uncommon that we
ever ran into one of Andrew's classmates, as the kids in his class lived
on the other side of town. I decided right then and there that it was time
for Andrew to come home to our neighborhood school.*

*At Andrew's next IEP meeting, I explained that we had no plans to
move and that because the neighborhood children would ultimately be
congresspeople, friends, employers, and neighbors in his future, he
needed to go to our neighborhood school. It wasn't easy, but the team
agreed. Andrew came home to our neighborhood school the following
September.*

In some towns a particular school is designated for all students who have
a certain disability, as the special education program at that school has been
designed for students with that label. This can be troublesome on many fronts
but is especially problematic when there is talk about student's being educated
in a general education classroom at that school. Instead, the student should
attend his or her neighborhood school. Although this point may seem obvious,
many schools have initiated great efforts at system change only to realize later
that a percentage of the students at their school belong someplace else.

Socialization

*When Andrew's principal asked me what I most wanted to achieve by
including Andrew at his neighborhood school, I told him that I wanted
Andrew to go to a birthday party. He replied, with his head in his hands,*

that he definitely could not guarantee that this would happen. Two
weeks later, I called him to let him know that we had achieved our goal.
Andrew was going to a party that weekend!

In the beginning, as advocates of inclusion, we tended to focus on the opportunities for socialization that the general education classroom provides. Our stance was, in effect, "It doesn't matter whether this student learns much of the academic content in the general education classroom, we just want him or her there to learn social skills." Over time this stance changed mostly because students with disabilities were gaining a lot of academic skills and knowledge in spite of low expectations. Classroom teachers also deserve credit for this shift, as many of them questioned the limited goals and objectives listed on students' IEPs. We realize now that no student should have to choose between learning to read and making a friend. We now know that both academic learning and social relationships are important and that for many students—both those with and those without disabilities—they are linked.

Communication

Speech-language therapy was part of Andrew's day in the classroom.
The therapist would observe what the class was doing and then deter-
mine (in collaboration with the paraprofessional and the teacher) how
Andrew could participate to the fullest extent while simultaneously
working on some of his speech-language goals. Andrew needed to learn
to communicate—and where better to learn communication than in a
classroom with his peers? Communication boards were developed, and
soon Andrew was able to make choices, indicate likes and dislikes, and
answer questions by pointing to pictures that corresponded to a variety
of events and activities.

Paraprofessionals

I had been questioning the wisdom of "attaching" an adult to my child
for several years, but ever since I could remember, Andrew had always
had an assistant assigned to him. It seems obvious that if an adult is con-
stantly with a student, there is the danger that both individuals will
become dependent on one another. At one point, the team decided to
increase the number of assistants who supported Andrew during the day
to reduce his dependence on one particular person. Andrew made the
transition beautifully and interacts well with many people, but the basic
problem still exists—dependence on adults!

Teachers of inclusive classrooms often say that the one thing without which they could not survive is the additional adult that often "comes with" a student with disabilities. The use of paraprofessional support, however, has been and continues to be an aspect of inclusive education that requires careful attention, long-term planning, even delicacy. When paraprofessional support is provided, the rate at which general education teachers welcome students with disabilities tends to increase. This allows for larger numbers of students with disabilities to be educated in general education classrooms. With paraprofessional support, however, there may be a future price to pay in terms of the teacher's sense of responsibility to and for the student, the degree to which inclusive curriculum is developed and used, and the student's friendships and social relationships. The use of paraprofessional support can at times adversely affect each of these, but the opposite is also true. The paraprofessional in the classroom may better enable the classroom teacher to know the student and may be an asset to both the development and the implementation of inclusive curriculum and instruction. The student's social relationships and friendships may also benefit from this person's facilitation.

This dynamic is with many types of supports, such as modifications to a math assignment, time with an occupational therapist, or use of a personal computer. Often the very elements that can make a situation work well are the very same elements that can make that situation problematic. The ways in which supports are utilized are equally as important, if not more so, as the kinds of supports we put into place.

For example, in one classroom a modified math assignment may be merely one assignment in a pile of many that have been individualized for students. The teacher sees his or her students as diverse, respects their unique learning styles, and carries on. The modified math paper in this scenario supports meaningful academic learning for the student with disabilities and does not compromise social inclusion or the student's self-esteem. Imagine a second scenario in which the rest of the class is doing a sheet of word problems and one student receives a modified math assignment. With the greatest of care, the student's dignity might be maintained in this scenario, but our experience tells us more than likely it is not. Perhaps the classroom teacher feels that the student's need for a different assignment is a nuisance. Unfortunately, there is arguably no such thing as the privacy of one's own mind when working with children, so of course the other children sense this and learn that this student's difference must be tolerated but not necessarily valued. What then happens on the playground later that day, when this same student with disabilities wants to play kickball but needs assistance to do so? Are kids going to see this as an opportunity for creative problem solving, or will they emulate their teacher's "Well, okay, I guess I've got to do this" approach? In this case, the modified math assignment—designed simply to address math goals on a student's IEP—presents a subtle but fundamental attitudinal barrier to the student's true membership in the class. In other words, what was designed to be supportive is not—and is in fact the opposite.

The supports we provide are simply people, things, and ways of thinking that we have determined will facilitate meaningful learning and social inclusion for students with disabilities. It is the way in which those supports are offered, utilized, and regarded that ultimately allows us to evaluate their—and our—effectiveness.

Looking Toward the Future

Will and I have the same hopes and dreams for Andrew that we have for our other children. We want him to be happy, healthy, loved, and accepted for who he is. We want him to have good friends, to have choices in his life, and to have the supports to make those choices possible. These choices include whether to go to college, what kind of work he wants to do, where and with whom he lives, and what he does for recreation.

For Andrew, we know the end we're traveling toward is more typical than special. There may be roadblocks along the way, but we keep in mind that wherever there is a roadblock, there is a detour. On some of these detours we find beautiful places that we might never have discovered otherwise. In the end, we know that Andrew's journey will have mattered and that he will have made a difference in the lives of everyone whom he has met along the way.

Andrew is now a sophomore at his local high school. He recently took his English class mid-term exam by answering the multiple choice questions by pointing to sections of a quadrant board. Andrew's classroom teacher said that he earned an *A.*

Parents often are the driving force behind organizational change because they are the ones who hold and articulate a vision for their child's future in the context of the family and the community. Whereas others come and go in the child's life, many times parents are able to hold a long-range view.

FROM VISITING TO BELONGING: A SPECIAL EDUCATOR'S STORY

In 1988, about the same time the Institute on Disability (IOD) at the University of New Hampshire began administering the New Hampshire Statewide Systems Change Project, I was working as a special education teacher. I would bring my special education class to the cafeteria against the wishes of the school's principal. According to the principal, my students had not yet demonstrated "proper eating skills." During that year and still today, the IOD provided intensive training and technical assistance to my school district in which families and educators were rethink-

*ing the ways in which students with severe disabilities were being edu-
cated in our state.*

*As a first-year teacher, I learned a great deal. Among other things, I
learned that "proper eating skills" are not a prerequisite for eating in a
school cafeteria. I also learned that if I merely taught my students the
skills on their IEPs, as I had been told to do, I would only increase their
proficiency in our special education classroom. My job, instead, was to
support these young children to work, play, and learn in the real world
of their school community. The only problem was that they had never
been invited to be there.*

It is interesting to look back at the late 1980s and recognize that the barrier being addressed at that time was basic physical access to general education. Today we fight that battle far less often and now face the challenge of
finding ways for students with disabilities to have access to the general education curriculum as well as to the social community of the class. Pearpoint,
Forest, and Snow (1993) framed this as shifting the agenda from "in" to
"with."

Early Mainstreaming Efforts

*I asked Mrs. Jackson, the first-grade teacher, if my students and I could
spend some time in her classroom. She would tell us when to arrive
(usually around noon) and when to leave (when one of my students got
noisy). I always knew that Bobby was going to get noisy because he had
a lot in his 6-year-old life to get noisy about. So, we'd go into the first-
grade classroom, hear the first page of a story or carve just one eye on
the jack-o'-lantern, and then turn around and leave. The next day I'd put
a note in Mrs. Jackson's mailbox thanking her for the "mainstreaming
opportunity." In the note I'd ask if she wanted me to take her recess duty
on Wednesday, if she wanted to borrow my math manipulatives, or if
she would like me to bring her chocolate or wine every day for the rest
of her life. I would have done anything to keep her classroom door
open for my students.*

In those days mainstreaming was a favor, and teacher deals were the cur-
rency of exchange. Spending time in a general education classroom was
thought to be a good idea for certain students at certain times, but not for all
students all of the time. We have since learned the crucial difference between
mainstreaming and inclusion and have learned that as long as eligibility criteria exist and a student can be "bartered" in or out of an inclusive setting, two
separate systems of education are operating in our schools.

Membership in General Education

Fairly soon after the school year had started, I realized that if I kept up with the food and the compliments, my class could continue to visit Mrs. Jackson's first-grade class. There was nothing, however, that I could do to ensure that they could stay. In response, I shifted my mission from "ensuring mainstreaming opportunities" for this year to ensuring first-grade membership for next year. I arranged a meeting with Mrs. Jackson and asked her to write down everything my students would need to know and be able to do before entering first grade. She gave me a long list, and I got to work right away.

With hindsight being 20/20, it is easy to realize that Susan could not teach her special education students everything that was on the first-grade teacher's list or guarantee their membership in the first-grade class. This was not due to novice instructional skills but instead to the fact that she had agreed to—and even asked for—a list of prerequisites for entering first grade. But what really are the prerequisites for first grade: Being able to be read to? Making a paper plate mask? Acting the part of the cranberry sauce in the Thanksgiving play? On one hand, Susan's question about prerequisites was an attempt at ensuring inclusion in general education, not just visitation rights, for her students the following year. On the other hand, Susan's question to the first-grade teacher revealed the reason that her students were segregated in the first place.

This incident exemplifies what has become a long-winded conversation among educators about what constitutes any child's "readiness" for first grade, second grade, eleventh grade, honor's English, or the school band. What is the purpose of education? To draw a line in the sand and determine who can jump far enough to reach it, or to draw a line in the sand and work hard to support all students to reach it? Our emphasis on educational outcomes and high standards makes this issue even more relevant.

Within educational circles professionals often agree on the value of high learning expectations for students. These standards often prevent educational discrimination. For example, we expect both male and female students to obtain a high level of skill in math and science. We expect students of all ethnicities to demonstrate sophisticated literacy abilities. Yet, thinking back to the first grade teacher's list of prerequisites, it has become apparent that there is also the danger that high standards in and of themselves are discriminatory. What if a student never learned to use scissors? Would that mean that he or she would never be ready for first grade? Would it mean that if the student were to participate in first grade, he or she would never be considered successful? As with the use of supports, the *ways* in which we utilize standards—not the standards themselves—matter most. Education is not a science, it's an art.

Quality Education for All

A fellow teacher once asked me whether I had a sibling with a disability. I answered that I did not, and she looked surprised. She wondered why I cared so much about students with disabilities and specifically about inclusive education. I did not know how to answer at the time. Today I realize that my passion for education is not limited to special education issues. I have realized that the inclusion of students with disabilities in general education often forces us to ask important questions about the education of all students. Sometimes these are questions we may not have otherwise thought to ask.

Special educators are in a unique position to support inclusion in a school, though for some, the inclusion of students with disabilities in general education classrooms may feel threatening. With time, training, and opportunities to observe inclusive classrooms, many special education teachers find ways to fit themselves into their new role of inclusion facilitator. They know their students well and are able to offer classroom teachers supports and strategies. For other special educators, the role of inclusion facilitator is one that they would rather not take, and it has become increasingly common for these educators to become general education teachers instead.

OPPORTUNITIES ARE THERE ALL ALONG: A GENERAL EDUCATOR'S STORY

As a general education third-grade teacher, my first direct contact with Marc was in the lunch room. I was on cafeteria duty and asked him to take his tray up to the counter. All of the second-grade children were cleaning up and getting ready to go outside for recess. At first Marc just looked at me, then he shook his head no. He proceeded to throw himself onto the floor. I reacted without the luxury of time to think the matter over. I immediately sat down with him and placed my arm over his shoulder so that he couldn't hurt himself or me. He was very agitated and started to spit. I think this is when I fell in love with Marc. Funny as it may sound, I felt a connection. I talked quietly to him.

Because Marc didn't talk, he made sounds to let me know that he was still upset. Eventually, his body relaxed, and I told him that he needed to take up his tray up before going out to recess. He nodded yes, took his tray up, and went outside. I went in search of our school's inclusion facilitator, as I wanted Marc to be in my third-grade classroom next year.

Regardless of personal opinions about inclusion, every teacher is faced with the daily incidents of school life and has to react quickly in a countless variety of situations. Grace handled the interaction with Marc by using respect for his dignity, not by using knowledge gained in a training session.

The Importance of Caring

At the end of the year, I attended Marc's IEP meeting and learned that I would, in fact, be Marc's third-grade teacher. I was thrilled and told Marc's parents that I had requested that their son be in my class. They were delighted and surprised to hear this. They told me that no teacher had ever requested to have Marc in his or her class.

Grace wanted this student to be a member of her classroom. She wanted to be his teacher, to teach and learn alongside him, and to play a significant role in his third-grade year. This desire is more significant than we have acknowledged in the past. Many parents of students with disabilities report that although they do want their son or daughter included in general education and although they do value the respectful provision of supports and services, the classroom teacher's attitude about their child's membership most affects their sense of how well things are going. A teacher who greets a child in the morning with a smile, who enjoys the gifts and talents the child has to share, and who truly likes the child and is comfortable being with him or her means more to many parents than inclusion advocates once realized. We should not be surprised. Hundreds of parents of children without disabilities would say the same—that they would prefer a teacher who really liked their child yet used instructional strategies with which they did not agree rather than a teacher who was at best indifferent about their son or daughter's membership yet used state-of-the-art instructional practices. It is possible that in our drive to get all of the inclusive pieces in place for students with disabilities, we have forgotten to attribute due importance to this matter.

The Other Students

Patting ourselves on the back because including Marc in our classroom was going so well, Leslie, the classroom assistant, and I were shocked one day when Marc appeared to be extremely upset right before art class. He really seemed to love art class, so we didn't understand what was happening. Before we knew it, Marc was on the floor, and Leslie was supporting him. I quickly lined up the rest of the students and had them go to art class. I'll never forget the look of fear on their faces—they just didn't understand what was happening. About half an hour later, I heard my students returning from the art room. I did not want them to enter the room and see Marc still on the floor with Leslie next to him, so

I met them in the hall and redirected them to the library. I asked them all to sit down.

As they took their seats, I held my breath because I wasn't at all sure what to say. (They never taught me this in college.) I decided to just tell them the truth as simply as possible. I asked them to remember a time when they were less able to communicate their feelings with words. We talked about what they had done in those situations, and I suggested that what Marc was going through today was similar to their experiences. He had become very frustrated and upset at not being able to explain what he was feeling. I asked them to remember how they felt after they had gotten very upset and had acted in a way that showed their frustration. Most of them agreed that they had been very embarrassed in those instances.

I asked them to respect Marc's feelings and to please go back into the classroom and start their reading assignments without staring at him. I assured them that Marc would be fine but that as his classmates, they had the power to make Marc feel like he was still a part our the class. When I felt sure that everyone was comfortable, we returned to the classroom. I could have kissed every one of those children—they acted like they did this every day.

In many of our earliest efforts to include students with disabilities, we seldom proposed changes regarding what children in general education classrooms were learning. Ours was a position of gratitude, and even as adults, we sometimes felt we had been granted only conditional membership to general education. We didn't want to rock the boat.

Some people might read Grace's account of handling this difficult situation as time "off task" for the rest of the class. They might be wary of the priority that was placed on having all students understand the feelings and behaviors of one student. They might ask whether time was taken away from "real" learning.

As advocates for quality education for all students become more knowledgeable, experienced, and confident, we become more comfortable questioning what all children are learning. Anyone who has read a newspaper in the 1990s could argue that lack of tolerance for diversity in American society is troublesome. With all due respect to the curricula operating in schools today, it is time to expand on what we teach our children. Educating students with disabilities in general education classrooms is not the reason that this expansion is needed—these students have simply helped alert us to an issue that we have sometimes pretended not to see. Along with teaching math, science, literacy, and the like, it is imperative that we help students learn to live and work with one another (which is exactly what Grace was teaching her students).

When taken seriously, this notion has systemic implications that reach much farther than the curriculum used in the classroom.

They Already Had It Figured Out

As I grew professionally and personally as a teacher that year, I often found myself holding my breath and saying a little prayer that I would be able to handle situations as they arose. One such situation involved a little girl named Rose and a cooperative learning lesson. Rose is a student who won't quit. She has Down syndrome and is well liked by her peers.

That day, the class was working in small cooperative groups in which their roles and responsibilities rotated. One of the roles assigned on this day was note taker. I remember well the moment that I realized that it would soon be Rose's turn to write, because in my mind, she wasn't yet able to do so. As I roamed around the room, I purposely saved Rose's group for my last stop. I didn't know what I was going to say or do. I was concerned about Rose's feelings.

My concern was unnecessary. When I walked over to Rose's group, thinking that I would simply have to ask another student to take on her job as note taker, one of the group members told me that the group had figured something out. "You see," he said, "Rose knows how to write the letters—she just can't spell the words, so we are going to spell them out for her while she writes them down." Kids are the best teachers.

I believe that my students sensed from the beginning that I was committed to making all students valued members of our class. When students without disabilities observed my interactions with students with disabilities, they saw no difference. Don't get me wrong, there were numerous times when I had no idea what to do and the only activity I could think of for a student with disabilities was something unrelated to what the rest of the class was working on. This was probably due to a lack of confidence left over from the days when I believed that special education teachers were magicians.

Our year together went well. All of my students learned, and I did too. I began the year both excited and anxious about educating students with disabilities in my classroom. By the end of the year, when a student with disabilities entered the room, I simply said hello.

General education teachers, as catalysts for change, represent the "typical" world and can approach situations without introducing a stigma of difference or specialness. Their impact is greatest when they take responsibility for each child's schooling and when they communicate that good teaching for students with disabilities is just that—good teaching.

CONCLUSIONS

What have we learned about creating inclusive elementary schools? Our answers fall into two categories. First, there are things we can do. Second, there are ways we can be. The list of things we can do—strategies that make inclusive schools more likely—grows everyday. We know the necessity of a school philosophy, administrative support, and common planning time. We know the value of technology, teacher training, and innovative instructional strategies. We have learned that the involvement of parents, inclusion facilitators, and paraprofessionals is vital. We know what we can do to create inclusive schools.

Our experience tells us that we must learn more about the second category. There are far too many schools in which a list of things to do to create an inclusive school is in place, yet students with disabilities are still offered a "continuum of placements," inclusion facilitators are seen as the enemy, classmates question the fairness of curricular modifications, and families feel segregated. Why? These situations may have more to do with who we are than what we do.

To varying degrees, inclusion is still seen as a mere option in many schools, even those we call *inclusive*. Membership in general education for students with disabilities may be their right, but it is not always an assumption. Although people value diversity more now than in the past, the belief still exists that although all children are unique and different, some children are *really* unique and different. Then, once again, these children are set apart from other children—perhaps not in our schools but in an even more powerful place, our minds. Change is in the air, and although we espouse to be proponents of it, it is by its very nature threatening. There is always the risk that we will change only to the point to which we still feel comfortable, and there is always the chance that the changes that matter most lie beyond that point.

We have learned that who we are matters greatly to the process of creating inclusive schools. This is both bad news and good news—bad news because orchestrating human commitment, building human community, and gathering courage are far more difficult than writing a school philosophy, scheduling common planning time, and providing teachers with training. Recognizing the essential role that our human integrity plays in the creation of inclusive schools is also good news—because the power is in our hands.

REFERENCES

Calculator, S., & Jorgensen, C. (1994). *Including students with severe disabilities in schools: Facilitating communication, interaction, and participation.* San Diego: Singular Publishing Group.

Coles, R. (1989). *The call of stories: Teaching and the moral imagination.* Boston: Houghton Mifflin.

Pearpoint, J., Forest, M., & Snow, J. (1993). *The inclusion papers: Strategies to make inclusion work.* Toronto: Inclusion Press.

5

Supporting Students with Emotional Disabilities in General Education Classrooms

Herb Lovett

Schools are faced with two conflicting impulses: to respect and support individual student and parent preferences, beliefs, and needs and at the same time to standardize academic and social expectations. Moving between these strong currents, the shift from special to inclusive education represents more than a change in educational policy—it reflects and typifies this larger crisis in educational philosophy and wider cultural concerns.

The University of New Hampshire's Institute on Disability (IOD), as part of its commitment to fully inclusive schools, has been working to support local school systems in developing flexible and comprehensive supports for students with educational disabilities. In collaboration with Keene State College in Keene, New Hampshire, and the state Department of Education, the IOD began the New Hampshire Statewide Systems Change Project, funded by the U.S. Department of Education. One aspect of this project involved developing and implementing proactive strategies and supports for those students identified as "seriously emotionally handicapped." Through ongoing training and technical assistance, schools throughout New Hampshire are developing a wide variety of student and teacher supports that allow them to successfully include identified students who are at risk of being placed in a separate classroom or school. The full inclusion of children with emotional disabilities represents a significant challenge for many schools. This project provides ongoing and systematic support to encourage systemwide change over time as opposed to a quick-fix mentality. Several districts receiving support have made long-term commitments to develop, implement, and monitor strategies and supports that enhance the social and emotional development as well as academic achievement of identified students.

There is no one answer as to what works, and no two schools have addressed the question of how to accomplish full inclusion of identified students in exactly the same way. This chapter presents case studies, based on numerous visits and in-depth interviews over a full school year, of four students in four different schools in four different areas of the state. Each school is deeply involved in the process of change and committed to inclusive education. Their experiences help shed light on the process and meaning of inclusion for individuals with behavioral difficulties.

BRIAN

Southwest Elementary School is in one of the wealthier communities in New Hampshire. This community of mostly white middle and upper-middle income families is committed to the importance of education and believes that directing local taxes to the schools is a good investment. As a result, the educational standards are quite high, and most children in the town attend public schools.

Much as one would expect, Southwest Elementary was clean, orderly, and quietly active. My visit felt like I was having lunch in a slightly pricey and popular restaurant. I met on a snowy, late winter morning with Brian's fourth-grade teacher and an assistant, both of whom had a warm, quiet way about them. When we began talking about Brian, their first words were, "He's a great little guy. And he's very intelligent."

Brian's mother was a single parent when he was born; he has never known his father. When he was of kindergarten age, his mother remarried and his stepfather is alleged to have abused him sexually and, inevitably, emotionally.

When he came into the first grade, he was kicking, biting, and spitting both at adults and at other children. His teachers are not quite sure what happened or why, but in the course of the next 2 years, Brian lived with his grandmother, at a group home for children with emotional disabilities, and with an aunt before coming back to Southwest as a fourth grader.

As part of this complicated life, Brian is legally the resident of another town but actually lives in the town of Southwest. Technically, he is a ward of the state, but his primary caregiver is his grandmother. The state pays for a psychologist to work with him at school for half an hour every week, but Brian works better when he has a full hour. Although it was recommended that he be seen by a psychologist for an hour each week, funding is only available for him to meet every other week for 1 hour. The compromise of 1 hour every other week is not the same as 1 hour every week. A full-time assistant works with Brian's class. Brian is still considered "explosive."

There have been days when Brian has broken pencils and chairs and then stormed out of the room when his teacher or the assistant have said "no" to him. Being in control is important to Brian, and he often has a hard time when told "no." Once he calms down he is expected to make up the work he has missed. As a consequence he often loses recess so that he may make up work that he has missed, but increasingly his teachers have been able to help him learn to make better choices by showing him alternative ways to deal with and talk about his anger and frustration. He is seen as gaining better control.

Brian's teacher thinks that his outbursts are sometimes connected to his diet and sometimes internally triggered by his difficult childhood. But for whatever reasons he gets upset, his teacher usually tries to get him to leave the room so he can yell outside until he has calmed down. She knows that talking with him when he's upset is useless but that he can be helpful in sorting his thoughts and feelings out once he's settled down again. Once Brian is calm, he is able to talk about what has made him angry and figure out alternatives to yelling or getting aggressive.

Like most children, Brian feels safe with clear boundaries, and his teacher's calm presence has helped him. As he starts to settle down, she asks him, "Do you want to go back to the classroom? Or do you want to walk more?" At first it would take him a good 15 minutes to wind down, but now it's more likely to take 5. Over time he has learned to recognize his readiness to return to structure and demands. Knowing that he has this choice gives him the sense of control he needs and helps him to deal more effectively with both the demands of school life and the internal stressors about which his teacher can only guess.

Brian's grandmother has petitioned the state for legal custody and has been encouraging more contact with his mother and his half-sister. The day I came to visit, Brian was planning to spend the upcoming weekend with his mother, his stepfather, and his half-sister on a trip out of state even though he has told his teacher, "Since I've been seeing my mother, I'm not doing the kind of work I was before." Staff who work with Brian recognize that disruptions in his life due to unstable and/or unsafe living situations often cause him to have more difficulty succeeding in school, and these staff members are able to adapt assignments and expectations when he is clearly too stressed to focus on these tasks.

An important factor in Brian's successful school experience has been the facilitating and trusting relationship he has had with his teaching assistant. When interviewed, the assistant reported, "I didn't have any special ed. background and, I [initially] turned the job down because I didn't know what to do.... But [the teacher] called me and told me I'd be fine. She told me 'He's wonderful. Wait until you get to know him.' The other teachers said, 'You're going to have your hands full. He's a monster,' but I decided to give it a try. When I met Brian, I realized his potential. He needs a lot of TLC, so that's what I give him."

Her positive vision of who Brian was and her high expectations of what he could become if provided with a safe and supportive environment have clearly contributed to Brian's performance in a typical classroom. The assistant said, "If he had a bad morning he couldn't turn it off. So I taught him to realize that [even] if he had a bad morning, afternoon [could be] different. I taught him to smile and [stay] calm as a way to do it. I don't like tokens. They're about being perfect. I think it's better to teach respect, trust, communication, and honesty. No one's ever going to be perfect."

Because the assistant started in Brian's class as a substitute teacher, when she came as a teaching assistant, the pupils saw her as she hoped to be seen— as an aide to the whole room, not an assistant to one child. She and Brian get along very well. During school vacations, Brian will drop by her house just to say "hi."

Lately, Brian's individualized education program (IEP) team has been talking of weaning him from what they view as his dependency on the assistant. This is an odd response for a child who has had so difficult a time trusting adults. Still, the assistant has not tried to distance herself from Brian so much as she has tried to give him more sources of support and more ability to monitor his own behavior. As the year has progressed, his classmates have been offering him more spontaneous assistance. As they are better able to act as natural supports, the assistant's role is changing to one of facilitator. If Brian still needs sustained daytime support when he is in middle school, he could have a system of planned peer support.

He is already making more friends at school. Last year a group of girls were like mother hens around him, and he often avoided playing with other boys because he would get into fights. But now he is fitting in better. He's doing well in karate, which gives him some status, too. Karate seems like a good way for him to connect socially because it has clear rules, boundaries, and a way to focus and direct energy positively.

In spite of all of this hardship for one so young, Brian has remained at grade level. His teacher says, "He does not need to perform at a certain level in order to get a passing grade. He enjoys being challenged, and our flexible grading system gives him some leeway in excusing his individual variation. Sometimes we accept the work, but [other times] we tell him, 'This is not the best you can do, so let's try it again.' I've been in the classroom 22 years. You can see challenge in a lot of different ways, and no two classes are alike. The trick is to make a class of so many individuals into a unified community.

"I was teaching third graders, and when I went to fourth grade, 18 kids came along. During that year, I began to think my discipline was too negative, and I didn't like behavior [modification]—it wasn't positive, and I was looking for positive discipline. So I put up signs like *We're here to help each other* around the classroom. I'm looking for ways to teach kids about looking for solutions, not blame.

"I also started having class meetings every morning. The agenda comes from a community problem book. The issues have ranged from minor ("Recess is too short") to serious ("I'm scared of this kid who kicks me"). These class meetings have really changed things for the better. Talking about these things has made all the difference in the world.

"Recently, the class had been in a debate because of what a boy had said and how a girl had reacted. What had started between two pupils became a major dispute. But in the class meeting, the kids themselves resolved the whole thing. They decided it's not a good idea to tell other people when someone is bothering you. It's a lot simpler to talk to the person directly. Brian had the last word on this. He pointed out that boys and girls see things differently and that it was important to remember this when talking things out. The other kids were impressed. Brian says he hates the morning meetings, but he likes the compliments he receives from the other students when he has something to contribute."

KEVIN

When Kevin started first grade at Northeast Elementary School, his teachers remember him crawling on the floor, barking, and destroying his work. He seemed to have mood swings from happy and giddy to seriously depressed within minutes. He was referred for assessment fairly quickly, was diagnosed as having attention-deficit/hyperactivity disorder (ADHD) and a major mood disorder, and was reassigned to the school's self-contained special education classroom.

But during second grade, Kevin was placed into the general education second-grade class at Northeast Elementary School, with a resource room available within the school as a back-up. He was considered one of the brightest kids in his room so his teacher focused on his academic ability. Originally, an assistant was assigned to work with him on arithmetic, but she decided it would be better to help the children who were struggling most with their work. As it turned out, Kevin was rarely one of them. As she described it, "He could do work well above grade level, but he couldn't do, 'What's your name? Can I play with you?'" Although academically bright, Kevin had problems using social skills to make friends, solve problems, and deal with frustrating situations.

When Kevin has a difficult time dealing with his emotions or needs to settle down, he goes to the resource room for a while. The resource room teacher has an open, sunny manner; and although we intruded on her fairly busy schedule, she matter-of-factly talked to us while she worked. "Our strategy has been to pull him out to the resource room when he's getting confused, give him some one-to-one instruction, and then get him right back into class to try it out," she explained. "I try to make a safe space here for *all* kids in the school. It should be a choice [for] all kids to say, 'I need a break, I need to go,' and not have to deal with emotional crisis in public or in front of a group. Sometimes teachers can get into a struggle with the child, and the only way they know how to deal with it is through public correction. I even have teachers who say public humiliation is good sometimes. But it is just inhumane for kids who didn't get dinner last night, whose parents were drunk, or who get beaten. This is not correction. For these kids it means, 'You are worthless.'"

By the second half of the year, Kevin, at 9 years old, was doing well as a full-time member of the second grade class. Kevin's teacher, with 18 years' teaching experience, had thought at the beginning of the year that having Kevin full-time in the class was going to be more difficult than it has turned out to be. As she began designing accommodations, she found that this process was not much different from how she had always adapted her methods in individual situations so that each student could get the most out of school. She had been individualizing her approach for pupils all along.

She said she believes that "maybe the real secret to our success had been having more people and the flexibility that gives us. Using the teaching assistants intelligently is work; I don't want someone just listening to me talking. Having the assistant makes planning more work, but because of the other adults in the room, I can have a group go out to do something while I get the chance to have five pupils in a writing lab. At that level of personal attention, instruction gets much more effective."

Her biggest challenge has been how to be fair but firm with Kevin. One of the difficulties of working with a student with neurological differences or emotional difficulties is sorting out when the child is overwhelmed, genuinely confused, or is just being a kid. "He will push and try not to be responsible. When he gets stressed or out of control, he cries or says, 'Everyone else is doing it!' I feel confident with the checklists we have developed to help remind him about work and conduct. And it helps having the safety valve of [the resource room teacher] and her room."

Both Kevin's school and the local mental health services agency recognize that a child is not just a "behavior problem" or a "difficult student" but a family member with a life beyond the school and that parents need (and usually want) to be part of their child's education in more significant ways than simply coming to an IEP meeting. The local mental health services agency has instituted a program of in-home therapy for children identified as having behavioral or emotional difficulties at school.

The director of this program said, "Many parents thought of the therapy program as 'They're coming to get me and take my kids away.'" Now, like good teachers, the agency staff meet families where they are most comfortable and allow trust, a critical variable in both therapy and education, to develop.

"Initially, I was only going to oversee this program," the director explained, "but it became clear that whoever was overseeing the program had to be involved personally. I wanted to create predictability and consistency. Relationships are critical, and I stay involved with every family. Ours is not a program where staff working with these families can come and go; every time a face changes, we set them back tremendously. Our hope is to carry over treatment into the home. For instance, if a child is learning to make friends, we figure out ways of helping school friends be a part of after-school life."

Kevin's family decided that participating in the in-home therapy program would be a good idea. One program staff member who works with Kevin said, "Home workers can take him and his friends down to the [arcade] to play computer games. The other kids' parents are comfortable with that, and Kevin gets to have his friends while doing something fun. Kevin has come through the same stages we have come through as a system. His mom was angry at the school, and she was right—we really were messing up. And now his mom has her own support group of other parents with kids with ADHD issues. She's listened to the other parents, and this has given her a way to work on her parenting skills."

Northeast Elementary is unique in its ability to gain access to community supports for students and families, which helps school staff extend support beyond the school day. Given the complexity of many of the students' problems, it is difficult for the school to provide all necessary supports in isolation from other professionals. Kevin's success is partially due to the school's ability to collaborate in providing comprehensive supports for him and his family.

Kevin is only 9 years old, but he has had a lot to cope with. Beyond the ordinary pains of growing most kids have and beyond having an unpredictable emotional life and adjusting to ADHD, Kevin had a hard time with his parents' separation. His big wish was that they would get back together.

Last April, Kevin spent part of his spring vacation week with his father, who committed suicide shortly after Kevin left. Kevin's teachers did not know how to talk to him about this, but they knew it was important that they do so. A clinical social worker who spends 2 days per week at Northeast Elementary School and who had been seeing Kevin at school was able to help them with their concerns.

The social worker said, "Kevin talked with the class about it: He told them he was having a tough time 'because my dad died over vacation,' and the kids asked, 'Are you okay?' The kids and the teacher understood, and he got a lot of support because of it. After this the kids were better able to accept him when he was difficult."

Success in school is only a beginning for Kevin, who will need significant supports as he continues to grow and develop. Social skills remain an area of concern. According to the social worker, "His relationship skills are weak. He gets depressed a lot, and he's hard to approach. If a kid asked him to play, he would appear not to hear [him or her]. And then if he did play, he would have a hard time understanding the rules or would have a hard time playing if he tried to join in."

The positive relationship between Kevin and his teacher will continue to be a key factor in making further growth possible. "I am his safety net; I am always here. He knows I will make good choices when he can't make them for himself and he knows I will never hurt him. I give him safety first and that is the biggest issue for kids who have been hurt." Helping kids be safe and successful is what it's all about.

ELIAS

I arrived at Central Elementary at the same time that another researcher was interviewing the teachers whom I was scheduled to meet. The teachers were answering this researcher's questions and talking to one another simultaneously. I waited for this to subside before jumping in with my questions about Elias, a sixth grader who was identified as having a "severe emotional disorder."

As I sat there, I was struck by the maxim "We are who we serve." These same teachers who spent much of their time each day organizing material so that children could be focused and attentive were, themselves, busily and noisily unfocused; were interrupting themselves and one another; and were distracted by everything going on around them. In the midst of this flurry, I started to piece together how life at Central Elementary might have been going for Elias and what it had been like before he had come to Central.

Elias started in parochial school and had a good first year but in the second grade began losing verbal control. He started swearing and was considered behaviorally difficult because of his resistance to direction and his argumentativeness with teachers. His mother was asked to take him out of the school.

Elias's mother took him to Central Elementary, where he was so argumentative and physically aggressive that he was assigned a one-to-one assistant. The assistant would take him out of the general education classroom for individual instruction in a room so small that his teacher said it was almost a closet. Soon after, Elias was diagnosed with Tourette syndrome and ADHD. The school district felt that it had little knowledge about how to deal effectively with a child with these diagnoses and was initially not willing to serve a child who was out of physical control. So, Elias was bused out of the district to finish second grade in a day school for children with behavioral and emotional disorders. This school did not use individual behavior plans but rather had a policy of sending disruptive students to a time-out room staffed with two assistants. Instead of teaching Elias more effective strategies to deal with his problems, he was punished for losing control. Elias spent more and more time in time-out and less and less time in class. As it happened, Elias came to enjoy socializing with the assistants, but they did not give any instruction. When his mother reported that she was having a hard time at home getting him to do the work he had missed in class, the school responded by no longer sending the work home with him. If his teacher asked him for his assignment, he would just swear and be sent to time-out for the rest of the day.

Not surprisingly, his academic levels at the end of the year were the same as at the beginning of the year, and by the end of fourth grade his behavior had deteriorated to the point where he spent large amounts of time angry and out of control. So, the out-of-district day school asked for additional funding. Confused and concerned by the school's inability to appropriately support Elias, his school district decided to develop an individualized transition plan to bring him back to Central. They decided that they could use the funding they were paying to the day school to provide better and more typical supports to Elias in a typical classroom environment. Initially, Elias came to school for just half a day, but he quickly complained that he was not really part of the class, and he was right.

When Elias began fifth grade, he was worried about math so he went to a tutor over the summer, and that helped to the extent that he came back with no academic lags. Now he has typical math skills, but his verbal abilities are very high. He began the year on a "diagnostic placement," which meant that for 45 days teachers would collect data and then develop a plan. They began with a tentative IEP until they could tailor it to him as they got to know him better.

Elias's initial behavioral goal was to control his speech volume, not the profanity (he would shout "yummy" or "f*** you," or make a clucking sound). The teachers did cue Elias to make him *aware* that he was swearing and give him 2 minutes to quiet down. If he didn't, they found his behavior would escalate and get very loud. For that reason, if he did not regain control in the 2 minutes, he earned a time-out, which meant he was sent to the resource room to regain control.

Once, when Elias failed to calm down in the resource room, the teacher called the special education van to remove him from the building. Elias was very upset and couldn't believe that he was being sent home. As the teacher explained, "I didn't know then how much control he had." A few days later she talked with Elias about the incident. She said, "I eventually asked Elias if he really wanted to be here at this school, and he said he did. So I told him, 'Then I expect you to be appropriate in the class and the hallway.'"

The point of time-out was not to be punitive but to give Elias a chance to calm down. Once calm, he was expected to plan a different way to deal with the next time he became angry or anxious. Elias was subsequently taught how to self-monitor his anxiety. When he found himself becoming anxious, rather than wait until he was out of control, he was allowed to quietly leave the classroom and go to the resource room until he felt he could return. But he still thought of this as a punishment. So, he and the teacher worked out a deal. In his classroom, he can say "I need to leave," or he can just leave without saying anything—and he can go where he chooses on school grounds. He usually chooses to go for a walk or to sit in the resource room.

The teacher reports that some of the other teachers are confused by this policy. They ask, "How does Elias get away with being out of class on his own like that?" Elias's teacher tries to help these teachers see this as not a moral lapse but rather an accommodation that Elias needs to successfully cope with school.

Elias regularly sees a local pediatric neurologist who has served on the multidisciplinary team that has been working on giving Elias specific behavioral supports and coordinating these with his medication. Recently, perhaps as the result of a medication change, he seems to be smiling instead of getting angry or only saying "yummy" rather than swearing noisily.

Elias has come to see the resource room as helping rather than punishing and as something available to anyone who needs it. He explained, "If there's a problem in a class, we can come down here where's its quiet, or they let [me] go outside to take a break. Or we can go walk around with the teacher in the school. We go back when we are okay." I asked him how he would know he needed to take a break. "If I get warm inside and if I can't concentrate, I can act really wild. I get warm inside my head, and I start fooling. I've learned to figure this out and take a break."

When asked what helps the most, Elias answered, "the teachers, because they understand me. I have had a tough time. They think of ways to help me and give me goals and stuff and help if I need it. They help me stay in class and with the homework and write home about what kind of day I've had. They don't say, 'He was bad today.' They don't use bad words. They write, *It's been a tough day.*"

Elias's sixth-grade teacher had worked in an automotive customer service department for 20 years when he decided to go back to school. He said, "I had always wanted to teach." He has a reputation of being very understanding but lets kids know when they are not acting as well as they might. "Kids may get crazy, but they are not all bad. I can gain the kids' confidence and that's reassuring to them. This year's class is an anxious group.

"I guess I have some structure, but it's flexible enough to make changes on the run. You can't go in straight lines; you may have to take a lot of detours. At the same time, you have to leave enough space for the kids. They have to be comfortable. If they aren't comfortable, nothing is going to get done. If they don't have that trust in you and what's happening, they will just shut down. To get that trust you have to be open and not assume things—actually see what's happening and respond to it. I help [each of] them find out what's going on, because sometimes the kid doesn't know either. I know this sounds vague, but that's the whole point—it *is* kind of vague."

CORY

The town of Southeast is a mixture of "haves" and "have nots." Approximately 12% of its population have college degrees, and 25% have not finished high school. A number of parents have a vision of education as a way for their children to advance. But another group, more vocal and active in local politics, have said, in effect, "I didn't have computers when I was in school, and I'm all right." A number of parents have chosen home schooling for religious reasons. One quarter of the homes in the community are mobile homes. After the IOD conducted a series of workshops for the Southeast school system, the town's high school embarked on a process of becoming fully inclusive.

First, I met with the principal of Southeast High. He had been described as young, caring, flexible, and supportive. He had arranged for students to take courses at the community college or for them to have personalized schedules so that they could graduate. Given the support of the superintendent, he worked to bring pupils who had been placed out-of-district back to their local schools.

He has a clear sense of what a school should be like and has worked to create a system in which experts support the teacher and the classroom rather than send the child to the expert. This way, he reasoned, a sense of ownership for each student's education would rest with a student's teacher. His goal is to create a culture where teachers have primary ownership and responsibility at every step.

Inclusion inevitably means more widely varying student needs. Students do not necessarily thrive simply by being included. The principal asked the faculty to design an approach to rule-violating behavior. He asked them how they could develop a consistent sequence of responses that would help students learn from their behavior rather than simply be punished for it. The results have been interesting, largely because of the way the issue was conceptualized. The principal might just as easily have asked, "How are we going to get kids to behave better?" This question would have led to a consideration of various strategies of cajoling, control, or coercion. Instead, by considering all of the staff in the school to be both stakeholders and resources, he invited them to have responsibility and investment in the result.

The faculty brainstormed about ways to address kids who break rules or do not make good choices and ways to give them more responsibility for their behavior, and how they could move from a punitive to a proactive learning system. They settled on an advisor–advisee program in which any adult in the building who wanted to work with kids would meet with a small group for half an hour once a month. The principal explained, "We use it mostly just to touch base with the kids. Every staff member agreed to be a part of it, though at this point it's voluntary, and some are better than others. We have all the teachers as well as people in food service, the secretary, the aides—they all have a group. This wasn't the point of doing this, but our school dropout rate fell from 8% to 2%. These sessions give kids a sense that if you're not here, someone will want to know why personally, not because it's their job to check up on you."

A technical assistance advisor from Keene State College also helped the school come up with a consistent system for responding to difficult situations.

Rather than send students directly to the vice principal, who is the administrator traditionally in charge of misconduct, the advisor suggested that students come to a planning room where they could identify what got them into trouble, identify their feelings, and think of different ways they could act in such situations in the future. The faculty feared that this would overwhelm the planning room and the specialists there, so the advisor's suggestion was to let this system develop over time as each teacher found a way to respond to difficult situations. In practice, the teachers have found that with consistency and predictability, the explosions are less frequent and kids are doing better.

Cory was identified as a student with educational disabilities by a student intervention team comprised of special educators, guidance counselors, administrators, teachers, and the school nurse. The team's function is to keep an eye out for kids who aren't succeeding or are at risk. The basic attitude of these teams is, "Something in this school is not working for this student, so what do we need to do?" Cory, however, was identified late and therefore was not provided with special education supports until his junior year in high school.

In his junior year at Southeast High, Cory dropped out but then decided to come back to graduate. He was missing 17 credits and needed to take three English classes, so he signed up for as many as he could in the fall. Teachers thought he would be overextended and were not optimistic about this plan. But he and his guidance counselor got along well, and she supported Cory in his plan. To almost everyone's surprise, he not only went to class and did his work but also passed all of his courses. Some of his teachers thought that a lot of this had to do with the counselor's faith in him.

By mid-year Cory got an after-school job and again enrolled in more than the usual number of classes for another ambitious semester. The job gave him some money, but it also added to his stress. Cory began spending his money on alcohol and drugs and started failing in his courses. At this point he started becoming defiant, saying, "I'm not listening to anyone anymore." His counselor wondered whether graduation meant that Cory would lose the structure and the safety that they had created at school.

Not far into the second semester, the principal noticed that Cory had a glass bottle in the cafeteria and reminded him of the rule forbidding glass containers in the cafeteria. Dealing with authority is, in the best of times, hard for Cory. In less time than it takes to read this, Cory lost control. He smashed the bottle and threatened to slash the tires on the principal's car, all the while menacing him with the jagged bottle neck. The principal knew that Cory needed time to blow off steam and process before he could talk rationally and that he had no skills of coping in the moment. The principal told him, "We know how hard you are trying, and we want to help you through." But Cory could only shout that the rule about glass containers was a stupid rule. Meanwhile, someone called the police, and as they removed him, they found a hash pipe in his jacket. (The school also has a rule forbidding drugs or paraphernalia.)

Cory went before the student board and negotiated his return. Given his difficulty in controlling his temper, his guidance counselor went over some options with him. The school rules, she explained, were not going to change for him, but he could make some choices about how he could live with them. She told him that if he felt stressed and needed to, he could walk around the school but that someone would need to know where he was, so one safe place would be to come to the planning room in the guidance department and calm down.

Sometimes, though, he would just walk to the restroom and smoke. He did this often enough to be caught six times, and the handbook on student behavior mandates suspension for 1 week after the sixth offense.

The day I came to Southeast High to meet Cory would have been the first day he was eligible to come back, but he had decided that it was hopeless. He was failing his classes and could not see how he could pass. His job, in a bottling factory, ironically enough, paid what seemed to him to be a comfortable wage. Compared with the structure and routine of his job, getting organized at school well enough to graduate probably seemed overwhelming to him.

I was curious about what kinds of clinical assessments Cory had been through. I was concerned that he had so many symptoms of a treatable neurobehavioral disorder that the school's accommodations, however well intended, simply missed the point. It made sense to me that the rules of the school would not change for him, and I admired the ways the adults in the school had worked so hard to be accommodating, but the difficulty, if my hunch was right, was not in Cory's intellectual grasp of success. Without having met him, I was sure that he knew very well what the rules were. I was concerned, though, that his highly variable capacity to gain access to that information, his impulsivity, his use of drugs, and his history of explosive behavior and substance abuse all might suggest that he had ADHD or a related disorder.

Just as Elias had Tourette syndrome but was not identified until it affected his academic work, Cory had not been identified as having educational disabilities until his junior year in high school, because he had been able to struggle along academically. Without any other way to understand him, and given his apparent intelligence, his behavior was seen as a lack of discipline or lack of regard for social norms. Without further clinical assessment, his underlying neurological condition could not be discerned or addressed, Cory would blame himself further and be more discouraged, and even adults who wanted to help would have to concede defeat in helping him.

It is difficult to strike the right balance. Because so much assessment focuses on what people cannot do (at least while being tested), some schools who have taken on inclusion have a justifiable suspicion of formal testing. Southeast High turned out to be one of these, and little assessment information on Cory was available.

Cory's girlfriend came to the guidance office to ask for the paperwork so that he could formally drop out. Perhaps with an accurate diagnosis and some clearer accommodation, he may yet be able to return to school eventually and graduate.

IMPLICATIONS

Each of these four students' schools is unique in it's ability to gain access to resources, train staff, develop schoolwide approaches that focus on discipline as opposed to punishment, teach social skills and problem-solving strategies as part of a general curriculum, and in general provide safe and supportive environments in which children can learn. Despite the diversity of communities, staff, and organizational history, certain similarities appear across all of the environments represented in these case studies. Each school not only initiated changes in their *responses* to challenging behavior but also addressed the need for the *system as a whole* to expand beyond traditional boundaries to enhance the school's ability to provide successful social and learning experiences. Some common themes from these four case studies have clear implications for policy and practice in the following areas:

- Labeling and diagnosis
- Discipline and assessment
- Supportive school cultures
- Teamwork and interagency collaboration
- Flexible curricula and scheduling
- Appropriate supports for students and staff
- Parental involvement

Implications for Labeling and Diagnosis

In watching teachers, administrators, and parents struggle with the issue of including all children, I have noticed that the one group that seems to have be the hardest to support are the children labeled "severely emotionally disturbed" (SED), which is defined in the *New Hampshire Code of Administrative Rules* (n.d.) as the following:

> A condition exhibiting one or more characteristics over a long period of time and to a marked degree, which adversely affects educational performance:
>
> (1) An inability to learn that cannot be explained by intellectual, sensory or health factors;
> (2) An inability to build or maintain satisfactory interpersonal relationships with peers and teachers;
> (3) Inappropriate types of behaviors or feelings under normal circumstances;
> (4) A general pervasive mood of unhappiness or depression or
> (5) A tendency to develop physical symptoms or fears associated with personal or school problems.

(6)   The term includes students who are schizophrenic.

The term does not include students who are socially maladjusted, unless it is determined that they are seriously emotionally disturbed.

This definition sounds as though it were a diagnostic category when in fact it is a social construct. "An inability to learn" might be expected among children whose teachers cannot teach. It would be hard, and by no fault of their own, for children from a feared or hated minority or even a low-income family to "build or maintain satisfactory interpersonal relationships." Section 3 leads one to question, "What is an inappropriate feeling?" It may not be "appropriate" to be tearful in geography class, but this obviously is not the case for a depressed child; it may not be "appropriate" to be rageful in algebra class, but it might be the best that a child with Tourette syndrome can do at the moment. This is not about blame. Children with "emotional disturbance" can come from chaotic homes; they can also come from homes where parents are doing as well as anyone knows to do.

I wonder who has more fun, logicians or lawyers, with the concluding sentence of the definition: "The term does not include students who are socially maladjusted, unless it is determined that they are seriously emotionally disturbed." In other words, children labeled "socially maladjusted" are not labeled SED unless they are SED.

The problem is that the term *SED* has pretensions to being a diagnostic label rather than the context-dependent, socially constructed expedient that it really is. No disability definition is—or even could be—about a child alone. To say a child has a body weight of 26 kilograms says nothing about the scale or the person who weighed the child, but to say a child has "an inability to build or maintain satisfactory interpersonal relationships with peers and teachers" necessarily says something about those peers and teachers.

The medical impulse to call children with difficulties in school by a name that was not pejorative, such as SED, was probably an attempt to describe, neutrally, a condition and not a child. But most schools talk about "EH [emotionally handicapped] children" or "SED children," so in effect the term has found its actual value. It has come to be used as a synonym for "crazy," "rebellious," or "troubled."

Children labeled SED often *do* have real difficulties in making friends with other children. It would be one strategy, albeit not at all useful, to say that those other children must lack in empathy if they are not able to embrace this child. But it is not a matter of blame. Some children baffle other children—and adults—not because these other people are uncaring or stupid but because they are just baffled. Similarly, if parents struggle to cope with a child whom they love more than they understand, they are at risk of being assessed as "dysfunctional." This tendency to blame, however, stops with professionals. If a therapist or a program has no effect, we professionals often console one another that these children must be, in effect, impossible.

Recognizing the mutuality of the problem children can present for schools invites us to ask honestly not just "What do we do about Brian (or Kevin, Elias, or Cory)?" but "What do all of us in this school need to support one another in creating a place where all can learn?"

Implications for Discipline and Assessment

These discussions of how difficult behavior is handled in schools have significant implications for what appropriate behavior is and what the consequences of inappropriate behavior should be. If we look at schools as factories making parts for the business world, then the emphasis on external appearance and conformity to social norms is well placed. But if we see schools as preparing children to feel like part of their communities, to make responsible decisions about themselves and their communities, and to continue learning and growing throughout their lives, then the focus shifts from appearances to understanding and accommodating each child's interior reality and needs. Without this feeling of understanding and acceptance, few children will be able to feel enough sense of belonging to care about social norms in the first place.

For example, one common misperception is that a child who is having tantrums or who is aggressive is angry. In reality, aggressive children are more often afraid. Typical discipline strategies may comfort the teacher and the class, but these responses can actually make matters worse for frightened children.

I suspect that routine disciplinary procedures are much more satisfying to the adults implementing them than they are instructive for the students on whom they are used. If, as a teacher, I have a student who for the first time is restless and is talking loud enough to disturb other students, I might try a gentle reminder. If the student escalates and tells me to back off, I might ask the student what is going on, with the implication that I'm really asking, "What's wrong? How can I help?" It might be that today this student is so anxious about something that he or she cannot say, "I'm worried about going home tonight." Or, this might be an anxiety attack that the child him- or herself poorly understands. Even a nonconfrontational and relaxed encounter can result in the student's blowing up and screaming threats or obscenities.

At this point, the class has a problem. Typically, the teacher is held responsible for managing a solution. Teachers choose, most likely, the route that seems to follow with what they think is the reason for a particular behavior. If they see disruptive behavior as coming from a "wild" kid who needs to learn that one doesn't talk and act like that in class, then sending him or her to the principal's office has a certain logic to it. If a disruption seems to be a chronic pattern, a teacher might want to put the student on a program where he or she can earn rewards or expect consequences depending on his or her "choices." If the teacher thinks the child is having a hard time at home and needs to cool off, then maybe offering 10 minutes somewhere quieter, not as a punishing time-out but as a break, would help.

If we take as our starting point that Elias, for example, is disruptive and perhaps aggressive when he is anxious, the addition of a punishment that is contingent on disruptive behavior, if he pays attention to it, will probably only increase his anxiety about how he is performing. Increased anxiety will almost certainly diminish performance. This will lead to more of the disruption or aggression and is likely to lead to an increase in the punishment he can expect. (For some reason, behaviorally based schemes almost always escalate punishments rather than rewards.) As these behavioral programs fail to work, they are shaped in ways that soothe the adult administering them rather than the child they purport to help.

Many adults mistakenly assume that these difficult behaviors are intentional and learned and that students can control them. One could just as easily reverse this vicious cycle with one that has more responsiveness to Elias and his teacher. Most of us prefer unconditional reassurance when we're upset. If Elias is in fact having an anxiety attack or is frightened that he will be discovered and ridiculed for his lack of information, then he might be so nearly out of control that the only thing that will help is a chance to go somewhere quiet and calm down. Some days he might need to sit and refocus with a computer game or to go out and walk around the school 20 times as fast as he can. In the ideal world, Elias and his teachers know that these stressful times can happen and have negotiated these options in advance. That Elias knows he has options when things start to be too much for him reduces his stress.

As Elias experiences less stress, he can be expected either to show less disruption or aggression or at least to begin to learn how to control those behaviors. With his stress level reduced and a relationship with adults that is supportive rather than competitive, he is in a better position to take in information. A relaxed atmosphere also allows both Elias and the teacher to be more creative about solutions. If walking around or computer games don't work, then maybe something else will. The point is not to expect Elias to be compliant to the program but for the program to be supportive of Elias. Instead of teaching him that "1) we don't care about your feelings; 2) you will have to sort things out within our expectations; and 3) if you don't, you will be punished," the school might teach him that "1) you already know—or can learn to recognize—your own feelings; 2) we trust you to tell us decent ways of helping you; and 3) if those ways don't work, we can trust one another to find something that might."

Students need predictability. Predictable consequences, though, are less supportive than a predictable process. Knowing that whenever I do something wrong a certain loss of privilege will always occur is less comforting than knowing that there is a process that will help me to take more responsibility. When punished, I resent and learn to avoid my punisher. When helped to take responsibility, I have greater skill the next time.

These kinds of negotiations subtly teach what is appropriate. By teaching Elias that we are working to make things safe for him, he learns that he can value this safeness because he has experienced it. Many students who are "emotionally disturbed" have received a great many lessons from adults on maladaptive behavior.

Implications for Supportive School Cultures

Just as the school systems' case studies represent different communities, they each have arrived at somewhat varying technologies of support:

- Brian's school uses class meetings and staff support team sessions to iden- tify pupils with difficulties and collaborate in supporting them. Support teams consist of trained school staff who meet on a regular basis and take referrals from school staff when any student is experiencing social or emo- tional difficulties.
- Kevin's school has collaborated with the local mental health services agency to bring supports to the school and to families with an emphasis on social skills development as well as collaborative problem solving. They also have brought in mental health consultation and increased adult assis- tance in classrooms in which kids need more support.
- Elias's school uses a planning room with in-school consultation for teachers.
- Cory's school has a planning room system as well as advising sessions for all students.

Given that inclusion is more of an attitude than a technology, it is not sur- prising that these schools had more similarities in their attitudes toward chil- dren than in the ways in which they implemented them. These attitudes were not just about children identified as having difficulties but about all children— as one school psychologist said, "We are trying to help all kids, coded or not."

This attitude—that everyone has value and needs to feel a sense of belonging—was a common characteristic among all four school systems. Often this came from what might be called *visionary leadership*.

In each school there was at least one administrator, but often several, who had a strong sense of what a school community should be like. These admin- istrators tended to work collaboratively and collegially. As Cory's teacher at Southeast High School put it, "[The principal] supported this change. And he asked us, 'What do you need to make this happen?' He kept saying, 'I don't know.' He's *still* not sure and is worried about the special education kids' academic progress." A different principal might have opposed these innovations, but by sharing his concerns and raising good questions, this principal has been able to develop as a leader and his faculty have developed as collaborators.

For example, the advising sessions at Southeast High School came about when the principal asked the school staff to consider ways for keeping students personally connected to and part of the school. By sharing a problem and asking the key players for ideas, he was demonstrating how these connections are made. He might just as easily have decided on a solution and held a staff meeting to announce how they would implement this. Instead, he created an environment in which the staff could be committed to the students first rather than primarily to him or his policies.

In all of the schools visited, administrators took a personal interest and personal leadership in creating inclusive environments, though how the administrators expressed this varied. The personalities of the people in the school appeared to be a more powerful factor in their success than did any one style of administration or set of policies.

Administrators also tended to see their schools as communities committed to personal growth, not just for their students but for their teachers and themselves. One principal said of his school's accomplishments, "The staff makes it all possible. When there is a conference they want to go to, I try to send as many as I can. It's important for them to go and part of my job to see their classes are covered."

It is not surprising that a number of the personnel involved in these schools had not always been educators or mental health professionals but had come into the field as part of their own personal or career growth. Some had been drawn to these innovations because they had family members with disabilities and felt strongly about the ways people with disabilities sometimes have been poorly treated in our culture.

A number of those interviewed mentioned that they spent some of their own time with families, working without pay. Although this voluntary contribution could be easily turned to exploitation, many of the teachers, consultants, and administrators talked about this work as something they found personally rewarding and engaging.

These administrators were committed to finding good staff, providing time for planning and professional development, and supplying information that teachers wanted. In turn, the teachers had some empathy for issues beyond their own classrooms. As one said of the school district's superintendent, "We have administrative support for our work. And we in turn are always looking for how we can consolidate to save money, but our administrator is not sacrificing quality for cost. In the long-term this kind of working relationship will pay off for everyone."

When matters did not go well, teachers saw this as coming from a breakdown in getting information, from not being listened to, or from working too much in isolation. As one administrator said, "The problem is that you can't mandate getting along."

These innovative administrators worked within a community that they had nurtured and helped to grow, not in a world they invented and whose values they established and enforced. This patient building and the need for wide ownership has significant implications for school systems that might attempt to replicate their work.

Implications for Teamwork and Interagency Collaboration

Given the number of social agencies and family members teachers might have to be in touch with, poor communication from system to system is a common complaint, even in schools in which things are going fairly well. Brian's service coordinator comes to school meetings but, for reasons of confidentiality, teachers have learned almost nothing about the facts of Brian's life beyond school. No one knows whether his stepfather was ever charged or how the allegations of his sexually abusing Brian have been pursued. Services coordinators, who change all the time, can keep teachers apprised of what is currently happening in a student's life but do not divulge history.

In Northeast, where Kevin lives, the good connection among the families, the schools, and the local mental health center has paid off. The mental health center has made a conscious effort to keep staff over time so that the relationships they make with children, their families, and school staff can have some stability and depth.

In one school system, the elementary teachers were concerned that so many children were showing up in first grade with unanticipated needs. By working with the private preschools (New Hampshire's public education begins with first grade), they were able to coordinate so that children who might have difficulty in school would have less difficulty. But this kind of thinking and planning helps all children and thus is not something that is done just for children perceived as different but for all children who are seen as needing some extra attention as they begin their school careers.

Implications for Flexible Curricula and Scheduling

There has been some confusion between the concept of individualized educational planning and personal planning. Just because a plan is for one child does not at all guarantee that it is suited to him or her personally. At some self-contained special education schools, all children have essentially the same individual plan of instruction, but this is all the children themselves have in common.

Good teachers have always tailored their methods to the student. As one teacher said, "Good teachers are sensitive to the needs of kids, able to communicate and problem-solve, and are not locked into one style. They're flexible." Teachers have some students with disabilities, though, are asked to stretch this flexibility even further. For example, Brian's teacher knows that writing can be frustrating for him. So she gives him the option of reporting orally to the class. If this is too stressful, then she and Brian can meet quietly in the hall. She uses a flexible grading system for him so that his differences don't translate automatically into poor grades.

When his class was preparing for a field trip to the opera, Brian found listening to the Italian words too difficult. So his teacher gave him two alternatives: going to the library and researching the opera on his own or listening to it during recess with an assistant. The point of giving him these choices was to let him know that he could in fact learn what others did and that his teachers could be flexible in teaching him. What is important to remember, though, is that without the mutually valued relationship he and his teacher had, this could easily have become a struggle of wills. Her way of working with him was to accommodate him with respect, and, fortunately, this was how he understood this process himself. Without this help, school staff might have been able to say either directly or with their own behavior, "You are not a good learner. If you can't learn with the others, then we should not expect you to keep up with the class." This would have been an especially difficult lesson given Brian's eagerness to learn. Instead of being discouraged and ostracized because of his differences, he was able to become a contributing member of his class.

Teachers need this flexibility as well as opportunity for real connection with other staff. In one school, all of the staff meet before school on Wednesday mornings to consider any child of concern. These meetings were called "child study groups," but teachers felt uncomfortable presenting a child in a case conference format. So, because the school took the idea of cooperation seriously, the same consultants—special education teachers, speech-language therapists, the school nurse, and so forth—who might have passed judgment contribute to the meetings and are now part of a conversation, admitting their own confusion, asking questions, and talking adult-to-adult with the teachers. When there is a culture of nonjudgmental support for teachers, making this culture available to pupils as well becomes easier. As one teacher put it, "Teachers are more confident to be creative; they are more able to focus on what they want to be creative about. When people are insecure, they focus on protocol, strict behavior programs, regulations." The success of these meetings is not just in the format but also in the relationships among school personnel. Because they generally like, trust, and respect one another, almost all school staff regularly attend these meetings, a sign that they find the meetings helpful.

Virtually everyone working in the four schools discussed in this chapter admitted a willingness to help one another, especially if asked. Although no one rationally expects any one teacher to be equally effective with each pupil, in many schools teachers act as if that were the case. In another school system, which was far less successful in including all students, I asked a teacher, "Can you go to the principal and say, 'This child and I are not a good match'?"

"Sure," she answered, "the principal has stated that kind of flexibility is school policy."

"Have you ever done it?"

"Oh, Lord no. It's bad form. It would mean you aren't a good teacher."

Implications for Appropriate Supports for Students and Staff

"A lot of teaching is very lonely," Brian's teacher said. "You are alone with the kids. Twenty-four kids can be hell on some days, and on other days they are the best thing that can happen to you."

Given this intense relationship that teachers have with their students and their work, it can be hard for teachers to ask for the help they need or even to consider that they might want it. As one school psychologist said, "You have to be so careful about how you enter that empire of the classroom. Teachers often need a lot of support for information and understanding, but they aren't entirely open to talking about things. A lot of teachers like closing the door and having that classroom as theirs."

The IOD has provided ongoing technical assistance to each of these schools. Given the voluntary nature of this relationship, these outsiders have been able to give new ideas. But most consultants can give new ideas. What is critical is that this outside help was offered in the sense of discovering together what this work could mean. Schools were more able to ask simple questions knowing that few of them had simple answers. A technical assistance consultant to a school said, "Every now and again, teachers wonder if all this planning and working actually has made any difference. I try to be their memory. I remind them what things were like a couple of years ago."

Good consultants don't strengthen dependency on them so much as help school communities develop their own strengths. Many teachers have found a reliable resource in their own network of informal support. As one teacher said, "I can just catch someone in the hall and say, 'I'm losing it with Terry.' And the other teacher will listen or even help me out herself. This doesn't go through formal channels, so we can help one another without having to call a formal meeting. Some administrators think a lot of requests for consultation is a sign of incompetence, and getting help for children can be made to look like—and feel like—professional failure."

Similarly, schools have developed ways for students to get help without making them feel like failures either. The schoolwide support teams at Southeast High make problem solving part of the school culture rather than something done only for "bad kids." The opportunities that students in the middle of behavioral difficulties get—taking a break, leaving the building for a walk, having a chance to talk to someone who knows them—are all ways of helping them to move from an escalating cycle of behavior to building a culture of accommodation and support. As one teacher said, "Having the backing of people familiar with the clinical pieces, having the support on a daily basis rather than a crisis, and having administrative support keeps this new for me."

Implications for Parental Involvement

Once someone said about children with emotional disabilities, "These are the kids no one wants. They are physically aggressive. They're not consistent. The parents are difficult to deal with." It is interesting to note that this was said by a psychologist who had spent a number of years in working to support children and their families. Having a child with a behavioral or emotional disability can be a stress on even the most stable and confident of families, and the schools did not pretend that parental involvement was simple and easy. They were committed to working in this way because it was the best they knew for their students.

Just as schools have historically tended to isolate and ostracize children with differences, so, too, have communities pulled away from their families. The collaboration with local mental health and family support services agencies evident in the four school systems described in this chapter helped parents to keep their connections or establish relationships that would sustain them.

In all of the schools studied, people mentioned the importance of sustained relationships. The wraparound services in one system did not work merely because the professional staff were so accomplished. It also worked because they understood the importance of coordinating their professional expertise in the context of a relationship in which all the players knew, trusted, and respected one another. This combination allowed families, schools, and professional service providers to work in a spirit of collaboration. Because there are no clear answers for most of the difficulties these children experienced, it was important for people to feel confident to guess as to what might help most. This way, the adults in the children's lives saw the children and their parents as people they were getting to know rather than as problems. As the local mental health director in one system said, "With the good case workers, there is a lot of communication among the players, so the families get clinical help they need or want. The clinical component often gets left out of most schools and after-school support. Lots of schools are still doing behavior control programs that assess the parents and hold them responsible for the child's progress. A lot of them are trying to get the parents under control as well."

One pupil's mother has mental retardation. His general education teacher said, "His mother does so well with most things that we forget how difficult life can be for her. She called the school for a meeting, but then when we sat down, she said things were fine, and there was nothing much to talk about. People wanted to blame her for being manipulative, but I think she was afraid that since her son was doing well at school and not at home, then we would think she was a bad parent. So the teachers spent time with her so she could trust that they did not want to judge her as a mother."

CONCLUSIONS

My own interest in the New Hampshire Statewide Systems Change Project has been as much in the adults in schools as in the children. Typically, we psychologists ask, "What's wrong with this child?" But this project allowed me the luxury of asking, "What makes this situation work so well? Why do you think you have these positive attitudes in working through difficult situations with children?"

I have been intrigued by the number of people in the helping professions who, when something goes wrong, are quick to find reasons in themselves and to take responsibility—"I'm afraid I failed Elias. He needed more than I could give." But when confronted to take responsibility for why things are going well or even outstandingly well, many teachers shift the credit: "Anyone would have done the same."

Teachers and administrators talked about this work of including students with difficult behavior as something that renewed them personally and professionally. It is interesting to note that many people talked about how their personal and professional growth became unified rather than parallel. Precisely because there is no one answer, the challenge of engagement never ends. The work can never become routine or stale. Listening to students with difficult behavior requires an attitude of openness, of looking from as many angles as it takes to develop a solution. Schools that have been successful have administrators who either allowed teachers to be creative or actively encouraged and supported them. Similarly, outside consultants were seen as helpers rather than rescuers. A sense of collaboration encouraged speculation and experimentation and gave people the security necessary for this to work.

Finally, the sine qua non of these successful experiments has been the relationships among all the players. Merely having good feelings about one another is no substitute for competence on the teacher's part and for availability for learning on the student's part, but without this primary and positive connection, education takes place in spite of the school rather than because of it.

It seems fitting to end with the wise words of two of the many people who gave their time and insight to this chapter. I asked Elias if he had any advice for teachers. He responded, "Talk nice. and don't give up on the kid. Try to understand what the kid is going through." A school psychologist said, "I know the kids, the staff, their families, the psychological umbrella that each child has. We do a lot of hand-holding, even if we call it coordination and consultation. But whatever you call it, when it works it means two human beings talking to one another compassionately."

REFERENCE

New Hampshire Code of Administrative Rules, Ed. 1102.31(j) (1999).

6

Turning Points

The Story of High School
Inclusion in New Hampshire

Cheryl M. Jorgensen and Carol Tashie

The story of high school inclusion in New Hampshire and the role played by the University of New Hampshire's Institute on Disability (IOD) is similar to any other "once upon a time" tale in three parts. In the first part of this story, we look back before any students with significant disabilities were included in general education classes. As the story unfolds, we show the relationships between the lives of individual students, the changes their schools were undergoing, the role of the IOD as the state's leader in systems change advocacy and action, and the educational and political contexts that were unique to the state. The second part provides insight into the IOD's effectiveness as a change agent by focusing on local schools' inclusion histories, both the good news and the disappointments. Our reflections are framed within the context of educational reform theory and experience. Finally, the third part describes systems change strategies for the future. The IOD's goal is to learn from the past, respond to the needs of today's students and families, and build New Hampshire schools' capacity to be true inclusive communities of learners.

LOOKING BACK

In June of 1997, Jocelyn Curtin graduated from Concord High School. Despite the fact that she has Rett syndrome, has others push her wheelchair, and communicates through facial expressions and body postures, Jocelyn was included in general education classes and a variety of extracurricular activities throughout high school. She starred in a nationally distributed videotape called *The Voices of Friendship* (Martin & Tashie, 1996), has a professional modeling portfolio, and has interviewed with a number of top agencies in New York. In the late 1980s, however, the vision that Jocelyn's parents held for her was very different from this reality, influenced by the separate educational experience that was typical of students with significant disabilities throughout the state of New Hampshire.

In September of 1987, Jocelyn was 8 years old. Her soft brown eyes were fringed with dark lashes, she had a smile that would melt your heart, and she had the ability to make you her ally from the moment you met. She lived in a close-knit family that included her mom, her dad, one brother, and one sister. Each weekday morning a small yellow school bus picked her up at her front door and transported her across town to the elementary school where she attended a self-contained classroom for students ages 6–21 who were identified as having "severe and profound disabilities." These students were among the school-age children who, just a few years before, would have lived at New Hampshire's state institution, Laconia State School and Training Center. Because Laconia was moving its adult residents into community-based programs, there would be no place for school-age students once they graduated. Thus, educational programs opened in local communities, administered by disability organizations (e.g., Easter Seals), educational collaboratives, and local school districts.

These new community-based educational programs grouped students by perceived functional capacity (e.g., "severe and profound") or disability label (e.g., "multihandicapped," "deafblind"), subscribed to a developmental approach to teaching (i.e., students' educational plans focused on early developmental milestones and foundational cognitive processes), and were separate from general education classes (if not outside the school building altogether). It was anticipated that someday these students would live in group homes, attend day habilitation programs, or be employed in sheltered workshops.

Jocelyn's class was composed of 12 students. Jocelyn and three of her classmates were elementary school–age, but there were also three younger students and five students ranging in age from 14 to 20. For Jocelyn and her classmates the school day began with a half hour of personal care routines that included toileting, taking medications, removing coats, and reading the notes written by their parents in a home–school journal. After all of the students had completed these arrival routines, they were gathered in a circle in the middle of the classroom while their teacher, aides, and therapists sang the "Good Morning" song. All 12 students were given hand-over-hand assistance to perform the motions that went along with the song, although none had a means of singing or signing the words.

Following this circle time activity, the students began their daily routine of therapy (e.g., speech-language therapy, occupational therapy, physical therapy), preacademic tasks (e.g., stacking blocks), snacks and lunch, and personal care routines (e.g., face and hand washing, toileting, toothbrushing). After lunch several students without disabilities visited the classroom to play with their so-called special buddies while these visiting students' classmates went outside for recess.

At the end of the day—15 minutes before the rest of the school was dismissed—the yellow bus returned to take the students home. Each student received a kiss and hug good-bye from an assistant, notes about the day were recorded in the home–school journal, and another school day was over.

Changing Vision for Elementary
School Students with Significant Disabilities

In 1988, as part of New Hampshire's first federal Statewide Systems Change Project (funded by the Office of Special Education Programs [OSEP]), Jocelyn's parents (and hundreds more from all over the state) learned about the possibility of a different kind of education for their daughter—education characterized by inclusion in general education classes in the neighborhood school, friendships and social relationships with classmates who did not have disabilities, and support from special education and related services to target individualized learning objectives within general education. In New Hampshire, prior to 1987, the majority of elementary age students with significant disabilities were educated in self-contained classrooms. By 1997, nearly 70% were receiving their education in inclusive general education classrooms (New Hampshire Department of Education, 1997).

As Jocelyn and same-age peers with significant disabilities moved through middle and high school, however, it became clear that an inclusive middle and high school education was not a given even though inclusion was becoming more the rule than the exception at the elementary level. In individualized education program (IEP) meetings all across the state, teachers and administrators argued that high school students with significant disabilities—even those who had received a fully inclusive elementary education—ought not be enrolled primarily in general education classes once they reached ninth grade.

Those who had been supporting inclusive education efforts through training and technical assistance were puzzled. Why were the same administrators who had embraced inclusion for elementary school–age students arguing for a separate education at the high school level? When we talked about visions, dreams, and beliefs in our workshops and summer institutes, we didn't remember saying "for young children only." Even some parents who had fought hardest for an inclusive elementary education for their sons and daughters were not sure what was right. They were confused when confronted with the question, "How else will your child learn the functional skills that he or she will need after graduation unless he or she experiences community-based instruction?" They didn't know how to respond when teachers asked, "What could your child possibly get out of sitting in a chemistry class?" In fact the whole system of secondary education—which relied on tracking and ability grouping for its typical students—seemed inhospitable to the idea of inclusion of students with significant disabilities.

A New Focus on High School

In the early 1990s—in response to the barriers that New Hampshire students were facing to being included in high school and because of an increased focus on transition in OSEP—the IOD initiated four projects focused on building the capacity of high schools to implement effective, inclusive secondary and post-secondary education for students with disabilities (see Table 6.1).

For each of the four projects, a detailed case study exemplifies a number of change strategies that were successfully utilized within and across all of the projects. Following these case studies, other related training and policy reform initiatives are discussed.

New Hampshire Statewide Systems Change Project: High School Reform in Moultonborough School District

Moultonborough School District is one of the smallest districts in New Hampshire, with approximately 700 students in grades K–12. In 1991, the district applied to become a project demonstration site for the New Hampshire Statewide Systems Change Project. Because the district had a long history of including students in its elementary school, one of its primary emphases was to look at ways in which the high school could restructure to support students with severe disabilities in general education classes and other inclusive school environments and activities. Project staff were quick to embrace this opportunity to further the state's efforts in high school inclusion.

The district's long history of inclusion at the elementary level proved to be both a benefit and a liability as the project began its involvement. The benefits were obvious—elementary school teachers and staff were familiar with students with disabilities and for the most part were comfortable with having them in classes and in the school. The liabilities were quickly discovered. Although most students were included through sixth grade, their participation in class was primarily through a parallel or alternative curriculum. Project staff discovered that educators and parents had some hesitancy to change from a

Table 6.1. Secondary and postsecondary inclusion initiatives of the University of New Hampshire's Institute on Disability (IOD)

Project name	Funding	Goal	Project initiatives
New Hampshire Statewide Systems Change Project (1993–1998)	$250,000 per year Funded by U.S. Department of Education, Office of Special Education and Rehabilitative Services (OSERS) Awarded to the New Hampshire Department of Education Subcontracted to the University of New Hampshire Institute on Disability (IOD)	To increase the permanent capacity of the state to implement recommended practices relative to the education of students with severe disabilities in general education classes in their neighborhood schools	Increasing local schools' capacity to serve students labeled severely emotional disturbed Increasing placement of young children with disabilities in typical community early childhood settings Increasing local schools' capacity to support students with chronic illness and long-term health problems Increasing local schools' capacity to include students with disabilities in general education classes Increasing the capacity of the state's Department of Education staff to support local schools' adoption of recommended practices Restructuring teacher education programs to better prepare teachers for all children

(continued)

135

Table 6.1. *(continued)*

Project name	Funding	Goal	Project initiatives
School Restructuring and Inclusion Project (1992–1996)	$150,000 per year Funded by OSERS, Division of Innovation and Development Awarded to the IOD	To investigate how students with disabilities can be included in systemic efforts to reform high schools	Conducting action research in a high school and a middle school regarding the participation of students with disabilities in school reform initiatives Disseminating project knowledge and products throughout the state and nationally Conducting leadership training for administrators
Turning Points Project (1991–1996)	$400,000 per year Funded by OSERS Awarded to the New Hampshire Department of Education Subcontracted to the IOD	To increase the capacity of secondary schools and communities to support students with disabilities in their high school careers and as they move out of high school and into the activities of adult life of their choosing	Increasing availability, access, and quality of transition assistance by developing and improving policies, procedures, systems, and other mechanisms Improving the ability of professionals, parents, and advocates to cooperatively implement strategies and procedures that promote successful transition from student to adult life

Establishing an incentive system for gaining access to and utilizing expertise and resources of programs, projects, and activities in support of quality outcomes in secondary special education

Evaluating the accomplishments of project procedures, activities, products, and outcomes

Postsecondary Education Project (1996–1999)	$150,000 per year Funded by OSERS Awarded to the IOD	To increase access and support for students with disabilities at New Hampshire's postsecondary schools	Establishing the Postsecondary Education Consortium of New Hampshire Selecting four postsecondary educational institutions as model demonstration sites Developing and implementing multicomponent inclusion model within each demonstration site Evaluating of each site Dissemination of project materials and information

parallel program to one of true inclusion. Also, because middle school– and high school–age students with severe disabilities were historically sent for schooling out of district, most teachers viewed inclusion as a viable option only in the lower grades.

To change these perceptions and bring inclusion to middle school and high school, the district sought the project's assistance to develop an inclusion leadership team. The team's membership was extremely strategic. Members included an outspoken high school teacher who was strongly opposed to inclusion; a parent of a high school student with disabilities who was not sure that her daughter could or should be included; and various teachers, administrators, parents, and students. With this team in place, the district was chosen as a project demonstration site, and project goals were mutually developed.

Project Goals　　Moultonborough identified six major project goals:

- Return all students from out-of-district placements to neighborhood schools.
- Provide technical assistance to classroom and special education teachers on all issues relating to inclusive education.
- Use recommended practices in education and related services.
- Involve school staff, administrators, school board members, family, and community members in professional development activities.
- Create a philosophy of inclusive education on which all future decisions could be based.
- Educate all students in age-appropriate general education classes.

Project Activities　　One of the first activities of the project was to support the return to district of high school students with severe disabilities. Initially, one student with a label of autism returned to the high school. Faculty and staff attended numerous training sessions, and project staff provided technical assistance. School personnel quickly became comfortable and confident in welcoming this student to their classes. More students quickly followed.

In addition to providing training to school personnel, a number of project activities focused on providing information to parents and community members. Presentations were conducted for the parent–teacher organization, and a large presentation was made to the school board in the spring. Presenters at all sessions were parents, teachers, students, and project staff.

Project staff provided faculty and staff with opportunities to discuss their teaching and support strategies with each other as well as with outside consultants and fellow teachers. Faculty members participated in a wide variety of strategic planning and reflective inquiry groups and met frequently to share frustrations and successes. A number of high school teachers were asked to meet with other stakeholders around the state to discuss strategies for high school inclusion.

Project Accomplishments   It was evident from the start that Moulton-borough School District had the commitment and the capacity to achieve its goals. Prior to participation as a project demonstration site, students with severe disabilities usually had been educated within the general education classroom with one-to-one assistants and parallel curricula until they completed sixth grade. At that point it had been determined that the district could no longer provide an appropriate education, and these students were sent to self-contained programs in neighboring districts. After the school district's participation in the project, however, all students with severe disabilities were included in general education classes in their home schools.

Parents in Moultonborough School District, for the most part, had high expectations for their children's education and demanded school accountability. Prior to the project's involvement, parents of students with disabilities remained in close contact with special education staff but had little or no involvement in general education. After participation in the project, parents increased their involvement in all aspects of their children's education and became strong proponents for the inclusion of students with disabilities in all areas of school life.

Personnel changes were an obvious result of participation in the project. An inclusion facilitator was hired to support faculty at the elementary school, middle school, and high school level, and classroom assistants were hired to provide additional support in classrooms. General education faculty were provided with training and supports so that all students could be successful in general education classes.

School Restructuring and Inclusion Project: Souhegan High School

In 1990, the Amherst and Mont Vernon school board met with their superintendent and expressed their wish to build a new high school so that students from their communities would not have to attend a regional high school that was growing in size and increasingly not meeting the students' needs. After much community dialogue and debate, development began on a "break-the-mold" school, dedicated to the preparation of responsible citizens able to compete in the world economy in the 21st century. Committees made up of school board members, at-large community representatives, and teachers from the regional high school met for 1 year to read the latest educational research and to describe the kind of school they wanted. Subsequently, a five-member planning team was hired, led by an incoming principal. The school applied for membership in the Coalition of Essential Schools, a national reform initiative. During the year prior to Souhegan High School's opening, the planning team considered issues of curriculum, school organization and governance, student support, and special education.

Because IOD project coordinators had provided technical assistance to students and teachers from some of Amherst and Mont Vernon's elementary schools, they were asked to work with the planning team to design Souhegan's special education model. The other coordinators talked with the team about the latest research on recommended practices in special education and presented a rationale for continuation of Amherst's elementary inclusion philosophy to Souhegan. Some teachers wondered whether a middle ground should be taken, in which most students would be included but also in which a small, alternative "school within a school" would be offered for those whose difficulties made their inclusion problematic.

A critical turning point in the discussions occurred during a presentation to the planning team made by Cheryl M. Jorgensen. One of Souhegan's incoming administrators (who had no experience with inclusive education or with students with significant disabilities) asked, "Isn't inclusion really just an extension of our commitment to nontracking? Isn't it really about creating a community of learners in which each student's talents are honored?" Souhegan's Information Center Director (the librarian) asked, "If we think inclusion is a desirable goal, why would we establish something [the alternative school] that we really want to eliminate as soon as we can? Why don't we just start with all students being included and then back off if we have to?"

Although it took a leap of faith for many people who were in the room that day, they decided to make Souhegan an inclusive school. Shortly after that meeting, an OSEP grant priority was announced that called for proposals to address how students with disabilities could be part of systemic efforts to restructure schools. Working closely with Souhegan's planning team, the IOD submitted a successful application for 4 years of research-to-practice funding.

In September of 1992, 550 students walked through Souhegan's front doors, all members of untracked general education classes. There were no separate programs, classrooms, or places just for students with disabilities. An academic support center stood in place of the proposed alternative school, where any student could go (or could be sent by a teacher) to receive tutoring in a challenging subject area. Three special education teachers were assigned to interdisciplinary 9th- and 10th-grade teams, and an additional teacher and full-time paraprofessional were assigned to the 11th and 12th grades.

Students with labels of learning disabilities and emotional disabilities composed about 10% of the student body, and four Amherst and Mont Vernon students had significant disabilities and had always been educated in out-of-district programs. The district's inclusion facilitator worked for several months with the students' parents and out-of-district program staff to plan for the students' transition to Souhegan.

From 1992 to 1996, Jorgensen served as Souhegan's "critical friend" (Olson, 1994) relative to inclusion of students with disabilities. Her role as action researcher included not only conducting qualitative research studies of individual students, teachers, curriculum, and policies but also working collaboratively with teachers to implement promising practices as identified by the literature and ongoing research.

This role as critical friend characterizes how IOD staff work with schools that are full-fledged project sites. Critical friends bring expertise to a school but do not present themselves as experts. Jorgensen's role was to be involved in all school conversations that related to general diversity issues as well as those that were disability specific. Examples of activities associated with this role are presented in Table 6.2.

Amro's Story

One student's story characterizes how Souhegan embraced the philosophy of inclusion and associated recommended educational practices. Amro Diab was one of the students from the Amherst community who had always been placed out of district. He attended a self-contained educational program for students with moderate disabilities, and his IEP

Table 6.2. Activities associated with critical friend role

Sitting in classes and providing direct support to students (with and without disabilities) to model recommended practices for teachers

Meeting with teams during their planning periods to discuss upcoming units and how materials, instruction, and assessments could be developed to address the learning styles and needs of all students

Giving presentations about inclusion at school board meetings

Attending meetings to assist in problem-solving about curricular or behavioral difficulties for individual students

Presenting schoolwide workshops on learning styles and inclusive curriculum design

Writing and publishing professional articles in collaboration with general education teachers

Presenting workshops with general education teachers at national conferences

Working with planning teams to design and implement policy statements, such as a new job description for special education teachers

Providing funds for substitute teachers to enable teaching teams and departments to take a day away from regular school duties to design long-term curriculum units or refine policies and procedures

Collaborating on individualized education programs for specific students

Supporting student leadership activities focused on inclusive education and on increased participation for students with disabilities

Hosting school visitors with a particular interest in inclusive education

Olson (1994) coined the term *critical friend*.

focused on functional living skills (e.g., cooking, making beds), academic readiness skills (e.g., counting, learning the alphabet), and communication skills (e.g., using sign language to express wants and needs). He was extremely shy and nervous, especially around strangers and in new situations. The first week that Amro came to Souhegan, he walked through the halls hugging the wall and looking at his feet. When he came to his IEP meeting, he sat close to his dad with his head down on the table, barely glancing up at the Souhegan teaching staff.

The inclusion facilitator knew that Amro's biggest hurdle in coming to Souhegan would be social and thus asked the football coach if Amro might be an assistant manager, responsible for carrying equipment, filling water bottles, and so forth. The football coach—a burly man more comfortable with diagramming offensive patterns than with social niceties—met Amro and immediately established a rapport with him based on playful teasing and gentle encouragement. At the end-of-summer practices, Amro quickly became an accepted member of the team. A number of seniors—athletic, popular, and socially connected—developed friendships with Amro. Several of his own ninth-grade classmates "showed Amro the ropes" at practice and in school. They supported him when he got anxious in new situations, but also kidded and joked with him mercilessly as they did with their other friends.

Amro came to Souhegan with no formal means of communication. He spoke only a few words (e.g., "yes," "no") and used a wide variety of facial expressions and informal gestures to make his wishes known. Without a way to participate in his academic classes, however, inclusion would have meant merely that he would be occupying a seat, not really participating. After about a month of school, an IOD consultant visited the school to introduce Amro to a new communication system. She invited Amro, a few friends, and teachers to an after-school meeting, at which she explained the system. After placing a paper letterboard in front of him, she gently supported his wrist and asked, "Amro, is there anyone you would like to talk to?" Tentatively, Amro spelled "KOCH." Everyone's eyes grew wide, and their mouths fell open. In none of Amro's files was there any indication that Amro knew how to spell! They knew that Amro understood much of what was said to him but until that moment, no one guessed that he might be able to spell. One of the teachers ran down to the gym, grabbed the football coach, and brought him to the meeting. The conversation continued.

"Hey, 'Ro, who did we beat last week?"

"LBNON." [Lebanon]

"Do you know who we play this week?"

"FLMTN." [Fall Mountain]

"Who is your best friend on the team?"
"LNDRY." [A teammate]
Over the course of the next month, the physical assistance provided to Amro when he pointed to letters on his communication board
was faded. Soon Amro was spelling independently with no physical support, although almost a year passed before he initiated use of the board
in all situations.

Over the next 3 school years, Amro's educational opportunities
and skills grew. He enrolled in four general education courses every
semester—English, social studies, science, and an elective. He learned
math skills by working in the school store and continued as assistant
manager of the football team. During his junior year he was no longer
content with managing the team and asked if he could play. On a cool
fall night in October of 1994, Amro suited up with his teammates and
executed four 35-yard, straight-up-the-middle kickoffs. Although everyone in the crowd knew it was a special occasion—surely no other students who used letterboards were playing in a varsity football game that
evening—the announcer simply said, "For Souhegan, that was number
70, junior Amro Diab, kicking off."

As a 12th grader, Amro sweated through his senior project and
presentation just like 170 other Souhegan students. He was asked to
go to the prom by one of his good friends and was even voted king by
his classmates. On senior awards night Amro received the Souhegan
Saber Award, given to that student who best exemplified the mission
of the school. Amro is currently working full time at a candle-making
shop in his community where he sees his old teachers and classmates
frequently.

As a result of the support given to Souhegan, a number of systemic changes
were made relative to recommended practices for students with disabilities:

- The school's mission statement was written to reflect a commitment to
  inclusion.
- A new job description was written for special education teachers that
  reflected their role as partners with general educators throughout the entire
  teaching process.
- The job description for general education teachers was written to reflect the
  use of teaching strategies that are effective for diverse learners, inclusive
  classrooms, and shared ownership for the education of all students.
- It is assumed that students with significant disabilities will attend
  Souhegan if they live in the school's district (the Amherst or Mont Vernon
  communities).

- Academic honors and awards recognize personal best achievements as well as talents in nontraditional areas.

- Social justice issues, including disability, are woven into the curriculum through the choice of novels and books (e.g., Steinbeck's [1937] *Of Mice and Men*) and the questions that guide some interdisciplinary units (e.g., "Is prenatal diagnosis and selective abortion moral?").

Transition Systems Change Project: The Turning Points Project

The Turning Points Project was designed to increase the capacity of high schools and communities to support students and young adults as they move through schools and into the adult world. Turning Points was committed to working closely with New Hampshire Department of Education staff, local educational and community support personnel, families, youth, and self-advocates to make sustainable change in secondary education and adult supports for individuals with disabilities. The project believed that simply developing and refining the *process* by which students move from school into adulthood was not sufficient. For this process to be meaningful, fundamental changes would have to be made both to the education system and to the adult support system. If transition was to be viewed as a bridge between school and adult life, the project contended that fundamental restructuring must occur on both sides of the bridge for it to truly support students while they are in school and as they become adults. The Turning Points Project's view of transition represented a departure from many current practices in transition. What follows is a brief description of some of the components of the project.

The Vision   The Turning Points Project promoted the principles of full inclusion, natural supports, youth and family leadership, and typical social and community connections for students and young adults with disabilities. The project's vision was to ensure that all students and young adults were supported to be full participants in typical school, community, and family life and to be true leaders in the decision-making process around choices and manner of supports. The project emphasized that individuals with disabilities must be valued for their contributions in school and community and must be rewarded for these contributions in a typical fashion (e.g., diplomas, salaried employment, career advancement) and took the strong position that there is a distinction between what a student's life (up to age 18 years) and a young adult's life (after the age of 18 years) should be, based on what is typical for any individual of the same age.

Full School Inclusion and Restructuring   The Turning Points Project promoted the notion that school restructuring efforts must enhance the educational experiences for all students, including students without disabilities, and that students with disabilities were to be neither under- nor overrepresented in these efforts. The project provided goal setting, training, and technical assistance to schools throughout New Hampshire to increase their ability to educate students with disabilities as participating members of all typical secondary school classes and school opportunities. It supported schools to embrace, in both philosophy and practices, recommended practices such as the following: enrollment in general education classes, including vocational education classes, with those courses chosen based on student choice and school requirements; students' movement through the grades in a typical fashion (i.e., 1 year in 9th grade, followed by 1 year in 10th grade, and so forth) culminating in completion of high school after the senior year; students' receipt of grades, credits, transcripts, and diplomas for class participation; natural supports; and natural representation of students with and without disabilities in school and community leadership activities.

Typical Social and Community Connections   Throughout all project activities, staff worked with schools, students, and families to ensure that students with disabilities were supported to develop typical social and community connections throughout their school careers. They assisted schools to actively facilitate the development of relationships between students with and without disabilities, both in and out of the school building, and to develop creative strategies so that students with disabilities would have full access to and support for all extracurricular activities. The project stressed that students with disabilities should never be removed from the mainstream of school or community life to participate in separate activities and that students' engagement in typical extracurricular and social opportunities should be based on individual *informed* choice.

Career Planning and Preparation   Although Turning Points was formally a transition systems change project, it worked with schools to develop systems to assist all students, including students with disabilities, and to begin thinking about and planning for future careers. The project promoted the idea that once such systems are developed, they can be augmented, supplemented, and individualized for specific students. Career and futures planning courses should be offered for all students to assist them in developing long-term goals, and school guidance counselors assist students with disabilities just as they assist typical students in doing so. The project asserted that students with disabilities, like their typical peers, should gain work experience and skills through after-school, weekend, and summer jobs; should have full access to all typical education classes, including vocational education classes, school-to-work experiences, internships, and apprenticeships; and should be neither under- nor overrepresented in these opportunities.

Youth Leadership   The developmental needs of young adults are related to their quest for identity and have implications for ways in which schools can provide conditions for students' learning and personal control. One of the needs that is most neglected by schools and communities, or that is reserved for those with the best scholastic achievement, is the opportunity to take a leadership role. Successful schools acknowledge the unique needs of students and find meaningful opportunities that enable them to exercise their leadership skills. Youth activities that solicit the opinions and ideas of young people and that involve them in planning and implementing programs that serve their needs build leadership skills that extend into their adulthood.

The Turning Points Project worked with schools to ensure that students with and without disabilities would be involved in local governance activities, including fuller participation in setting and carrying out local youth agendas through membership on school boards and on governmental and advisory boards. Students with disabilities should be neither under- nor overrepresented in all established leadership organizations (e.g., student government councils, judicial boards, community service projects), where they should practice leadership skills that will serve them throughout their lives.

Graduation   One of the policy barriers that continues to exist is in regard to the ways in which students with disabilities exit from high school. State regulations in New Hampshire and other states mandate that students with disabilities are entitled to special education supports and services until the age of 21 or until they receive a diploma (New Hampshire Department of Education, 1997). Thus, many students with disabilities must choose between graduating from high school with their peers or continuing to receive school district support until their 21st birthday. The Turning Points Project worked closely with local school districts and statewide policy makers to determine how students could continue to receive supports and services from their local school districts—outside of the high school building, in age-appropriate postsecondary experiences—while not forsaking the rite of passage of high school graduation.

Ideally, all students would be awarded standard high school diplomas that reflect a typical high school curriculum that may or may not have been modified to reflect individual goals and achievements. Ideally, graduation would occur after the student's senior year in high school (usually at age 18). For students with severe disabilities, school districts would continue to provide support to them on the basis of student and parent choice, outside of the school building, through the age of 21. Coordination between the school and the community will ensure that uninterrupted supports are provided so that the graduate can engage in postsecondary education, work, and community opportunities of his or her choice. Although unsuccessful in bringing forth policy change in this area, the project was able to bring the issue out in the open and continues to work both locally and statewide on this issue.

Postsecondary Education Project: A Choice for Everyone

Systems change often goes full circle, and so the discussion of New Hampshire's commitment to postsecondary education for people with severe disabilities can be illustrated by revisiting Jocelyn Curtin's story. As a primary "mover and shaker" in the world of inclusive education (Jocelyn was one of the first students with severe disabilities to become fully included in her neighborhood school), Jocelyn continues to compel us to examine and expand our beliefs about recommended practices for individuals with severe disabilities. While planning for high school graduation, Jocelyn, along with her family and friends, decided that college would be the next logical step in her life. Her mother, Marlyn, approached several IOD staff members to discuss strategies to support Jocelyn in college. Coincidentally, the IOD had recently been awarded a new model demonstration project grant designed to increase the capacity of New Hampshire colleges and universities to enroll and support people with severe disabilities. This project began working with Jocelyn and the school of her choice (New Hampshire Technical Institute in Concord) to ensure that her educational and career goals would be supported. Jocelyn enrolled in classes in the summer of 1997 and successfully completed both a biology and a psychology course. She planned to continue taking classes at this 2-year college, with the possibility of transferring to a 4-year college the following year.

For students with severe disabilities, postsecondary education at a college or university may seem like an unreachable possibility. Few high schools encourage these students to think of college as a viable extension of their educational experience, and few parents are supported to help their sons and daughters with severe disabilities to continue their education beyond high school. Using the Americans with Disabilities Act (ADA) of 1990 (PL 101–336) mandate of "otherwise qualified" as a criterion for admission to college, colleges and universities generally view people with cognitive disabilities as unqualified for their schools. The Postsecondary Education Project was established to identify and address these barriers.

The project engaged individuals with disabilities, their families, high schools, postsecondary institutions, and support providers in three ways. First, the project developed long-term relationships with four colleges within the state's postsecondary system. These four schools made a commitment to examine their practices to enhance the participation of students with disabilities. Each of these four schools developed a set of goals and activities unique to their individual system. Strategies employed to assist the schools in achieving their goals included the following: faculty training sessions and retreats, leadership advisory committees, administrative training, and examination and refinement of support roles on and off campus. Results of these activities included a marked increase in the number of students with disabilities attending these four colleges and an increased knowledge and skill base among faculty and support providers.

Second, the project engaged in broad-based training and dissemination of information about postsecondary education to families, students and adults

with disabilities, high school faculty, provider organizations, and other interested stakeholders. This training and information provided participants with
a greater understanding of and increased commitment to the benefits of postsecondary education, as well as a general sense that it would be possible. After
hearing testimonials and strategies from the speakers, participants in these
training sessions expressed sentiments ranging from amazement ("My daughter could really go to college?"), to anger ("Why didn't anyone ever encourage
me to pursue this for my son?"), to concern ("How can we really make this
work?").

Third, training sessions and retreats were sponsored by the project. These
included leadership seminars for college disability support coordinators, planning retreats for college personnel and adult service and support personnel,
and futures planning workshops for high school inclusion and transition facilitators. Because the training sessions and retreats increased interest in and
knowledge of postsecondary education as an option for people with disabilities, the project also offered technical assistance and support to individuals in
their quest for a college education.

As Jocelyn Curtin and numerous other young people have shown, recommended educational practices must always include any and all options that
are available to others in the community. Although many barriers remain, they
will tumble as more and more people demand their rightful places in postsecondary institutions.

Related Training, Technical Assistance, and Leadership Initiatives

Although each of the projects just profiled made a significant contribution to
the districts and organizations that were directly involved, the IOD also implemented a comprehensive and coordinated array of training workshops, school-
site technical assistance, and leadership training related to the adoption of
inclusive education values and practices in high schools. The nature and
variety of training and technical assistance offerings—depicted in Table 6.3—
provided opportunities for the IOD to approach and influence people who represented all stages of knowledge about and attitudes toward inclusion of high
school students with disabilities. One systems change effort that was not
specifically related to a funded project but that made a significant impact on
local high schools' capacity to include students with disabilities was related to
the restructuring of the state's Secondary Discretionary Project initiative. A
description of this effort and its impact follows.

Secondary Discretionary Projects: Sowing the Seeds of Innovation   In
the late 1980s, the New Hampshire Department of Education established the
Task Force for the Improvement of Secondary Special Education with a primary role of administering a yearly grant competition for small discretionary
grants that was entitled "State Grants to Support the Development, Expansion,

Table 6.3. University of New Hampshire's Institute on Disability (IOD) systems change activities related to high school students

Dissemination	Technical assistance	Staff development and training	Project sites	Leadership development	Policy restructuring
Petroglyphs photo essay *Equity and Excellence* newsletter *The Voices of Friendship* videotape (Martin & Tashie, 1996) *High School Inclusion: Equity and Excellence in an Inclusive Community of Learners* videotape (IOD, 1999) Career planning manual *Petroglyphs* videotape	On-call technical assistance was available to all high schools. An average of 20 schools received at least one technical assistance visit each year.	Statewide and school-based workshops dealing with topics such as • Introduction to inclusion • Extracurricular activities • Curriculum design • Natural supports • Friendships • Career planning • Changing roles of paraprofessionals in classrooms • Person-centered futures planning	Each major grant-funded project selected multiple project sites to receive intensive training and technical assistance. A total of 30 individual high schools and four community/technical colleges participated as project sites.	The New Hampshire Leadership Series (first conceived as family leadership) graduated several parents of high school students as well as several students themselves. Youth Leadership Series for 40 students with and without disabilities. Leadership development among key postsecondary personnel.	New Hampshire Department of Education was restructured. Policy forums and task forces convened. Standards-based educational reform occurred. Discretionary funding initiatives, such as secondary discretionary grants, consolidated applications, Goals 2000, and Technology Literacy grants, were put in place.

149

and Improvement of Supports and Services for Students with Disabilities in Regular Middle and High Schools." The grants awarded in this competition, totaling $200,000 per year, have been given to schools in two categories: planning grants ($3,500 per year) and implementation grants (more than $3,500 per year). Over its lifetime, the task force has made available more than $1 million to middle schools, high schools, and postsecondary education programs. These funds have served as a catalyst for some innovative collaborative projects that have substantially influenced secondary special education and graduation planning for students with disabilities.

Collaboration between the IOD and the task force resulted in significant changes in the design of these grants, the ways in which they are administered, and the dissemination process. Five major changes occurred in the design and implementation of the program in the areas of the definition of innovative educational practices, the requirements of grantees, the educational agencies eligible for funds, the composition of review and technical support teams, and the financial resources available.

Definition of Innovative Educational Practices   Grant priorities were rewritten to reflect current recommended practices in secondary education and futures planning. Most notable were priorities that required grantees to address students with and without disabilities. Grant priorities now include the following:

- Education of students with disabilities in age-appropriate general education environments
- Development of support to facilitate relationships between students with and without disabilities
- Participation of students with disabilities in extracurricular and after-school opportunities and/or development of support for students with disabilities to work after school, on the weekend, and during the summer
- Development of a leadership team to align school restructuring and inclusion reforms
- Development of supports to achieve student-directed futures planning for students with and without disabilities
- Development of comprehensive faculty development programs
- Development of recommended practice supports and services for students ages 18–21
- Development of community bridge-building strategies, mentorships, internships, and apprenticeship programs for all students

Grant Requirements   Criteria for proposals were rewritten to reflect recommended practices in staff development and systems change. Grant criteria now include the following:

- Demonstration of how grant activities will positively affect all students (those with and without disabilities) as well as the entire school community
- Inclusion of parents, students with and without disabilities, general and special educators, and administrators on grant planning and implementation teams
- Allocation of a portion of grant funds for ongoing staff development opportunities

Eligible Educational Agencies   Educational agencies eligible to receive funds were expanded to include middle schools in 1995. At this time awards also became available to secondary schools that were collaborating with postsecondary educational institutions.

Composition of Review Team   The task force revised its membership to include students with and without disabilities, parents of students with disabilities, general educators, and administrators.

Financial Resources   In 1995 there was a 100% increase in the department's contribution to grant awards, which now total $200,000 per year.

Addressing Organizational, Policy, and Practice Barriers

Although the IOD's systems change strategies have been effective in changing school practice relative to individual students, time and time again the same barriers have stymied efforts to effect inclusive high school educational programs for all New Hampshire students with significant disabilities. These barriers have included 1) tracking and ability grouping within general education, 2) debate over community-based instruction, 3) lack of agreement concerning recommended practices for students ages 18–21, 4) standards-based reform and implications for graduation and receipt of a high school diploma, and 5) outdated certification systems and teacher education programs. A discussion of each barrier and the IOD's response to it is presented next.

Tracking and Ability Grouping within General Education   IOD staff members have participated in countless IEP and placement meetings for high school students in which the most heated discussion was in which "level" of general education class the student should be placed. Often such questions arise as "Should he or she be in an honors or college prep class where the other students can provide models of appropriate behavior and curriculum support? Might a general track class be better because the teacher uses more hands-on teaching methods? Perhaps the student ought to be in a low-level class because it is offered at a time when the special education teacher can be there for support?"

At the heart of this discussion is the continued reliance on tracking and ability grouping in most high schools. Although a large body of research documents the lack of benefit of tracking for most students and negative consequences for many students (e.g., Oakes, 1985; Wheelock, 1992), high schools still place students in tracks. Thus, inclusion represents a challenge not only to special education practice and values but to the basic foundation on which *general* secondary education is structured!

Rather than mount a strategy against tracking based on the research evidence, the IOD has focused its efforts toward increasing teachers' ability to design curriculum that is effective for heterogeneous groups of students that include students with significant disabilities. Jorgensen has written extensively on inclusive curriculum design and has coordinated the IOD's efforts in this area by 1) offering statewide workshops on curriculum design; 2) conducting staff development workshops for individual school faculties; 3) providing in-school technical assistance to teachers and teaching teams on inclusive unit design; and 4) disseminating information about inclusive curriculum design through newsletters, book chapters, and journal articles. These efforts represent a long-term investment of IOD resources in which the outcomes are not immediate but rather accrue gradually over time.

It is important to note that the utilization of IOD resources to support activities such as inclusive curriculum design are not always related to the goals and objectives of a specific, IOD-funded project. All IOD staff have areas of expertise and passions that they nurture, regardless of the project under which they are primarily funded. This practice allows them to initiate new areas of inquiry and action in the absence of a major grant, to work on pet projects, and to stay on the cutting edge of educational reform in the state.

Debate over Community-Based Instruction   In 1979 Brown and colleagues described a curriculum model for students with severe disabilities based on instruction in natural community environments outside the school building. This practice, termed *community-based instruction,* was proposed as an alternative to students' spending their entire school days in self-contained classes and segregated schools learning "prevocational," developmental skills, such as sorting, counting, object permanence, and so forth, devoid of a functional context. Brown and colleagues believed that as students with severe disabilities grow older, they should have increasingly frequent access to their local communities during the school day. Hailed as a revolutionary educational practice, community-based instruction was introduced by special educators throughout the country, and students with disabilities began to spend their days learning skills such as bus riding, grocery shopping, and ordering fast food.

Today, this practice continues, despite the fact that inclusive education has long since become the standard bearer of recommended educational practices. Students with severe disabilities in high schools (and even middle and elementary school) are being taken out of general education classes and away from their classmates without disabilities to engage in community-based instruction. This practice is antithetical to the goals and values of inclusive education. What follows is an analysis of the dangers of separate community-based instruction for students with disabilities and some alternatives.

Access to all school and community opportunities should be independent of a student's abilities and/or disabilities. Whether a school requires all students to spend their entire school day within its walls or embraces a free-flowing partnership with community businesses and organizations, expectations and access should be the same for all students. Someone's disability or label should not increase nor decrease access or opportunity. As schools throughout the country develop philosophies and policies that merge the dual systems of education for students with and without disabilities, they often continue to perpetuate the separate system that exists for middle and high school students with significant disabilities. Secondary students with disabilities, even those who have been fully included in elementary school, are expected to gradually move away from their peers during their middle and high school years. By leaving the school building—when all others remain—students with disabilities become physically segregated and socially isolated from their peers. Typical relationships are impeded, peer contacts are minimized, and the notions of separate and different are reinforced.

The segregating outcomes of community-based instruction during the school day for students with disabilities is but one reason—albeit very significant—to discontinue this standard practice. This social inequality, however, is coupled with academic inequality as well. Many schools are moving toward a belief in the ability of all students as learners because of reports of literacy and competency in individuals with labels of mental retardation. It is clear that students with disabilities can and should have access to the learning that occurs in typical high school classes. Limiting a student's time in the school building necessitates limiting the number of classes that compose the student's school career. A society that values a well-rounded liberal arts education for its students cannot exclude students with disabilities. Long-held beliefs that students with disabilities cannot learn nor benefit from the knowledge and skills taught in high school classes have set up an endless cycle of low expectations and minimized outcomes. Middle and high school classes offer all students opportunities to gain knowledge that assists them in making present and future life choices as well as in developing interests and community connections. These same classes provide students with life skills such as communication, cooperation, problem solving, and organization—skills and habits of mind valued by teachers and employers alike. It is this knowledge and skill, coupled with strong social networks, that helps to prepare students for a well-rounded life after school.

In addition to the traditional courses that most middle and high schools offer students, many schools are broadening their curriculum by offering applied technology or vocational education classes. These courses are designed to provide students opportunities to acquire knowledge and gain skills in a variety of vocational and technological areas. Traditionally, students with significant disabilities did not have access to these courses. Today, students with disabilities are taking these courses to develop competencies in a wide variety of career-related areas. These courses, coupled with full scholastic expectations, support students in their present and future endeavors.

In our argument against separate community-based instruction experiences for students with disabilities, we are not dismissing the value of instruction and experiences in students' lives in their local communities nor in their opportunities to gain job experience. Instead we hope to raise the question of the appropriateness of this approach for students with disabilities when all other students are in school. The issue is more one of equality and inclusion than about the specifics of a student's individual goals. The question then becomes "When and where do students with disabilities gain experience and skills in areas that are not traditionally covered in high school classes or curricula?"

The answer lies in the basic principles of inclusion. Students with disabilities must have the same opportunities as their peers to develop skills and experiences in relationships, at school, in the community, and on the job. Students without disabilities usually venture into the community not during the school day but after school, on the weekend, and during the summer. Students explore the full gamut of community resources (e.g., shopping malls, movie theaters, recreation centers), as well as work a variety of jobs when school is not in session. Students combine their school day with a rich array of out-of-school experiences.

Knowing this allows one to determine where and when students with disabilities should have access to this rich array of experiences. A student who desires to gain job experience can be supported in an after-school, weekend, and/or summer job. A student who needs experience in ordering and purchasing in a restaurant can be supported to join peers at the local hamburger joint. Support for this instruction and experience occurs in the typical places that students use for recreation, social connections, and work experience. For schools that embrace the value of community connections for all students, this support can also occur during student apprenticeships, community service projects, and school-supported cooperative work experiences.

The provision of these supports outside of the school day requires that school staff, families, students, and communities work together to ensure that all students can fully take advantage of these typical opportunities. It is important that everyone move away from the question of "Why?" and move quickly toward the question of "How?"

In addition to being supported while not in the school building, young adults with disabilities can be supported to develop increased competency and experience in the community on completion of their senior year of high school. Adoption of this practice requires a significant change in the way education typically has been structured for students ages 18–21 with severe disabilities.

Lack of Agreement Concerning Recommended Practices for Students Ages 18–21   Recommended practices for educating older students who have significant disabilities have gone through many changes since the mid-1970s. When students with significant disabilities were educated in self-contained programs, grouped according to their "developmental age" rather than their chronological age, it was common for preschoolers and 21-year-olds to be in the same classroom. As mentioned previously, in 1979 Brown and colleagues introduced the notion of a functional, community-based curriculum, and it became common practice for all students with significant disabilities to spend a portion of their time outside the school building, learning independent living and work skills in those community environments in which they would be after high school.

Ironically, the trend to include high school students more fully within the general education curriculum led to the practice of keeping those students in the school building until they aged out of the special education system at 21. This practice takes on several different configurations. In some school systems, students with significant disabilities are retained a few times throughout the elementary and middle school years so that their senior year corresponds to their 21st birthday. In others, students stay in school as second- and third-year seniors and do not actually go through the graduation ceremony until they reach 21. Yet a third iteration is a mixed schedule of academic classes and community-based work experiences so that students might be on the school campus two periods and in the community on a jobsite for the rest of the school day. In a few districts in some states, students between the ages of 18 and 21 are educated on community college campuses although the staff are hired and paid for by the local school district (D. Fisher, personal communication, June 19, 1997).

During the mid- to late 1990s, parents and professionals began working to create an educational experience for students with severe disabilities ages 18–21 that included the same options available to students without disabilities. The IOD has been a leader in this movement and has worked closely with a number of school districts and colleges, developmental disabilities services agencies, and vocational rehabilitation agencies to design individualized experiences for young adults ages 18–21. Instruction and support in the community can now occur to assist a young adult with disabilities in setting up an apartment, attending college or adult education classes, joining a local health club, and/or working a full- or part-time job. Paul's story is an example of the administrative, financial, and support considerations that must be addressed.

Paul's Story

Paul, who is 19 years old and has a label of severe disabilities, is a student at a small community college in southern New Hampshire. He currently takes classes in computer science, sign language, and literature;

participates in AmeriCorps activities and mentoring experiences; and is an active member of the college's community service club. Going to college was always Paul's dream, and he graduated from high school with a sound idea of how to make this a reality.

High School Supports

While still in high school, Paul was afforded numerous opportunities to develop his plan for the future. His weekly advisory classes used a student-directed futures planning process to help students determine their interests, talents, and desires and to develop an individualized plan for the future. Through this process, Paul was able to articulate his desire to attend college and his interest in studying computer science. Paul's guidance counselor was instrumental in providing him with information about different local colleges and the programs and supports they offered. She encouraged him to attend college fairs and ask hard questions of college officials about their school's capacity to provide supports for both classwork and college life. And Paul's circle of support—several teachers, friends, and family members—met regularly to help him refine and implement his personal plan. Paul's family and friends took the lead in supporting him to choose a college that would meet his interests and needs. In addition, throughout his high school career, Paul took all general education classes, which had been chosen based on the requirements and electives available to all students at his grade level. This helped him to prepare academically for college, as well as to develop the self-advocacy and independence skills that are so essential for a successful adult life.

Graduation

Although it was decided early on that Paul would leave high school after the completion of his senior year, there were many decisions that still had to be made. One of the biggest was determining whether Paul would receive a standard high school diploma on completion of his senior year. In addition, there was a great deal of discussion regarding the appropriateness of a standard diploma versus a certificate of completion (IEP diploma). In many schools, certificates are still used instead of diplomas for students with significant disabilities. According to New Hampshire regulations, the certificate would enable Paul to receive supports from the school district until age 21, whereas the receipt of a standard diploma could result in a curtailment of school services. Paul was adamant that he deserved a standard diploma to recognize the hard work he had done; however, he felt that he needed continued support from the school district to successfully pursue his goals.

Although Paul, his family, and school staff felt that there was no perfect solution, they all agreed to a compromise. Paul "graduated" from high

school without any diploma at all. He participated in all graduation activi-
ties, including the ceremony and will receive a standard diploma on his
21st birthday. Until that time, Paul will no longer attend high school but
will receive financial support from the school district for college and a job.

Financial Support

Although Paul will continue to receive support from the school district,
neither he nor his parents believe that the school district should be
expected to pay college tuition. Because tuition is an expense common
to all students, financing for tuition will occur through a combination of
scholarships, school loans, and family help. With the assistance of his
guidance counselor, Paul learned that he is eligible for a Pell grant. In
addition, Paul has applied for support from the state's Department of
Vocational Rehabilitation to pay college tuition. Supplemental Security
Insurance (SSI) or Medicaid benefits will be used to pay for personal
care support. The remaining typical college expenses will be paid for
through Paul's personal savings (accrued through his part-time employ-
ment), his part-time job, and support from his family. Financial support
from the school district will only be used to help Paul with the costs
associated with the additional supports he requires to be successful.

College Supports

Paul has been well supported by teachers and classmates throughout
high school. There is every reason to believe that these same kinds of
supports will be equally successful in college. Paul and his family are
meeting with both school district and college personnel to determine
how Paul can receive the supports he requires. Paul has decided to use
the support from the school district to pay for an employment consultant
and for two college students who will provide outside tutoring for the
classes he is taking. In addition, because Paul would like to live in the
dorms someday, an occupational therapist will coach him as he learns a
variety of independent living skills. The school district's inclusion facilita-
tor will provide Paul with academic supports and will work very closely
with the college disability support coordinator to determine appropriate
class accommodations, modifications, and supports. The college will
provide supports such as peer tutoring, facilitating access to accommoda-
tions and technology, social connections, and career counseling.

The Future

For most students, college is a stepping stone to a career and an adult
life filled with opportunity, challenge, family, and friends. Paul views his
college years as an opportunity to gain knowledge and skills, make new
friends, and further develop his career goals. One of the first services
Paul will use in college is the career counseling center, where all stu-

*dents are assisted in selecting meaningful courses and activities. He will
also continue to meet with his circle of support as necessary. Although
there are no guarantees in life for anyone, Paul and his family know that
Paul is headed in the right direction—a direction that he is controlling
and that others are helping him map. Where will Paul's life eventually
lead? No one can say for sure, but with the supports and plans that are
in place, it is certain that Paul's life will be led by Paul's dreams (Tashie,
Malloy, & Lichtenstein, 1998).*

**Standards-Based Reform and Implications for Graduation and Receipt
of a High School Diploma**   In the early 1990s the New Hampshire legislature
voted to establish a statewide testing system for its school children on the basis
of voluntary curriculum frameworks. Within the original intent of the law, the
system was meant to apply to all students. A list of approved testing accommodations and a rigorous procedure to request exclusion for testing has helped
to ensure that more than 95% of New Hampshire students take the test. After
2 years of gradual introduction in the mid-1990s, all 3rd, 6th, and 10th grade
students now participate in the testing program in the areas of language arts,
math, social studies, and science. Test results, reported as the percentage of all
students in each school scoring at the novice, basic, proficient, and mastery
levels, are publicly available. Although low test scores do not generate negative consequences (at least from the New Hampshire Department of
Education), districts take the assessment program seriously, and many have
mounted efforts to improve their scores by aligning district curricula with the
frameworks and changing educational practice.

Paralleling this standards-based reform at the state level are individual
districts' efforts to identify what students ought to know and be able to do in
order to receive a high school diploma. Across the state, committees made up
of teachers, parents, administrators, community representatives, and sometimes even students are trying to establish broad learning goals and periodic
benchmarks through which to evaluate not only student learning but also the
effectiveness of teaching.

The issues of learning standards, standardized assessment testing,
performance-based diplomas, and other practices designed to elevate student
performance have always sounded an alarm among parents and professionals
who represent students with significant disabilities (Fried & Jorgensen, 1998).
To these people, such initiatives sound like one more way to restrict students'
access to the general education curriculum; to assess them relative to unreachable standards, resulting in a lifetime of Fs, incompletes, and novice labels;
and to deny them a high school diploma on completion of their publicly supported educational careers.

In fact, even a cursory reading of statewide curriculum frameworks and
sample test questions reveals that although the intent of the law was to assess

all students, the writers were not thinking about most students with significant disabilities in their definition of *all*. The average exclusion rate in 1996 was 5%, and students with more significant disabilities compose most of that group (New Hampshire Department of Education, 1996). New Hampshire is currently developing an alternate form of the New Hampshire Educational Improvement and Assessment Program (NHEIAP) for students with severe disabilities, based on the same curriculum standards as for students without disabilities.

Until 1996, the IOD raised a cautionary voice whenever the discussion of standards or testing arose. Students' IEPs were used to provide a safeguard against placement in high school classes where students weren't being expected to meet the same academic standards as students without disabilities.

As special educators across the country began to take a more active role in the standards discussion and as IOD staff began to hear of students being denied a diploma even after a fully inclusive school career, the IOD increased its involvement in standards discussions and activities. Since 1996, the IOD has sponsored an annual national conference titled "School Reform and Inclusive Education: Equity and Excellence for All" whose purpose is to expand the school restructuring conversation in a number of areas (curriculum and instruction, school climate, governance, standards and accountability, and teacher roles) to include students with disabilities. Teams of teachers, parents, and administrators from schools already engaged in school reform have attended and made a commitment to continue their reforms with all students in mind. IOD staff have worked closely with the New Hampshire Department of Education to develop the NHEIAP–Alternate test so that assessment data on students with the most significant disabilities contributes to school reform initiatives.

Because granting a diploma is still a local school decision, IOD advocacy with regard to graduation has necessarily occurred one student at a time. Some schools have informally adapted the performance requirements for students with significant disabilities so that they could receive a diploma at graduation (or at age 21), whereas other schools have been more rigid and have awarded certificates of completion. If the state ever links a minimum level of performance on the NHEIAP with the receipt of a high school diploma, IOD staff will advocate the development of an equitable and inclusive policy.

Outdated Certification Systems and Teacher Education Programs
General education teacher preparation programs in several of New Hampshire's institutions of higher education are divided into early childhood, elementary, and secondary divisions, but most special education programs have only early childhood and K–12 concentrations. At the University of New Hampshire, for example, prospective special education teachers take one course in curriculum design and instruction that addresses elementary, middle, and high school students. Likewise, New Hampshire's special education certification system centers on grades K–12 both for teachers of students with mild disabilities (general

special education certification) as well for teachers receiving specialty certifications (e.g., mental retardation certification, learning disabilities certification).

This lack of focus on high school students in both teacher education and the certification system has many programmatic consequences at the local level. First, some teachers view older students with severe disabilities as developmentally younger than their peers without disabilities, perhaps because their teacher education program emphasized elementary special education topics such as child development, early literacy experiences, and family adjustment issues that are prominent during the preschool years, and elementary school organization. Many special education teachers currently teaching in high schools completed only an elementary school student teaching or internship experience. Second, most special education teachers know little about general high school curricula and are intimidated by the prospect of supporting a student in an upper level science or math class. Third, the focus of elementary school is to prepare students for middle and high school, whereas the goal of high school is to prepare students for adult life. If teachers have never learned about community living options for young adult students with disabilities, they tend to focus their efforts on the high school experience rather than provide a balanced emphasis on high school and what comes after it. Fourth, most teachers of young children have strong nurturing and caregiving attributes—wonderful characteristics for a kindergarten or first grade teacher but detrimental for a teacher of older students, given these students' need to develop autonomy, self-reliance, and self-determination as they move through adolescence into adulthood.

Since its beginning the IOD has played an active part in restructuring both teacher education and the state certification system to reflect recommended practices that include knowledge and skills related to high school students with disabilities. Several IOD staff members managed a state-funded contract that developed a new special education teacher certification system based on age divisions of early childhood, elementary and middle school, and secondary school. The competencies required in the secondary school category address not only access to the general education curriculum and the development of academic and independent living skills but require teachers to support students' postgraduation plans, including work, technical education, or 4-year college as postsecondary options.

Beginning in 1994, the Statewide Systems Change Project and state-funded higher education projects have awarded small innovation grants to faculty from the state's colleges and university to promote greater collaboration between general and special education, grounded in inclusion philosophy and recommended practices (Jorgensen, 1996). Although these grants have supported major changes in early childhood and elementary teacher education, efforts by the colleges to restructure secondary teacher education were just beginning in 1997. Influencing the attitudes and skills of future high school teachers is essential to the IOD's mission of increasing local school capacity to create a seamless system of inclusive education from preschool through college. During 1999 and 2000, IOD staffperson Cheryl M. Jorgensen served as a coordinator of the state's efforts to revise all certification standards, including those for general and special education teachers.

INCLUSION HISTORIES OFFER INSIGHTS INTO THE CHANGE PROCESS AND THE INSTITUTE ON DISABILITY'S ROLE

Analyzing the IOD's effectiveness in initiating change and in creating sustainable change is a difficult task. Although the IOD is the major organization in New Hampshire involved in systems change activities that affect high school students with significant disabilities, its efforts have always existed within an everchanging milieu of local, state, and federal educational initiatives. So, to isolate the IOD as *the* major contributor to positive changes (or conversely, to a lack of positive change) seems spurious and self-important. It is useful, however, to describe New Hampshire's achievements relative to creating fully inclusive high schools; to provide a comprehensive description of IOD activities that, at a minimum, influenced this picture; and to analyze the IOD's role in the success stories and in goals not yet realized. This analysis may be helpful to others currently engaged in similar efforts.

As the IOD approached its 10th year of existence in 1997, several respected colleagues were invited to study the organization's accomplishments, offer insights into the reasons behind disappointments, and make suggestions as it moved past infancy into organizational adolescence. Our conversations with these thoughtful colleagues (among them Valerie Bradley, Doug Fisher, Jo Krippenstaple, John O'Brien, and Jeff Strully) and the subsequent discussions that IOD staff have had among themselves highlighted both the organization's strengths and weaknesses as a change agent in the state. With particular regard to the challenge of changing schools, IOD staff came to realize that its greatest strength is the ability to effect first-generation changes in schools that might be characterized as "early adopters" of inclusive education values and practices (Fullan & Stiegelbauer, 1990). The districts that were part of our first model demonstration and systems change projects—Concord, Hampton, Hudson, Lebanon, Moultonborough, Somersworth, Windham-Pelham, and Woodsville, to name just a few— quickly embraced the values behind inclusion, developed action plans to include students with significant disabilities in general education classes in their home schools, and made the necessary changes in staff roles and instructional practices that yielded early successes. The data on student placement collected at these early project sites showed dramatic results of the IOD's work. In a typical district prior to participation in an IOD inclusion project, 90% of students with significant disabilities would have been placed in self-contained classes in or outside the district with 10%

participating in some general education classes. Following a year or two of intensive training and technical assistance from the IOD, most districts' placement statistics flip-flopped—90% of students were then included full time in modified general education classes, and only 10% were still in self-contained classes.

If we were to judge the IOD's effectiveness based on data gathered from these sites immediately after their participation in a project or even a year or two later, we would be overjoyed. Over time, however, a bit of slipping was apparent in some of these districts. A student here or there was sent to an out-of-district placement. A few students were spending time in a resource room or out in the community with other students who had disabilities. A center-based preschool program remained open in lieu of integration of all students in community child care and preschool settings. The IOD closely examined these phenomena by talking to administrators, teachers, and parents, and discovered that five different inclusion histories emerged:

- Some districts, representing project sites from both the IOD's early years (1987–1992) and more recent efforts (1992–1997), made rapid changes in their programs for students with significant disabilities, maintained their commitment to inclusion and recommended practices, and continued to grow in response to evolving notions of promising inclusive practices.
- Some districts' inclusion rates experienced a small but significant decline that began about 3 years after the districts' initial restructuring efforts and stabilized at a level far above "pre-IOD" association but did not increase to 100%. (Inclusion rate represents the percentage of students with significant disabilities whose placement was in modified general education classes plus a measure of the actual time that students were spending in those classes or in other inclusive environments.)
- Some districts maintained their commitment to inclusion and 1980s recommended practices but never progressed to adopt a second generation of values and practices that reflected the evolving definition of inclusion.
- Despite IOD's repeated efforts to offer technical assistance or provide staff development, a few schools in the state continued to resist inclusion mightily.
- A few districts experienced a dramatic return to separate placements for students with disabilities after the project had finished focusing on these districts.

A careful consideration of each prototypic history yields some interesting insights into the IOD's role and effectiveness, the change process itself, and areas for future growth.

Early Commitment to Inclusion and Continued Growth:
Inclusion Leads the Way for Restructuring at Pelham High School

When Robert Pedersen, principal of Pelham High School in southern New Hampshire was asked about the major restructuring efforts underway in his school, he cited inclusion as one of the reasons the faculty and community is committed to and energized by these changes. "When we began including students with disabilities in our general education classes, teachers began to take a look at the ways in which they taught all students," he said. "Inclusion helped teachers realize that there were strategies they could use to ensure that all students could learn. This eased the way to implementing major restructuring in our school and district."

Pelham High School is home to more than 400 students. In 1989, along with the elementary and middle schools in this district, Pelham became a fully inclusive school—all students with disabilities in the district returned to their neighborhood schools and began attending all general education classes. Through a 2-year participation with the Statewide Systems Change Project, faculty and staff received training on how best to educate all students in their classes, families received information on recommended practices in education and community living, and students received all of the supports necessary to be successful in those general classes. Pelham was viewed by many as a school worthy of replication for their success with inclusion.

Today, Pelham is still viewed as a model of a fully inclusive high school, but people are also taking note of the numerous changes in curriculum, scheduling, support, and community involvement that have occurred since 1989. For example, in 1995 the high school converted to a four-by-four block schedule (each semester students enroll in four classes, each of which is 90 minutes long), and many classes use an interdisciplinary curriculum design model. Pelham's principal stated that having students and teachers spending longer periods of time together has allowed for a more comprehensive and hands-on approach to the curriculum. "All students benefit from a schedule that allows for practical applications of the material being covered," he said. Pedersen also said he was excited about increased flexibility in support services that began in 1998. In addition to the support that is now given to students and teachers in the classroom and during students' study periods, the school will offer support to students before and after school.

Many of the changes in the basic structure of the school are guided by the school council, a governing body made up of representatives from the student body, faculty, administration, school board, and community. The school council meets on a monthly basis to propose changes and support ideas. One of the proposals to come before the council was the development of a comprehensive career/futures planning process for all students. Pelham High School developed such a process for students that involves career portfolios, community service, and the development of strong school–community partnerships that would support apprenticeships and internships. All of these opportunities are available for all students, with additional support provided to any student who requires it. Pelham's principal explained, "Students with disabilities are a part of our school, and, of course, they are included in all typical career and futures planning processes. The only difference is in the amount of support that an individual student might need."

Pelham High School is an example of a high school that continued its systems change efforts beyond general inclusion. What has been essential for Pelham High School is that they have not engaged in school restructuring efforts separate from inclusion. Instead, they continue to ask themselves the question, "How can our school be restructured in order to support the best education for all students?"

Decline in Inclusion Rate

The full-time inclusion rate in many of the districts with which we worked so intensively during the late 1980s and early 1990s began to drop within 3 years of their participation as a systems change project site. The principals and special education directors in those districts offered several explanations for this phenomenon. They said that as students got older, inclusion was harder. They pointed out that the first students they included were elementary school age and that inclusion became more difficult when students reached middle and high school. The state special education data reflected this phenomenon. In 1997, approximately 70% of elementary school–age students with significant disabilities were included in modified general education programs compared with 36% of high school students (New Hampshire Department of Education, 1997).

Administrators at the schools whose inclusion rates declined perceived that the students who were the first to be moved from self-contained classes or out-of-district placements were "easier" to include in general education. These administrators told us that the success of the first few years of students' inclusion was judged by gains in social skills but that as time went on, teachers (and sometimes parents) became concerned when students did not receive direct instruction in independent living and "functional" skills. (It is important to note that most of the concerns expressed by teachers and parents were not a reaction to empirical evidence that students *weren't* learning these skills but a reaction to the absence of focus on them in students' IEPs or daily schedules.) Because of a shift in the desired benefits for students' inclusion from mostly social gains to social, academic, and functional gains, teachers and parents opted for a mixed school program and schedule. High school students with disabilities were spending part of the day in general education classes to gain social benefits and part of the day in special education classes or in community-based instruction to reap the perceived academic benefits. Despite the fact that the

IOD conducted extensive staff development training to demonstrate to people how students could learn academic and functional skills in general education classes, the organization was not effective in convincing others to share this belief or change practice.

Commitment Maintained but Not Updated

The third phenomenon that characterized how inclusion at the high school level has changed over time is represented by districts whose commitment to inclusive values has remained steadfast but has not been refreshed. These districts adopted recommended practices that existed when they participated as an IOD project site, but as time went on they never adopted newer practices that were being written about in the literature or that were being promoted in IOD-sponsored staff development workshops.

One district that exemplifies this phenomenon comes to mind. In this district, five elementary schools, two middle schools, and one high school participated in a variety of IOD projects for a 7-year period during the late 1980s and early 1990s. To this day, the district's superintendent, special education director, and several principals willingly speak on behalf of inclusion at state and national conferences, the IOD is positively regarded throughout the district, and parents are very satisfied with their children's education. Yet if one visited a school in the district and closely observed the day-to-day lives of students and teachers, one would notice several practices that were common and acceptable in the 1980s but are not representative of recommended practices in the 1990s.

For example, special education teachers and general education teachers collaborate to write students' IEPs, but curriculum is still planned by general education teachers and modified by special education teachers; in contrast, 1990s recommended practice calls for curriculum to be designed inclusively, with modifications reflected simply as demonstrated performance options available to all students. Students with significant disabilities are included in general physical education classes, but instead of being members of school sports teams, they participate in Special Olympics. At the preschool level, the "reverse mainstream" model that brought typical students into the district's early childhood classrooms has not been replaced by a community-based model of parental choice of programs and children's inclusion in local preschool programs. Finally, at the high school level, students with significant disabilities enroll in a few nonacademic general education classes (art, music, computer, theater) but still spend part of their day engaged in community-based instruction with other students who have significant disabilities.

Resistance to Inclusion Efforts

The fourth observation about inclusion histories is that the IOD experienced difficulty in facilitating significant changes in schools that were not early adopters of inclusive principles and practices. It seemed that the strategies that were effective for the IOD's first cohort of project sites (approximately 1987–1992) were not as effective with the new group of schools who were project sites after 1992. IOD staff neglected to understand that not only were these schools "middle and late adopters" of educational innovations—by their very nature more cautious about giving up old practices and instituting new ones in any area—but also that the IOD's understanding of inclusion had changed as had the national climate.

Whereas IOD staff talked about vision, friendships, and participation with the first group of project sites, the requirements that were imposed on the second group of project sites included not only those original elements of an inclusive school but also utilization of natural supports, a commitment to literacy development, access to assistive technology, grading of students' work in the same manner as typical students, and the integration of related service learning objectives (e.g., communication, movement) into every lesson plan. It is no wonder that these schools were less willing to take the plunge toward full inclusion!

A changed political climate also may have influenced the second group's reluctance about inclusion. When inclusive education was first introduced in the late 1980s, resistance came from individual administrators and a few disability-specific organizations. In 1995, however, the president of the largest teacher's union in the United States issued a statement against full inclusion! On the legal front, several court decisions in the early 1990s supported inclusive placements (Lipton, 1994), but later in the decade the decisions were less favorable (e.g., *Kari H. v. Franklin Special School District*).

Dramatic Return to Separate Programs

In a very small number of districts who had been early adopters of inclusive practices, a dramatic reversal of policy and practice occurred, in which placement data showed an almost complete return to restrictive placements for students with disabilities. Three districts that had achieved modest success as part of a systems change project experienced a turnover among key staff people. When individuals who had been part of the district's inclusion team left the district (e.g., principal, special education director, inclusion facilitator), new staff who had not been part of the project reinstated self-contained classes and out-of-district placements.

Analysis of These Phenomena Based on Education Reform Theory

Before engaging in a critical reflection of the IOD's effectiveness as a change agent, it is prudent to consider whether the innovation being promoted—full inclusion of students with significant disabilities in general education classes—is a more unique challenge than is, for instance, gaining acceptance for a new math curriculum or even revising a grading system.

Is Inclusion Unique as an Educational Innovation?   Perhaps inclusion is unique as an educational innovation in that it requires people to make radical changes not only in their beliefs about the value of people whose contributions to society are not self-evident but also in the basic assumptions that underlie learning and teaching. The contrast between what most people believe and the belief system of inclusion illustrates the paradigm shift that the IOD tries to help people make (Onosko & Jorgensen, 1998; for more discussion on paradigm shifts, see Chapter 2).

For example, many teachers believe that a few students are gifted, that most are "average," and that the remainder are somewhere "below average," whereas inclusion is based on the belief that all students have value and unique gifts to offer their school. Many teachers believe that thinking and learning at high levels of performance can occur with only select students, whereas inclusion is based on the belief that all students can think and learn, regardless of their label or ability. Many teachers believe that diversity among students ought to be minimized in the classroom through ability grouping or tracking, whereas inclusion is based on the belief that diversity within a learning community ought to be embraced and that all students can actually learn more in a quality inclusive classroom. Many teachers believe that students with different learning styles and disability labels need separate, specialized instruction that is inappropriate for typical students, whereas inclusion is based on the belief that effective teaching for students with disabilities is actually good teaching for all students. Many teachers believe that a back-to-basics approach to curriculum and instruction yields high levels of achievement for all students and condemn attempts to make education relevant to students' interests and real-world issues, whereas inclusion is based on the belief that all students learn best when studying interesting and challenging topics that they find personally meaningful. Many teachers believe that they possess a body of knowledge that can be directly conveyed to students through lecture, whereas inclusion is based on the belief that students learn best when they are actively and collaboratively building knowledge with their classmates and their teacher.

Not only are there basic differences in the beliefs that underlie inclusion compared with those underlying the special education continuum, but also even the organizational structure of schools is antithetical to the creation of a unified system of education (Skrtic, 1991). Organizational and systemic barriers to the creation of inclusive schools include the following: 1) a perceived threat that special education teachers and administrators will lose their jobs in a merged system; 2) entire university training programs for special education teachers that are separate from general teacher education programs (Pugach, 1988); 3) local and state funding structures that reward restrictive placements and penalize schools for supporting students in general education classes; 4) regulations that prohibit the use of special education personnel to support students who do not have disability labels; and last, but not least, 5) the real threat of being out of compliance with the Individuals with Disabilities Education Act (IDEA) Amendments of 1997 (PL 105-17) that require that schools maintain a continuum of educational placement options including choices other than general education. Recognizing that creating inclusive schools has these unique challenges ought not diminish anyone's commitment to the goal but should inform the standards by which the IOD judges its effectiveness and the achievements of participating schools.

Reasons for Failure of Education Reform Efforts   Michael Fullan and Matthew Miles, thoughtful scholars of educational reform, warned that "reform will not be achieved until [new] orientations have been incorporated into the thinking and reflected in the actions of those involved in change efforts" (1992, p. 215). The five inclusion histories just described—a mixture of successes and failures—can be analyzed relative to Fullan and Miles's reasons for the failure of most educational reforms and by their seven propositions for success that "form a set and must be contemplated in relation to one another" (p. 215).

Faulty Maps of Change Are Used   Unless the IOD draws an accurate map of change relative to inclusive high schools, it will make wrong turns, be unprepared to forge into deep rivers or survive inhospitable climates, and even arrive at the wrong destination. One faulty assumption is that schools need a concrete mission statement and action plan to guide every step of change along the way (Fullan & Miles, 1992). Everyone has his or her own pet theory (map) about changing schools that is reflected in familiar propositions such as "Every school is unique" and "Full participation of everyone involved in a change is essential." Although empirical research has debunked all these propositions, the IOD has used each at one time or another to design technical assistance or training strategies. In fact, schools participating in IOD systems change projects were required to write Inclusion Action Plans! Everyone has a different map of change, and to survive the journey together everyone must agree to use just one.

Solutions to Complex School Reform Problems Are Not Easy or Are Not Known   Fullan and Miles described the complex nature of educational change:

> Even if one considers only seemingly simple, first-order changes, the number of components and their interrelationships are staggering: curriculum and instruction, school organization, student services, community involvement, teacher in-service training, assessment, reporting, and evaluation. Deeper, second-order changes in school cultures, teacher–student relationships, and values and expectations of the system are all the more daunting. (1992, p. 212)

Although they were not referring specifically to reform in special education, the relevance to inclusion efforts is clear when their passage is reworded like this:

Even if one considers only seemingly simple, first-order changes, the number of components and their interrelationships are staggering: *tracking and ability grouping, the existence of separate special education administrative services, parent participation in the IEP process, grading of students with IEPs, and the roles of related service professionals in the general education class.* Deeper, second-order changes in *school cultures, general/special education teacher relationships, the value that we place on students with extraordinary differences,* and the values and expectations of the system are all the more daunting.

Thus, because of all of these complex components in the education process, it is impossible to arrive at simple solutions to inclusion. When working with a high school to help them include students with disabilities fully within general education, inclusion facilitators need to recognize that predicting the course of change or even trying to describe exactly what the new system will look like is an exercise in futility and, more important, that doing so actually prevents teams from putting into place a reflective change process that can be constantly fine-tuned based on experience.

Symbols Are Valued over Substance   When educational reform is promoted by politicians at the local, state, or federal level, one must be wary of people who play along with reforms simply to garner positive press or to amass political capital. In New Hampshire, where most educational decisions (and more than 90% of funding) occurs at the local level, school administrators must be particularly responsive to their most vocal constituents. When the loudest voices are from parents of students with disabilities who want inclusion, and administrators respond quickly without making the necessary investment in building support among all community members, the following year's voices protesting just as loudly against inclusion can cause an equally precipitous turnaround. Although the IOD effectively uses symbols and rituals through its publications, videotapes, and visible presence in the educational community, it must ensure that these symbols are just one part of an overall commitment to sustainable change among constituents.

Hasty and Superficial Solutions Are Devised   Remember the school districts that jumped into inclusion with both feet and just as quickly reversed their placement practices when staff changed? This phenomenon is an example of how superficial reforms (e.g., merely changing the classroom to which students are assigned) rarely result in changes in the underlying culture of the school and the organizational structures that support effective inclusive practice. Because inclusion in those districts relied on the commitment of just a few key people, their departure guaranteed that inclusion would falter.

The IOD has shifted its resources dramatically over the years from a primary focus on training and technical assistance to emphasis on policy change, teacher education, leadership development, and cultivation of long-term relationships with schools that have demonstrated a history of deep commitment to educational reform. Although all IOD consultants know the importance of a quick-response technical assistance capability in the state, they also know that too large a proportion of those technical assistance visits are merely Band-Aids providing some relief to the immediate situation (e.g., teacher burnout, difficult student behavior, parent–school disagreements) but not resulting in a cure of the underlying problem that prompted the call (e.g., lack of qualified staff, no administrative vision, antagonistic attitude toward parents, no time for collaborative planning).

Of critical importance is learning how to better assess which schools are good candidates for large investments of time and resources. Also, technical assistance must support such schools' adoption of the internal processes that not only move students from segregated to integrated classes as rapidly as possible but also develop their *own* capacity to manage the inevitable problems that will arise.

Resistance Is Misunderstood   Although IOD personnel write journal articles, conduct training workshops, publish newsletters, and teach academic courses, most of the personnel spend the majority of their time in the field working with the people who are responsible for making inclusion work. IOD staff get to know them personally—their educational backgrounds, philosophies, how they conduct their classrooms—and they quickly discover that IOD staff are members of the "100% club" with regard to inclusive education. Under these circumstances it is not difficult to understand how difficulties in the introduction or refinement of inclusion can appear to be personal. Although some individuals lack any sort of belief in the humanity of people with significant disabilities, the resistance offered by most teachers is probably due more to real problems of implementation, such as "diffuse objectives, lack of technical skills, or insufficient resources for change" (Fullan & Miles, 1992, p. 214). Blaming lack of success on people's attitudes simply immobilizes and prevents one from seeing what can be done to make a situation better.

Pockets of Success Fade   Although local innovators may be successful in the short run because of an extraordinary commitment of time and energy of a few key people, Fullan and Miles explained that

> They may burn themselves out or unwittingly seal themselves off from the surrounding environment. Thus schools can become hotbeds of innovation and reform in the absence of external support, but they cannot stay innovative without the continuing support of the district and other agencies.... The failure to institutionalize an innovation and build it into the normal structures and practices of the organization underlies the disappearance of many reforms. (1992, p. 214)

Unless the IOD becomes more skilled at demonstrating that educational practice reforms associated with inclusion and better outcomes for students with disabilities also are related to better outcomes for all students (and thus should be made part of standard district policy), exemplary school models will experience the slip in commitment and practice described previously.

Knowledge About the Change Process Is Misused Finally, understanding the reasons for failure and knowing something about the many individual components that are related to success are not enough to guarantee the sustainability of an innovation (e.g., inclusion). We must continually study what is being learned about the change process itself, respect the interrelatedness of the many variables at play, and understand that change is systemic and involves not only students with disabilities but also the foundations and practices of general education itself.

SYSTEMS CHANGE STRATEGIES FOR THE FUTURE

The beginning of the new century offers opportunities and challenges to the creation of successful inclusive high schools. The following strategies (representing the third part in the high school inclusion story) offer one possible new map of change. Organizations working toward inclusion must share this map with their constituent groups and must make frequent course corrections based on shared experiences, while keeping the destination clearly in sight.

Learn More About the People Involved in Change

In 1998 the IOD sponsored a 1-day workshop for special education administrators and parents involved in advanced leadership training on the topic of social marketing—the use of business marketing strategies to get people to change their behavior to create positive outcomes for their communities (Andreasen, 1995). The speaker talked about the different responses of various constituent groups to the question, "What would it take for you to include all students with significant disabilities in the mainstream of high school academic and social life?" and IOD staff realized that there was much to learn about change. They realized that they have been using the same menu of change strategies—appeal to people's sense of justice, provide them with curriculum ideas, take them to visit schools that are a step ahead of them, and so forth—for just about everyone. When a strategy didn't work with a particular group or school after one try, IOD staff members simply went back and tried again with more enthusiasm or stronger arguments! In the past they had not systematically learned about the beliefs, motivations, and investments of those people who were involved in change nor had they designed information or educational campaigns accordingly. *Learning more about various constituent groups and designing educational programs and initiatives accordingly should be a major focus of efforts to support and facilitate inclusion as the 21st century begins.*

Become Scholars of the Process of Change

As mentioned previously, Fullan and Miles suggested that a number of themes or lessons derived from current knowledge of successful change "form a set and must be contemplated in relation to one another" (1992, pp. 215–218). These themes include the following:

- *"Change is learning loaded with uncertainty."* Ownership of a change process and the commitment of the resources necessary for its longevity comes after people have learned new information about the innovation and linked it to their self-interest and better outcomes for students. When innovators expect people to change long-held beliefs and practices without teaching them the reasons behind a different model of education, they are likely to arouse fear, resistance, and avoidance.
- *"Change is a journey, not a blueprint."* Although writing district goals and objectives relative to school reform and inclusion is a useful exercise, the resulting document should only serve as a guide, not as a prescription for change. Perhaps the largest number of objectives and action plan statements ought to refer to the *management of the change process itself* rather than to the details of how curricula, assessment, or teachers' job descriptions ought to be restructured.
- *"Problems are our friends."* When the IOD is called in to provide student-specific technical assistance or to provide training in curriculum modification, success is usually judged by the disappearance of the problem that prompted the call to our office! So, it seems antithetical to approach change looking for problems rather than trying to eliminate them. Yet, unless innovators are willing and even aggressive in looking for the problems inherent in inclusive education—and then in providing resources to help solve them—problems will crop up sooner or later, innovators will not be in a position to help a school muster their coping resources for an effective response, and the status quo will be maintained.
- *"Change is resource hungry."* Although IOD staff understand this tenet well and budget considerable funds for districts while they are full-fledged project sites (e.g., for teacher workshops, for visits to exemplary schools, for substitute teachers to provide teachers with days away from school to work on curriculum development, for books and videotapes about inclusive practices), only a handful of school districts in the state have barely adequate staff development budgets and time. All organizations advocating inclusion need to see their role as working with schools to assess outside funding for continuous quality improvement in addition to allocating funds that exist in the overall school budget.

- *"Change requires the power to manage it."* As long as the power to effect inclusion rests with an agency's staff person, a parent of a student with a disability, or one administrator, there will be a power vacuum when a project or program is over, the parent runs out of energy, and the administrator is faced with new challenges and priorities. The power to manage and sustain change must be seated within a much larger, representative group of people in a district who are vested with decision-making clout.

- *"Change is systemic."* As stated before, reform must focus on the development and relationships of all of the main components of the system simultaneously and must address both the culture and the structure of the system. Placing a student with significant disabilities in an upper-level science class necessitates a careful look at standards, which has implications for assessment and grading, which prompts a look at tracking and grouping practices, which leads to an investigation of school culture and values, and so forth.

- *"All large-scale change is implemented locally."* The IOD's mission and operating practices match closely what we know about the necessity of focusing on local change. Although the IOD will always invest in making changes in state policies that affect local educational practice, its first commitment is to develop relationships with parents, teachers, and administrators in local New Hampshire communities. *All of an organization's major activities should be based on these lessons about change so that investment of time and resources results in sustainable change.*

Increase Investment in Initial Teacher Education

Every time an IOD staff member visits a school to conduct a workshop with veteran teachers, he or she thinks, "We must put more effort into changing the way that teachers are prepared so that we don't have to start with Inclusion 101 every time we go out to do a workshop!" Yet, because of the IOD's unique position in the university system—it is not an academic department and thus does not grant degrees or teach its own courses—influencing teachers-in-training depends first on the establishment of a positive working relationship with university departments of education. The IOD has taken a number of steps in that direction, such as working with the University of New Hampshire and Keene State College to establish a teacher education program in severe disabilities. It is extremely difficult, however, to do 100% of the work of coordinating a federal grant and to teach university courses at the same time. Although IOD efforts to influence teacher education have focused on early childhood and elementary education programs, the next focus area will be secondary teacher education. *In the future, one way for innovators to encourage inclusion is to be committed to being closely associated with teacher education programs and to finding creative ways to manage project and course instruction responsibilities.*

Become Aligned More Closely with General Education Reform

If one asked 100 principals from high schools in New Hampshire whom they would call if they needed consultation and technical assistance for a student who experiences significant disabilities, 9 out of 10 would probably name the IOD. If one asked the same 100 principals whom they would call to learn more about portfolio assessment, new math standards, innovative guidance programs, block scheduling, or designing a community service program, it is unlikely that any of the principals would mention the IOD. Yet, the future of inclusive education amid the everchanging educational landscape depends on its linkages with those general educational debates and reforms that affect all students, not just those with disabilities. Even as the IOD maintains its strong identity as an organization with particular interest and expertise relative to students with disabilities, it must become more knowledgeable about general education and develop collaborative working relationships with its leaders. *One helpful factor in an organization's efforts to promote inclusion in schools is for its staff to strengthen their credibility in general education and develop collaborative relationships with school leaders.*

Put More Resources into Building Leadership
Capacity in People Outside the Institute on Disability

Each year IOD project coordinators invite respected colleagues from other universities and organizations to evaluate its projects. Program staff are less interested in getting feedback on whether they achieved each minute objective on the management plan in a timely fashion than they are in discovering whether they have truly met the goal of increasing the capacity of others to advocate for students with significant disabilities. Through these impartial evaluations, those who work for the IOD have come to realize that they are constantly exposed to experiences that solidify their beliefs in the positive value of people with significant disabilities, provide new educational techniques to make students' inclusion richer, and allow the luxury of time to sort through difficult organizational and policy issues. Yet, many of the people in the field who are actually responsible for administration, teaching, and policy have at most three or four opportunities each year to build their skills, talk about barriers and solutions, and receive collegial support. Thus, although IOD staff are constantly bringing new ideas to the table, those in the field barely have time to try out and evaluate last year's innovations! First and foremost, the IOD needs to be more sensitive to the demands that are faced by people in the field. The IOD's values and commitment to inclusion should be unwavering but must realize that the road toward it is winding, filled with potholes and unseen obstacles around every bend. An important shift in efforts must occur relative to the amount of time spent introducing innovations, raising standards, and solidifying beliefs and practice innovations among a larger group of practitioners who can then serve as allies in the field. *To expand the network of experts beyond people who work for a specific agency or organization, efforts around leadership development for families, consumers, administrators, teachers, and policy makers need to be increased.* To accomplish that goal, for example, the IOD may need to identify additional resources so that technical assistance and training continue to be available for people who are just beginning to learn about inclusion while the organization concentrates more of its time and effort on leadership development.

CONCLUSIONS

The IOD's vision for *all* students is their *full* inclusion in *all* aspects of school and community life. Although holding fast to that philosophy causes some people to label the IOD as inflexible, idealistic, and radical, program staff will continue to accept the consequences of their beliefs because the stakes are so high for the students for whom they advocate. A parent of a student with significant disabilities who has sometimes disagreed with the IOD over means (but not ends) offered the following reflection on the organization's role in the state, and inclusion advocates can draw support from her comments when deciding to take a similar and sometimes difficult course: "I have found myself disagreeing with the Institute on a variety of issues here and there over the years. But when all is said and done, I guess I see the necessity for an organization that takes such a 'hard line' stance. It's comforting, somehow, to know that amidst changes in the political climate, the fads of the day, or the whims of public officials, you can always count on the Institute to never change what it believes in—the right of all people to carve out for themselves a life in the community where they are valued for the gifts that they have to offer, not discriminated against because they have a label. I guess disagreeing with the Institute's positions now and then is a small price to pay for what we get in return."

REFERENCES

Americans with Disabilities Act (ADA) of 1990, PL 101-336, 42 U.S.C. §§ 12101 *et seq.*

Andreasen, A. (1995). *Marketing social change: Changing behavior to promote health, social development, and the environment.* San Francisco: Jossey-Bass.

Brown, L., Branston, M., Hamre-Nietupski, S., Pumpian, I., Certo, N., & Gruenewald, L. (1979). A strategy for developing chronological age-appropriate and functional curricular content for severely handicapped adolescents and young adults. *Journal of Special Education, 13*(1), 81–90.

Fried, R.L., & Jorgensen, C.M. (1998). Equity and excellence: Finding common ground between inclusive education and school reform. In C.M. Jorgensen, *Restructuring high schools for all students: Taking inclusion to the next level* (pp. 15–28). Baltimore: Paul H. Brookes Publishing Co.

Fullan, M., & Miles, M. (1992, June). Getting reform right: What works and what doesn't. *Phi Delta Kappan, 211*–218.

Fullan, M., & Stiegelbauer, S. (1990). *The new meaning of educational change* (2nd ed.). New York: Teachers College Press.

Individuals with Disabilities Education Act Amendments of 1997, PL 105-17, 20 U.S.C. §§ 1400 *et seq.*

Jorgensen, C. (1996). *Teachers are for all children: Restructuring teacher education for today's diverse classrooms.* Durham: University of New Hampshire, Institute on Disability.

Kari H. v. Franklin Special School District, 23 IDELR S 38 (M.D. Tenn. 1995).

Lipton, D. (1994). The full inclusion court cases: 1989–1994. *Bulletin: National Center on Educational Restructuring and Inclusion, 1*(2), 1–8.

Martin, J., & Tashie, C. (1996). *The voices of friendship* [Videotape]. Durham: University of New Hampshire, Institute on Disability.

New Hampshire Department of Education. (1996). *New Hampshire educational improvement and assessment program.* Concord: Author.

New Hampshire Department of Education. (1997). *Special education information system.* Concord: Author.

Oakes, J. (1985). *Keeping track: How schools structure inequality.* New Haven, CT: Yale University Press.

Olson, L. (1994, May 4). Critical friends. *Education Week, 20*–27.

Onosko, J., & Jorgensen, C.M. (1998). Unit and lesson planning for the inclusive classroom: Maximizing learning opportunities for all students. In C.M. Jorgensen, *Restructuring high schools for all students: Taking inclusion to the next level* (pp. 71–106). Baltimore: Paul H. Brookes Publishing Co.

Pugach, M. (1988, May–June). Special education as a constraint on teacher education reform. *Journal of Teacher Education,* 52–59.

Skrtic, T. (1991). The special education paradox: Equity as the way to excellence. *Harvard Education Review, 61*(2).

Steinbeck, J. (1937). *Of mice and men.* New York: Covici, Friede.

Tashie, C., Malloy, J.M., & Lichtenstein, S.J. (1998). Transition or graduation planning?: Supporting all students to plan for the future. In C.M. Jorgensen, *Restructuring high schools for all students: Taking inclusion to the next level* (pp. 233–260). Baltimore: Paul H. Brookes Publishing Co.

University of New Hampshire, Institute on Disability. (1999). *High school inclusion: Equity and excellence in an inclusive community of learners* [Videotape]. Durham: Author. (Available from Paul H. Brookes Publishing Co., P.O. Box 10624, Baltimore, MD 21285-0624; 800-638-3775; www.brookespublishing.com)

Wheelock, A. (1992). *Crossing the tracks: How "untracking" can save America's schools.* New York: New Press.

7

Postcards on the Refrigerator

Changing the Power Dynamic in Housing and Assistance

Jay Klein, Barbara Boyd Wilson, and Debra Nelson

When we first met Ken Forché, he was living in a group home on Willowrun Drive in a small town in New Hampshire. He had been there for 7 years. For 6 of those years he had been saying he wanted to live somewhere else. It took another 26 months, a number of false starts, and a tenacious team of stalwart supporters, but finally, on April 12, 1996, at age 61, Ken Forché moved into the first home he had ever been able to call his own.

Through the story of Ken Forché and through those of Greg Garvey and Jolene Harris, all three of whom participated in New Hampshire's Home of Your Own Project, this chapter chronicles the early stages of a profound change in the way in which people with disabilities are supported to live in

---

This chapter is dedicated to Butch Gagnon, who was able to move into a home he owned after years of living in a variety of institutions, nursing homes, and group homes. A little over 1 year after moving into his own home, Butch had a massive heart attack from which he never recovered. Butch's vision of homeownership and his life will continue to inspire many more individuals to reach their dream of owning a home.

their communities: through homeownership and control of personal assistance. This change is not merely a shift or a shuffle but is a true metamorphosis in assisting people to have control over their own lives in their own homes. It is a change that requires the debunking of myths, the reengineering of bureaucracies, and the rethinking of priorities and values. It is a growing grass roots movement that can be understood best through the personal experiences of the individuals who are championing this change—the homeowners themselves and the people who assist them. The differences in the three individuals' stories that follow are variations on a theme. These three people eventually accomplished their dream of owning a home, but the routes they followed were as unique as they were.

Throughout the nation, individuals, advocates, and innovative service providers have made significant progress in creating housing and assistance that permits all people, including those with the most intensive support needs, to live in homes that they own and control. This trend is part of the broader shift away from traditional, agency-dominated services toward support resources that encourage personal control and full community participation.

This chapter examines what it takes both for individuals and for the community to move away from institutions and group homes toward individually owned and controlled homes with personalized assistance. The first section reflects briefly on the history of residential services and homeownership, typical approaches today, and the need for dramatic change. Ken Forché's story illustrates how one person and his support team collaborated creatively and employed innovative strategies to overcome formidable barriers and enable him to become a homeowner.

The second section calls for person-controlled assistance, which represents a major departure from the traditional way of providing services to individuals with disabilities. Through the experiences of Greg Garvey, who now owns a home and controls all aspects of his personal assistance, this alternative approach is illustrated. The third section explores the forces in New Hampshire that have provided a solid foundation for the homeownership initiative. To illustrate how a coalition succeeded in overcoming barriers and roadblocks to personal control, this section contains the story of Jolene Harris and recounts the history and successes of New Hampshire's Home of Your Own Project. This 3-year demonstration project resulted in a host of significant changes in housing and assistance, which are summarized in this chapter's fourth section. Finally, an initiative known as the National Home of Your Own Alliance is described. The Alliance has become a major force in influencing national housing policy and creating opportunities for individuals with disabilities to own and control their homes.

THEN AND NOW: WHY A "DAY ROOM" IS NOT OKAY

Like most adults, people with disabilities typically want and need a home of their own where they can be themselves and make choices about what they do, with whom, and when. Choosing and controlling one's home is a basic act of personal autonomy. The reality, however, is that most people with disabilities who receive residential services are rarely afforded such basic rights.

Until the early 1990s, there were virtually no opportunities for thousands of individuals who depended upon public assistance and required significant personal assistance to own their homes. The barriers to homeownership and control were formidable, including 1) systems and attitudes designed to limit personal choice and favor programs, providers, and buildings over individuals; 2) criteria used by lenders to determine qualifications for a mortgage; and 3) the limited financial resources of most people with disabilities.

Programs, Providers, Buildings, and Attitudes

Calling for change in the provision of residential assistance for people with disabilities is not new. Nationwide efforts have focused on the deinstitutionalization of people with developmental disabilities since the late 1960s, and the number of individuals in large institutions has declined steadily from a peak population of 194,650 in 1967 to approximately 63,250 in 1994—a decrease of 67% (Braddock & Hemp, 1996). Despite this dramatic reduction, however, the work is far from complete. In 1992, for example, 346,619 individuals received residential services in the United States. Only 14,841 of these individuals received supported living services. (Supported living involves housing that is chosen by the individual and shared with others at the person's discretion and that is not owned by the service provider. Supported living also ensures that each person is a member of his or her community and has a personalized assistance plan that can accommodate changing needs and abilities [Braddock & Hemp, 1995].) Therefore, almost 332,000 individuals who received residential services in 1992 either remained in large institutions or were provided residential services through a state service system in homes that they did not own (Braddock & Hemp, 1995). This approach to housing clearly limits the capacity of service providers and people with disabilities to design innovative housing and assistance options. Thus, the lives of most individuals with disabilities receiving residential services in the United States are still controlled by somebody else.

The United States has no comprehensive and coherent national long-term care policy focusing on affordable, community-based housing and assistance for people with disabilities (Litvak, Heumann, & Zukas, 1987). Legislative efforts in the 1990s have been driven by the goal of balancing the federal budget. As a result, more and more of the authority for managing increasingly limited financial resources is being shifted to individual states. Still in effect, however, is a federal policy that offers substantial incentives to states' choosing services that establish professional domination over people's lives (O'Brien, 1994). Funding sources favor service providers over individuals. Present policies, both at a federal level and at a state level, predominantly finance programs, providers, and buildings instead of services, assistance, and individuals with disabilities.

Within the existing system, administrative structures for community services often perpetuate this systems-driven approach, choosing congregate and agency- or provider-controlled residential and related services over services based on the needs and desires of individual people. Agencies that can deliver both housing and assistance as one service fit most neatly into these administrative and funding structures. As a result, most people who have been moved from large institutions will continue simply to be moved into smaller institutions.

The traditional approach to residential services reflects a long-standing cultural bias that must be addressed. Our culture has thought for decades in terms of housing rather than houses and of group homes rather than homes for most people with disabilities. Although the difference in terms may appear to be semantic and subtle, this way of thinking often results in a self-fulfilling prophecy of where people ultimately live. The term *housing* itself implies a locus of control that is outside the individual. It implies a congregate living situation with financial management by someone other than any of the several individuals who live there. *Group home* implies that decisions at all levels are to be made on behalf of the group by whomever is "in charge"—from the color of the building exterior, to the art hung on the walls, to the brand and style of refrigerator that is bought, to the materials adorning its doors.

The simple example of the refrigerator is very illustrative. In most people's homes, refrigerator art ranges from children's masterpieces to dental appointment reminders. It may include postcards from friends, photographs of sisters' babies, and clippings of comic strips. In most group homes (the kind of community-based housing to which people with disabilities typically have been assigned), however, refrigerator art is replaced by messages of instruction—dietary restrictions, medication schedules, staff rosters, and daily or weekly agendas.

As impersonal as the refrigerator art of a group home is, so too is the communal living space. The family room is not called *the family room,* for example; it is called *the day room.* Often no one is there in the evening because it is not an especially comfortable place to relax. Similarly, the living room is not called *the living room,* it is called *the activity room.* The living room art is not welcoming to friends and many times does not reflect people's lifestyles. Where people end up living is in their bedrooms. That's where their personal possessions are crammed—all of those would-be refrigerator photographs, the television, and the compact disc player. Certainly, it may be called a "group *home*," but the members of the group each "nest" separately, tucked away in their own rooms. Members of the group home frequently do not entertain friends or family or have overnight guests because of lack of privacy and space.

People do come together at meals. In the best of places, residents have some input into meal planning, but this is not always the case. Sleeping in and wanting to eat brunch instead of breakfast and lunch is a challenge if all of the other residents are not so inclined. Wanting to eat an hour earlier or an hour later than usual can disrupt residents and staff alike. Padding barefoot to the kitchen for a midnight snack may or may not be allowed. These simple things adults take for granted in their own homes often do not exist for people with disabilities when their homes are group homes, when their homes are not under their own control, in short, when their homes are "housing."

Mortgage Lending Criteria

The second substantial barrier to homeownership is the criteria used by most lenders in the United States to underwrite mortgage loans (in which a loan application is evaluated to determine the risk involved for the lender, taking into account the borrower's creditworthiness and the quality of the property itself). These criteria disqualify the majority of people with disabilities from homeownership:

- Individuals who receive Supplemental Security Income (SSI) and Medicaid dollars cannot accumulate savings without jeopardizing the benefits that would fund their mortgage payments. Because of resource restrictions, recipients of public benefits do not have the ability to accumulate enough money for down payment and closing costs. For example, people who receive SSI benefits may not have more than $2,000 in cash and other financial resources in their possession at any time. Individuals who receive Medicaid funds have resource limitations ranging from $1,000 to $2,000, depending on the laws of the state in which they live.
- Many individuals who receive SSI and Medicaid benefits also have wages from employment. For these people, a standard formula is used to determine the amount by which their benefits are reduced because of the wages they earn. Because both of these public benefits are means tested, benefits would be discontinued if an individual's income were more than the amount determined by that particular state. Therefore, anyone who receives public benefits has a very limited ability to contribute toward down payment and closing costs.
- When individuals have funds from grants, secondary loans, or gifts, many lenders are unwilling to accept them in lieu of a borrower's contribution.

- In determining a borrower's credit status, a lender requires (established) good credit as well as information regarding how any past credit problems may have been resolved. An individual who has lived in his or her family's home, in foster care, in a group home, or in a nursing home is not likely to have established a credit history. Because the utilities, lease or mortgage, and perhaps even the mail are in someone else's name; the individual has little opportunity or experience to demonstrate credit reliability.

Financial Resources

A third major barrier to homeownership concerns financial resources for people with disabilities. Historically, people with disabilities have been unemployed or underemployed and have received poverty-level income. Despite significant progress in expanding work opportunities during the 1980s and 1990s through the supported employment movement (Sowers, McAllister, & Cotton, 1996), as recently as 1990, fewer than 10% of people with significant disabilities had access to employment in the community (Mank, Buckley, & Rhodes, 1990). The mean weekly wage for people who participated in supported employment as reported by 36 states was only $107.21 in fiscal year 1993 (Wehman & Kregel, 1995). Thus, the challenge remains to examine sources of financial assistance available to people with disabilities and to use these sources in creative ways that enable these people to become homeowners. (For more information on finances, see Klein & Black, 1995, which offers a summary of financial data of 16 participants in New Hampshire's Home of Your Own Project.)

Ken Forché's story, as told next, illustrates a typical lifelong experience with housing and residential services. This story describes how Ken, with assistance, overcame each of the three major barriers to homeownership—systems design, lending criteria, and a lack of financial resources—to buy his own home.

Ken: Just One of the Neighbors

"I was just going to crack a beer, Ken. Would you like to join me?"
                                                               —Ken's neighbor

After his parents died in the late 1950s, Ken Forché was moved from his family's home to a state hospital at the age of 23. From his mid-20s to his early 50s, he lived in hospitals and nursing homes. In 1987 he was the first resident to be moved into the group home on Willowrun Drive.
Ken's first impression was that the group home was a great improvement over his experience in a large institution. But in less than a year's time, he began to voice his growing dissatisfaction with his living situation. What

he wanted was not a small institution but a home more like the one he remembered from his youth—a home with a living room, a home of his own. For Ken and many other people, having a day room was not okay.

A support team made up of Ken, his service coordinator and other representatives of the area agency, and individuals from the agencies that provided his residential and vocational assistance was formed. Ken's first planning session was held at the end of January 1994. The team discussed Ken's ideal home, neighborhood, and assistance. They covered everything from the color scheme Ken imagined for his new home to his desire for a fireplace and a neighborhood with children and little traffic. Because Ken used a wheelchair, he needed an accessible home and a live-in personal care attendant who was strong enough to lift him.

When asked about any other needs he might have, Ken named three items: new shoes, a motorized wheelchair, and, because of the lack of accessible public transportation in his rural community, a van. These items may not seem directly relevant to a homebuyer's planning process. However, the fact is that for most people with disabilities, moving into homes of their own involves much more than simply the right real estate. They require a system of assistance and resources that ensure their safety, health, and comfort.

It took 2 years of searching for the right combination for Ken to move out of the group home and into his own home. Separating his finances from those of the other three people who lived at the same group home was one of the challenges. Once Ken's budget was separated out and clearly delineated, planning and progress were possible. The financial manager for the residential assistance agency informed Ken of the amount of money the agency currently received on his behalf for his living expenses in the group home. The area agency agreed to reallocate those dollars to Ken for his personal living expenses and monthly mortgage payments. During that 2-year process, Ken made other important progress. First, with Medicaid funds, he was able to acquire a motorized wheelchair and new orthopedic shoes; second, members of his support team helped him to obtain a grant to buy a used van.

As in all of the situations in which individuals have worked with support teams to muster resources and find a home, Ken and his team discovered many new ways of working together and in concert with other individuals and agencies. One specific example of creative collaboration was Ken's negotiation with his employment support agency. In exchange for needed van repairs and upkeep, Ken granted the agency use of his van on a temporary basis. This arrangement essentially expanded their motor pool at minimal cost. The agency was able to use the van to transport Ken and other people to and from work and on job searches until Ken moved into his home and needed the van for himself.

This win–win exchange is typical of the new type of collaboration that people around the country are discovering is an essential element of their success in finding homes of their own. They are redefining the relationship that traditionally existed between an agency and the individuals whom it served. People are coming together as individuals with the common goal of helping one of them to find and settle into a home of his or her own choosing. Such collaboration results in a new urgency and a new enthusiasm for innovative allocation of resources and a renewed sense of purpose that benefits all.

A big challenge for Ken, exacerbated by the length of time it took to find the right house, was finding someone to share that house with him. "Marie's little, but she's mighty," Ken said. He smiled when he referred to the young woman who, with her 2-year-old daughter, was now sharing his home. "She used to work at the group home, so she knows me. That's important. When she heard I was looking for a new home and a housemate to be my personal care assistant, she said 'What about me?' Once we decided to go for it, she really took the bull by the horns."

With Ken's permission, Marie spent weekends and evenings scouring the neighborhoods in search of "For Sale" signs, following up on promising leads in the newspaper's classified ads, and checking out referrals from friends and acquaintances. She would call Ken and tell him about a place, and he would instruct the van driver to cruise past the address for a drive-by assessment on their way home from Ken's job at a local store. If the house looked like a real possibility, Ken would ask Marie or Abe, his service coordinator, to make an appointment and arrange for a ramp to be set up, if necessary, so that he could look around inside. Ken finally found a small home that met his budget needs and his definition of an ideal neighborhood. An additional benefit was the minimal amount of renovation necessary to meet his accessibility needs.

Within the first few weeks of moving into their new home, Ken and Marie had met their three closest neighbors. One man just down the street had done some of the renovation work on Ken's house, and his wife invited Ken and Marie over to pick flowers from her garden to brighten their living room.

"When we got there," Marie said with a smile in her voice, "her husband invited Ken onto the porch to show him around. He said, 'I was just going to crack a beer, Ken. Would you like to join me?' Ken's smile lit up the whole neighborhood. For the first time in his life, a neighbor invited him over for a beer. That never happened in the group home. Finally, he is what he always wanted to be—just a regular neighbor."

Ken's story illustrates the multiple layers and connections, affiliations and partnerships, and collaborations and negotiations that are involved in the process of individuals' obtaining control over their homes and assistance. Success in this venture requires the collaboration of state, federal, and local agencies; the alliance of private and public entities; and the partnership of individuals, their personal assistants, bureaucrats, service providers, family, and friends. Both on an institutional level and on a personal level, champions of change emerge. These champions are individuals with and without disabilities who are willing to take risks and agencies that are willing to bend or change the rules. Everyone is willing to do whatever it takes to support homeownership and person-controlled assistance, as is discussed next. They are willing to try something new and different, to defy the obstacles, and to succeed.

PERSONAL ASSISTANCE: FROM READINESS TO RIGHTS

*"How many 27-year-olds have to go to their rooms at
9 o'clock at night?"*
—Shana Greely

In addition to simply facilitating homeownership, effecting change in community living requires that everyone dramatically change their approach to personal assistance and the management of related resources. When moving into his home, Ken chose, for the first time in his life, the person (Marie) who would help him with his basic and personal needs, such as getting in and out of bed and getting dressed. He also chose Marie as his housemate.

Overall, states invest more than 95% of their developmental disabilities resources in facility-based services, with few dollars allocated for personal assistance (Braddock & Hemp, 1995). Few states organize their personal assistance programs to allow control by the people who actually use the services. Even individuals with severe physical disabilities who are very healthy are typically required to become home health care patients or clients of some professionally controlled agency in order to obtain assistance (O'Brien, 1994). In addition, some states' income assistance policies actually serve as disincentives, offering higher payments when individuals live in a congregate setting than when they live on their own.

The Case Against "Readiness"

We venture to say that virtually everyone, like Shana who was quoted previously, would prefer to decide for themselves what and when to eat, when to go to bed, when to get up, and in what room they put their television set and favorite chair. Of course, some people may need some assistance to stay healthy and safe. But this needed assistance should only be related to health and safety needs. How people choose to manage their lives and decorate their homes is up to them. The traditional, well-meaning social services approach, however, has been based on the notions that a basic level of competence is associated with many aspects of daily living and that such competence can and should be measured before people are "allowed" to live in their own home or apartment. As a result, processes have evolved to assess a person's "readiness" to live independently.

This readiness filter, at best misguided and unnecessary, is often arbitrary and inflexible. For example, the requirement that a person must make his or her bed every morning; do his or her own laundry; balance a checkbook; take public transportation to and from work; or accomplish other specific, measurable tasks presumes that any or all of these activities represent some standard to which all people must adhere. In fact, there is no such standard, and many people without disabilities live very happy and fulfilling lives despite their unmade beds. Many people ask their spouses, partners, friends, or hired help to assist them with laundry, checkbook balancing, or transportation to work. Lack of ability or interest in any or all of these activities does not add up to disqualification for a home of one's own. Individual ability to perform each of these tasks is not the issue. Mustering the resources to accomplish the ones that can be accomplished is the issue.

If, however, the goal is neither checkbook balancing and bed making nor homeownership per se but rather enhancing individual quality of life, then this goal and value should fundamentally shape the structure and delivery of service (Sabatino & Litvak, 1992). To a large extent, however, services for people with disabilities have been organized around the concept of a continuum, providing the least restrictive residential environment that is conducive to individuals' well-being (Hitzing, 1980; Hoggs & Moss, 1990). Once they are accepted into programs, which traditionally have linked services to residential facilities owned and operated by service provider agencies, people must progress through the continuum. That is, the professionals involved put together a treatment plan and training schedule said to be designed to help people attain the skills necessary to move to the next, less restrictive setting in the continuum. If matters do not go well for people in such programs, the usual response is to move them back to a more restrictive environment (Klein, 1994; Taylor, 1988).

Instead of fitting individuals into a preexisting static program of services, a more malleable service delivery system that is controlled by individuals themselves must be embraced. The concept that people with disabilities have as much right as anyone else to the safety and security of their own home and should be able to decide where and with whom they live is relatively straightforward. The obstacles to realizing that goal, however, are multiple and complex. Service providers are faced with the challenge of rethinking and redesigning the delivery of assistance to people with disabilities and, more pragmatically, also are faced with the question of how to redirect funds to assist individuals rather than institutions. Essentially, a person becomes responsible for hiring the program to meet his or her needs rather than for allowing the program to be responsible. Greg Garvey's story is a case in point.

Greg: A Home with Hardwood Floors

"Life is a chance you have to take!"
—Greg Garvey

At age 6, Greg Garvey was placed in a rehabilitation hospital in Laconia, New Hampshire. At age 19, he "graduated" to a group home. He spent his days at a sheltered workshop and passed his evenings and weekends at the group home. After 3 years at the group home, Greg decided he was ready to move into an apartment of his own and sought a live-in personal assistant who could help him with personal care and household management. The state and federal funding that paid for Greg's personal care needs through the group home was re-directed through the Granite State Living Foundation, the state's independent living center, and the adult care services division of the state's Department of Child and Family Services. In this way, Greg was able to hire a personal care assistant of his choice. About this time he met Donald, a young man who worked at the sheltered workshop. Donald, who was living at home with his mother, welcomed the opportunity to move in with Greg and work as his personal care assistant. Greg requested that his SSI payments now come directly to him rather than to the group home so that he could pay for his own rent, food, clothing, and other personal expenses. For the next 9 years Greg and Donald lived in a small town, but then together they decided to make a radical change.

In December 1990, Donald and Greg moved to a large city in New Hampshire. "We realized there was a lot more going on in [the city] than in Laconia," Greg explained. "It's more accessible and there are more things to do." A three-room apartment in a tenement building was all they could afford on Greg's SSI benefits and Donald's wages, but they were living in a city of their choice. They were making friends, had a social life, and felt connected to their community. Because neither of them had a driver's license and because Greg used a motorized wheelchair, they were very concerned with public transportation and accessibility. Greg soon became an active member of the Handicapped Advisory Committee of the city's transportation authority. He also became involved with a regional action committee for the Americans with Disabilities Act of 1990 (PL 101-336) through a self-advocacy and disability rights organization. This committee offers members opportunities to talk with and educate people about accessibility. Each election day, Donald and Greg have helped ensure polling places are accessible for people who use wheelchairs or have other mobility challenges. They began to feel like a part of their new community.

One day Sunita Lee from the Carroll Agency, a service agency for people with disabilities, told Greg about a new project that was accepting applications from people with disabilities who were interested in owning their own homes. Greg submitted his name but did not get his hopes up. In fact, he barely gave it another thought.

"The day Sunita called me and told me I had been picked, my jaw dropped! I had forgotten all about it!" Greg laughs as he recalls the surprise telephone call that changed his life. "First, we had to fill out a bunch of paperwork to make sure I was qualified for a mortgage. Then we looked at 35 houses before we found this one." "This one" is a two-story single-family dwelling on a narrow street only a few blocks from the downtown area.

"A lot of my friends said, 'You should look for a place in the country, Greg.'" He shook his head. " I would just look at them and say, 'Now why would I want to live in the country?' I don't drive. I don't exactly enjoy the woods or fields. I wanted a place with big rooms, near the bus line, close to a store. And I found it. After looking at 34 other places first, that is!" What Greg found was a home and a location that met his needs, not what other people thought he needed. He really was not interested in much of a yard. But when he found a place with a large deck on the back, it was a bonus.

Donald was particularly interested in a place that had room for their own washer and dryer. "We shared a washer and dryer with 16 other units where we lived before," Donald recalled. The stackable washer and dryer located in their spacious kitchen was one of the first purchases they made after moving in.

If the millions of homeowners nationwide—people with and without disabilities, single people, families, men, and women—were polled about what it is that they like best about their own homes, it is likely that it would come down to something as simple as space for a washer and dryer, a backyard for the children, a second bathroom, a study, a spacious kitchen, the view, closet space, or a front porch. These seemingly simple matters of personal preference are the real indicators of individual control and personal satisfaction, and they differ widely from person to person. That is why it is so important to listen to people, to hear what it is that they want and do not want in a home, and to help them figure out how to acquire it.

What was Greg's favorite aspect of the house? He said it was the hardwood floors. "The night before we looked at this place," Greg admitted, "I had a dream about hardwood floors. The next day Sunita called to show us this place. Our real-estate agent talked about how it fit all the requirements—close to the bus line, a store right down the street—but as soon as I saw the paneled walls and hard-

wood floors, that's what did it. I knew this was it. I said to Sunita, 'I'll take it.' She said, 'Go home and think about it.' But I said I knew this was it."

Over the course of the next 6 months, Greg and Donald cut back on all of their expenses. They saved every bit of Donald's income and lived frugally on Greg's SSI. By the time they closed on the house on Valentine's Day 1995, they had saved enough for the down payment. Because of their substantial down payment, they were able to keep their monthly mortgage, including taxes and insurance, to an amount only slightly more than they had been paying for the three-room apartment they hated, where they had to share a washer and dryer and wait for a landlord either to make repairs or not, whichever suited him.

Once the papers were signed and the house belonged to them, some repairs and renovations were necessary before they could move in. Sunita helped Greg obtain a one-time grant from Medicaid to cover the needed renovations to make the house accessible. They added a ramp up to the deck. They converted the shower so that it would be flush with the bathroom floor. Greg can roll right into it, and Donald can lift Greg from his wheelchair into the special shower chair. At the back door they installed an automatic opener so that Greg can enter or exit on his own with just a push of a button. New kitchen flooring and a rearrangement of appliances finished the renovations.

Looking back at Greg's young adulthood once he left the group home, his story is in many ways remarkably similar to those of his peers without disabilities. In his early 20s, he established a partnership with Donald. After a few years in their hometown, they took off to make a life for themselves in the big city. Greg established himself as an integral part of the community through his volunteer work and activism. Finally, in his early 30s, he became a homeowner.

Greg's and Ken's stories are not stories of independence. Rather, they are stories of interdependence. For example, by working in concert with the available support system, Greg has been able to achieve his dream of owning a home and his goal of a self-directed lifestyle. In the rehabilitation hospital he was a patient. In the group home, he was a resident. Now, he is a neighbor and a contributing member of his community as a volunteer, a consumer, an employer, and a taxpayer.

The convergence of several forces in New Hampshire made possible the dream of homeownership for Ken, Greg, and at least 30 others. These forces are described next, including a shift in the developmental services system, the Comprehensive Housing Affordability Strategy (CHAS), and the Home of Your Own Project.

A MOVEMENT IN NEW HAMPSHIRE

Although New Hampshire's struggles with homeownership issues are not unique, this state may be considered unique in its conscious commitment at all levels to assist people in individualized ways. This commitment is expressed in state government policy, by the attitudes and actions of professionals in local communities, and through the efforts of families and advocacy groups. For example, a regional area agency system was developed in the 1980s as a means of returning people who had been living in institutions to their communities of origin. This community-based service system facilitated the closing of the Laconia State School and Training Center in 1991, making New Hampshire the first state in the country without a public institution for people with developmental disabilities. The area agencies are governed by citizen boards primarily consisting of people with disabilities and their family members—further expression of New Hampshire's commitment to meaningful and individualized assistance.

While the developmental services system was shifting in the 1980s, simultaneous developments in the banking industry and housing market motivated New Hampshire to prioritize the housing needs of people with developmental disabilities in the state's first affordable housing initiative. The CHAS program, created in 1991 by the U.S. Department of Housing and Urban Development (HUD), required states to draft a policy and planning document (with extensive public input) to receive specific federal housing and community development resources. CHAS listed federal, state, and other private funds available for state investment in housing. It also provided a comprehensive set of priorities, goals, and objectives to ensure that housing needs identified in the state are addressed in a coordinated manner.

New Hampshire's Home of Your Own Project

The forces just described positioned New Hampshire to receive an award on homeownership and control from the U.S. Administration on Developmental Disabilities (ADD) in 1991. The primary charge from ADD was to demonstrate new and expanded approaches to community housing that would 1) separate where one lives from the services and assistance one receives and 2) tailor assistance to the individual's preferred residence, whether it be a purchased home, rented apartment, or some form of shared housing.

The University of New Hampshire's Institute on Disability (IOD) served as the lead agency in a unique 3-year model demonstration collaboration that pooled the resources and experience of both the public and the private sectors. This partnership involved agencies, organizations, businesses, and people with broad-based homeownership concerns, including the New Hampshire Housing Finance Authority; neighbors; real-estate agents; lenders; affordable housing agency staff; staff at the state's community loan fund; community leaders; and those concerned with disability issues, such as the New Hampshire Developmental Disabilities Council, the New Hampshire Division of Mental Health and Developmental Services, the Disability Rights Center (New Hampshire's designated protection and advocacy agency), area agency staff, people with disabilities, friends, and family.

Each of these natural partners for the New Hampshire Home of Your Own Project, as the initiative came to be known, contributed time, funding, and/or expertise to promote the vision of homeownership and control. The Developmental Disabilities Council provided staff and council member expertise and $10,000 per year to offset the cost of ongoing project research. The Disability Rights Center contributed staff and intern time and legal research on issues of guardianship, trusts, future planning, and labor laws related to personal assistance services.

The New Hampshire Housing Finance Authority (NHHFA), the state-mandated agency that spearheaded the CHAS process, was the most critical contributor to the success of the Home of Your Own Project. The NHHFA finances single- and multifamily housing for people with low and moderate income and makes direct loans or purchases mortgages from the state's lending institutions using proceeds from the issuing of bonds. The Home of Your Own Project initially was presented to the NHHFA as a vehicle that could affirmatively address the NHHFA identified priority of affordable housing for people with developmental disabilities. In September 1991, the board of the NHHFA reserved $1.8 million to be used for mortgage loans at 1% below market interest rates. In addition, they set aside $100,000 in no-interest forgivable loans on the recommendation of the NHHFA's executive director. The no-interest forgivable loans were earmarked for closing costs, renovations, and down payments (as much as 2% of the purchase price) and were to be distributed over the 3-year model demonstration period with the stipulation that the Home of Your Own Project secure $100,000 in matching funds for the same purposes. This mutually beneficial relationship between the NHHFA and the project was enhanced when NHHFA staff agreed to offer extensive technical assistance to the project, to participate in numerous meetings, and to co-present with project staff in training sessions throughout the country.

The $100,000 in matching funds were contributed by the New Hampshire Division of Mental Health and Developmental Services. The division, which contracts with 12 area agencies to oversee community services and to provide service coordination and family support, encouraged all 12 area agency directors to participate in the project. The division also assigned a staff person to work specifically with the project to assist in the homeownership process for participants. Each of the 12 agencies was given $8,000 from the Division's match pool to be used as unrestricted grants for down payments, closing costs, renovation, and long-term maintenance and selected two participants who were seeking homes.

By the project's end in 1994, 20 Home of Your Own Project participants had purchased their own homes. In addition, the original state funders had allocated a substantial amount of money to continue the initiative for 3 more years, including $4.5 million from NHHFA and $350,000 from the New Hampshire Division of Mental Health and Developmental Services and the area agencies with which the division works. Through direct experience, the Home of Your Own Project had developed viable strategies to overcome common barriers to homeownership pertaining to programs, providers, buildings, and attitudes, as well as to financial resources and lending criteria, as described later in this chapter. By focusing on individuals' needs, desires, and preferences, the Home of Your Own Project also demonstrated that service funds and disability-related entitlements could be used imaginatively to enable people to purchase a home, as Jolene Harris discovered.

Jolene: "Lakeshore Vista Association—Members and Guests Only"

"I was afraid I was going to be broke all the time. I figured I'd be constantly scrounging. But that didn't happen."
                                                            —Jolene Harris

Jolene Harris might be one of those people with disabilities who "slipped through the cracks." Jolene's family moved frequently when she was growing up. She didn't spend very much time in any one school, but attended a number of them in Maine, New Hampshire, and Massachusetts. As a result, it appears that no one detected her developmental disability. By age 14, shortly after her mother's death, she was having so much trouble in school that she just stopped going.

By the time Jolene was 30 years old, she was living in Massachusetts, had three children, and was struggling to survive on Aid to Families and Dependent Children (AFDC, now called Temporary Assistance to Needy Families) and food stamps. The only places Jolene could afford to live were crowded, low-rent apartment buildings where she was often the victim of crime and felt surrounded by too much drinking and drugs. After her television and food stamps were stolen in 1989, she decided that she had had enough. She lived with her twin sister for a short time until she became eligible for HUD Section 8 rental assistance and then found an apartment for herself and her children. Her daughter Teya was 10, William was 8, and Kevin was just over 1 year old.

As she settled in to a new community in a new state, some things changed. Others did not. The community felt safer, but Jolene still found herself moving frequently. Busy streets were dangerous for the children. They had no place to play. They always seemed to be getting into trouble and often were accused of mischief they hadn't done. Nobody in the Harris family was very content with the living situation. Two more years passed.

When Kevin was 3 years old, a neighbor of Jolene's suggested that she check out a program that was helping this neighbor with her own son. Kevin was soon enrolled in an early intervention program to encourage his development. Jolene, now pregnant with her fourth child, also enrolled in a parenting class to enhance her parenting skills. After a while, the parenting class staff suggested that Jolene might wish to apply for services from the local agency that provides assistance to people with developmental disabilities.

Once Jolene became eligible for developmental disabilities services, she qualified for assistance from a service coordinator and a personal assistant. Unlike Greg Garvey and Ken Forché, she didn't need someone to live with her and provide personal care. Jolene's personal assistant worked with her 40 hours a week in areas identified by Jolene, including meal planning, money management, parenting skills, and personal development.

Jolene's living situation was still a challenge. She was so concerned about the welfare of her children and so preoccupied with the continual search for a better place to live that her own personal growth took a back seat. She wanted a stable home and knew her children did, too. She remembered how it felt for her as a child to move from place to place, from school to school, and to never have a place that really felt like home. When Terri O'Connell, Jolene's service coordinator, learned about the new statewide effort to assist people with disabilities in purchasing homes, she immediately suggested that Jolene apply.

"At first, I thought she was kidding," Jolene recalled 2 years later. "Me? Own my own home? She must be kidding! But here I am. And I love it!"

"I was afraid I was going to be broke all the time," Jolene said, recalling her initial reaction to Terri's suggestion of homeownership. "I figured I'd be constantly scrounging. But that didn't happen." The reason it didn't happen was that Jolene and her support team made a concerted effort to carefully explore the amount of money Jolene had available and to find a house that met her needs on all counts—financially, geographically, and architecturally. In the small community where Jolene lives, a three-bedroom apartment averages $550–$600 per month. Jolene had never been able to afford more than a two-bedroom place.

"Jolene's very good with figures," says her personal care assistant. "She would be able to calculate in her head whether she could afford a place or not. She knew her budget and the team concentrated on helping her to find a place that fit it."

The search began with a planning meeting with Jolene, Terri, and other agency staff who offered assistance to Jolene. With help from Terri, Jolene had carefully reviewed her financial situation. Jolene used the money she received from SSI and AFDC to pay her bills and other expenses. She received grocery assistance through food stamps and $50 per month of child support. The remainder of her child support money was paid directly to the state to subsidize the AFDC payment.

With the help of her team, Jolene determined that she could afford up to $525 per month to cover mortgage, taxes, and insurance. The next task was to define the type of home Jolene wanted to live in. Not surprisingly, Jolene's personal planning map had a distinctly children-centered focus. She wanted to make sure she found a home within the same school district so that the children would not have to change schools. She also wanted a quiet neighborhood where children and pets could play safely outside. As for the home itself, she envisioned a two-story home with three or four bedrooms and one or two bathrooms. She wanted a dining room, a big kitchen with a dishwasher, gas or oil heat, a washer and dryer, a porch, a finished basement for a playroom, and a fenced-in yard with a swing set.

Once her dream house had been defined, Jolene needed to talk with the banker to determine how her income translated into purchase price. Also to be taken into consideration were the down payment assistance through the NHHFA and the matching funds from the New Hampshire Division of Mental Health and Developmental Services. Jolene was preapproved for a purchase price between $50,000 and $55,000.

What Jolene had wanted most of all was a place for her children to be safe and content that was within walking distance of shopping. What she found was a small A-frame house with three bedrooms and a bathroom on the first floor and the living room, dining room, and kitchen on the upper floor—all for $52,000. "I like the bedrooms downstairs," Jolene said. And she said that in the big open living space upstairs, "you can eat and watch TV at the same time. Plus it's quiet. I like that."

She laughed about the 1970s-era orange shag carpet that she hopes to replace soon. The front half of the large room, she pointed out, will be carpeted with a blue-green Berber that she has already picked out. The back half, which is the kitchen and dining area, will be covered with linoleum. "No more Cheerios in the carpet," she said with a smile to her youngest child. She happily took visitors outside to show off the portion of the quarter acre of wooded property that she had begun to clear to make way for a swing set.

Jolene is able to walk downtown on a few quiet streets and across a small footbridge. A personal assistant drives Jolene to the supermarket for weekly grocery shopping and is available to accompany her to

*parent–teacher conferences at the children's school if the need arises.
Now that Jolene doesn't have to worry about a house, she can get on
with other priorities. Her personal assistant is helping her learn to read.*

*Less than a half mile down the road from the Harrises' house,
there's a turnoff on the right. At the end of the short driveway, three
large granite boulders, three pine trees, and a small white birch mark
the edge of a private beach. A sign posted there says this:*

LAKESHORE VISTA ASSOCIATION
Members and Guests Only

*This private beach with a view of hills and mountains in the distance is on
the shores of a small lake. It's a swimming hole that any child would love.
But the beach and the lake is reserved for residents of Lakeshore Vista
only, a neighborhood that the Harris children can now call their own.*

NEW TRADITIONS IN OLD INDUSTRIES:
SIGNIFICANT CHANGES IN HOUSING AND ASSISTANCE

Through the stories and experiences of three determined people, this chapter
has illustrated how individuals with disabilities can realize their dreams of owning a home. Innovative solutions to traditional barriers have been presented,
which were discovered through the Home of Your Own Project in partnership
with the participants and numerous collaborators who dared to debunk myths,
reengineer bureaucracies, and rethink priorities and values. In the process of becoming homeowners, Ken Forché, Greg Garvey, Jolene Harris, and a score of
other participants overcame difficulties with lending criteria, down payments
and closing costs, restrictions in definition of borrowers' contributions, credit
status, and approaches to community development services that combine
homeownership and personal assistance. These people, with the help of their
support teams, championed significant changes in both the housing industry
and the approach to community developmental services and, in the process, often improved their living situations without financial hardship. In Jolene's case,
for example, although $531 per month covered principal, interest, taxes, and in-
surance for a home that she owned, that amount was not sufficient to rent even
the least expensive three-bedroom apartment in her community.

As illustrated throughout this chapter, a number of significant changes are
taking place in industries related to homeownership (e.g., real estate, lending),
as well as in the developmental disabilities services approach to residential
assistance. Among the more noteworthy changes are the following:

1. Homeownership has given people an opportunity to make living and assis-
    tance choices that reflect their unique needs and preferences. For some

individuals, it is the first time they have had a voice in where the furniture goes, which pictures and decorations are on their walls and their refrigerator, who comes through their door, and, most important, who shares their space and their lives.

2. Assistance has become more personalized when it is not dictated by the rigid protocols required when numerous people live together in one facility. With homeownership, the agency responsible for providing assistance no longer owns or leases the house; the individual does. As needs change, assistance can be modified accordingly in the person's home. People are not moved when the need for a new service or assistance arises and therefore are able to sustain stable and typical connections to their new communities. Ownership serves as the platform for community membership.

3. Lenders are beginning to recognize most forms of public benefits as borrower income. Traditional underwriting criteria looks at income-to-debt ratios of approximately 30%. Accepting that many borrowers receiving public benefits do not have an employment history, lenders allowed the use of a budget-based approach rather than an income-to-debt ratio in determining the borrower's ability to pay the mortgage. Lenders in determining credit status consider individuals' prior living histories. That a prospective borrower has not had an opportunity to establish credit does not automatically prevent him or her from qualifying for a mortgage.

4. Budgets are being personalized and restructured such that an agency can commit a line item of the budget for housing to mortgage payments (principle, interest, taxes, and insurance). In making this commitment, agencies have found that in addition to homeownership's stabilizing effect on people's lives, it offers a constancy in housing costs not always available in the fluctuating rental market. In dedicating a housing budget line item to homeownership versus other forms of housing, individuals, lenders, and service providers are locking into a cost and a source of payment that remain more constant over time.

5. Participants are using agency budgets to verify their income and to demonstrate an ongoing commitment of assistance to obtain mortgages. In some cases, agencies, families, and friends contribute money toward down payments, closing costs, and long-term maintenance. Agency staff, family members, and friends have been closely involved in assisting people to choose and purchase homes and in planning for and ensuring personalized assistance. Through this process a greater respect and understanding of the person searching for a home is gained by all individuals providing assistance.

6. Lenders acknowledge that people receiving public benefits do not have funds from savings because resource limitations prevent them from accu-

mulating significant savings. Down payments and closing costs are being accepted from sources other than the borrowers. A mix of private, local, state, and federal funds are becoming available through grants and low- or no-interest loans. Funds for down payments, closing costs, renovations, and long-term maintenance are being made available to borrowers.

7. Lenders are becoming familiar with nontraditional income streams, different procedures, and new forms of documentation and by doing so are tapping a new market of highly motivated home buyers. What these new borrowers bring to the mortgage process are stable income streams in the form of public benefits and ongoing assistance from social services agencies, friends, and family. This assistance can include monitoring of home maintenance, help with paying bills, and guidance and intervention before problems arise. This collaboration among the banking industry, individuals, and the human services system has proved mutually beneficial.

In facilitating these changes, the Home of Your Own Project applied numerous successful strategies, including the following:

• *Begin with a pilot program.* This approach offers policy makers, moneylenders, and service providers an opportunity to test the program on a limited basis, for a defined number of people, and under safer conditions. Requesting "only $1 million" of a $280 million budget to assist "only 20 people," as opposed to "everyone," enables programs and agencies to participate at a lower level initially. A pilot program may be appealing due to the short-term nature of the commitment. Once homeownership has been demonstrated successfully, formerly reluctant stakeholders may be more amenable to commit their resources on a long-term basis.

• *Involve key partners from the beginning.* People with disabilities and their families, state housing authorities, developmental disabilities councils, real-estate agencies, banks, independent living centers, community development organizations, disabilities rights organizations, advocacy groups, state service agencies (e.g., mental health, public health), and low-income housing organizations all are key players in promoting homeownership.

• *Develop personal relationships with individuals* within policy-making, lending, and service organizations or institutions. Such relationships offer both parties an opportunity to learn about common interests, visions, and goals and to facilitate collaboration.

• *Understand the goals and objectives an individual has for his or her job,* and help him or her to meet these goals and objectives. Point out ways in which promoting homeownership for people with disabilities relates to outcomes expected in their jobs from both a practical and civic standpoint, and collaborate on mutually beneficial areas of interest.

- *Ensure that people have a vested interest* in the success of the program by giving them "a piece of the pie." For example, invite all agency heads to serve on the program's steering committee and meet quarterly over lunch. Through the composition of the committee and decision-making authority of the group, ensure that everyone has a compelling reason to attend.

- *Learn what motivates people,* and build these incentives into the collaborative process (e.g., positive publicity for the agency/organization).

- *Understand the issues related to homeownership.* For example, familiarity with the lending industry process, the real-estate purchase/sales process, and income sources for people with disabilities enables planners to work knowledgeably with all involved parties.

- *Leverage resources.* Common sources of funding for states engaged in homeownership activities include the following: Fannie Mae and local lenders (mortgage purchase commitments); state housing finance authorities (down payments, operating funds, low-interest mortgages, renovation assistance, closing costs); Federal Home Loan Bank (down payment assistance, closing costs assistance, renovation assistance); HUD's Home Investment Partnership Program (also known as HOME) funds (down payment assistance and renovation assistance); developmental disabilities councils (operating funds and down payment assistance); and other sources (e.g., state agencies, bank waivers of fees, bank "match" assistance).

NATIONAL HOMEOWNERSHIP INITIATIVE

Beyond the borders of New Hampshire, the tremendous success of the original demonstration project piqued the interest of the ADD. This agency continued its commitment to homeownership when it funded a 5-year cooperative agreement with the IOD to create a national technical assistance center called the National Home of Your Own Alliance. Through this center, 23 states received technical assistance to develop local homeownership demonstration sites and to build coalitions of homeownership and disability organizations led by individuals with disabilities, their families, their friends, and advocates. Each state assists a specified number of people to own or lease their own homes through a pilot project. In addition, the center operates a national information clearinghouse and is engaged in research on policy and homeownership control issues.

One of the more significant lessons about homeownership is that no single approach can or should be prescribed. Just as there is wide variability in individuals' preferences for homes and assistance, states are choosing a variety of creative approaches to address their homeownership needs. Russ Pitsley may have said it best when asked what model they were using in North Dakota for 598 people to receive funding for supported living: "We have 598 models" (Klein, 1994).

The National Home of Your Own Alliance works with each state through a steering committee comprising representatives of the coalition with strong participation from people with disabilities. Alliance members assist states in developing a technical assistance plan that represents the unique culture of each region. The hope is that states will allocate technical assistance resources toward certain parameters that are believed key for successful initiatives: intensive planning with individuals and agencies; collaboration of the organizations and individuals in the housing arena; flexibility in underwriting loans; and having access to funds for down payments, closing costs, renovations, and long-term maintenance.

The work of the National Home of Your Own Alliance has spurred the creation of initiatives on homeownership control throughout the country. The locus of control is with the person with a disability, who directs what goes on in his or her home. The state initiatives offer an unprecedented opportunity to understand more about the impact homeownership control can have on the lives of people with disabilities and the systems that assist them.

The National Home of Your Own Alliance has also influenced national housing policy in ways that create opportunities for individuals with disabilities to own and control their homes. In particular, the organization has had major success in its work with Fannie Mae, the nation's largest secondary mortgage lender (lenders who sell existing mortgages into the secondary market, in which mortgages are bought and sold by investors), and was instrumental in helping Fannie Mae shape the first national secondary market mortgage product targeted exclusively to the needs of borrowers with disabilities. This $50 million single-family underwriting experiment, called HomeChoice is designed to accommodate the needs of individuals with disabilities and families who have a child with a disability. HomeChoice will initially be piloted in 16 states and the District of Columbia. The underwriting criteria combines underwriting flexibility never seen before in the lending industry. During every stage of the product's development, the National Home of Your Own Alliance offered ongoing consultation, linkages with state coalitions, and the technical expertise of housing experts.

The homeownership initiative was created to develop, implement, evaluate, and disseminate an approach to assist individuals with disabilities in buying their own homes and fully participate in their communities. The process is slow, but policies and program practices are changing throughout the nation. Service systems built around specialized residences are giving way to a new concept—the delivery of needed assistance to individuals. There is growing assistance for people with disabilities to secure tenure—the ownership or lease of a home of their own. During the 1990s, understanding of and confidence in assisting people with disabilities outside the confines of congregate facilities has grown enormously. People who have secured tenure are reporting that it means they lead more self-determined, self-sufficient, and stable lives. They have better connections to their communities (Smith, 1995). Robert Williams, the commissioner of ADD, in summarizing the homeownership movement in the United States, made the following remarks:

> We have the opportunity and responsibility to use what we do here to reinvigorate the American dream we all call homeownership. People with disabilities for far too long have been denied the right and opportunity to chart and control their lives and futures. The Home of Your Own initiative is about changing the power dynamic.

REFERENCES

Americans with Disabilities Act (ADA) of 1990, PL 101-336, 42 U.S.C. §§ 12101 *et seq.*

Braddock, B., & Hemp, R. (1995). *The state of states in developmental disabilities* (4th ed.). Washington, DC: American Association on Mental Retardation.

Braddock, B., & Hemp, R. (1996). Medicaid spending reductions and developmental disabilities. *Journal of Disability Policy Studies, 7*(1), 10–13.

Hitzing, W. (1980). ENCOR and beyond. In T. Apolloni, J. Cappucilli, & T.P. Cooke (Eds.), *Towards excellence: Achievements in residential services for people with disabilities.* Baltimore: University Park Press.

Hoggs, J., & Moss, S. (1990). Social and community integration. In M.P. Janicki & M.M. Seltzer (Eds.), *Aging and developmental disabilities: Challenges for 1990s: Proceedings of the Boston Roundtable on Research Issues and Applications in Aging and Developmental Disabilities.* Washington, DC: American Association on Mental Retardation, Special Interest Group on Aging.

Individuals with Disabilities Education Act Amendments of 1997, PL 105-17, 20 U.S.C. §§ 1400 *et seq.*

Klein, J. (1994). Supportive living: Not just another "rung" on the continuum. *TASH Newsletter 20*(7), 16–18.

Klein, J., & Black, M. (1995). *Extending the American dream: Homeownership for people with disabilities.* Durham: University of New Hampshire, Institute on Disability. (Available from the Institute on Disability, 7 Leavitt Lane, Durham, NH 03829-3522; 603-862-4320)

Litvak, S., Heumann, J.S., & Zukas, H. (1987). *Attending to America: Personal assistance for independent living.* Berkeley, CA: World Institute on Disability.

Mank, D., Buckley, J., & Rhodes, L. (1990). National issues for implementation of supported employment. In F.R. Rusch (Ed.), *Supported employment: Models, methods and issues* (pp. 289–300). Sycamore, IL: Sycamore Publishing Company.

O'Brien, J. (1994). Down stairs that are never your own: Supporting people with developmental disabilities in their own homes. *Mental Retardation, 32*(1), 1–6.

Sabatino, C.P., & Litvak, S. (1992, Winter). Consumer-directed homecare: What makes it possible? *Generations,* 53–58.

Smith, G.A. (1995). *Supporting Connecticut citizens with disabilities to have a home of their own: State policy review and recommendations.* Durham: University of New Hampshire, Institute on Disability, National Home of Your Own Alliance.

Sowers, J.-A., McAllister, R., & Cotton, P. (1996). Strategies to enhance control of the employment process by individuals with severe disabilities. In L.E. Powers, G.H.S. Singer, & J.-A. Sowers (Eds.), *On the road to autonomy: Promoting self-competence in children and youth with disabilities* (pp. 325–346). Baltimore: Paul H. Brookes Publishing Co.

Taylor, S.J. (1988). Caught in the continuum: A critical analysis of the principle of the least restrictive environment. *Journal of The Association for Persons with Severe Handicaps, 13,* 41–53.

Wehman, P., & Kregel, J. (1995). At the crossroads: Supported employment a decade later. *Journal of The Association for Persons with Severe Handicaps, 20,* 286–299.

8

A Multielement Approach to Creating Change in a State Employment System

Jo-Ann Sowers, Kim Milliken, Patty Cotton,
Shawna Sousa, Leslie Dwyer, and Kris Kouwenhoven

During the 1980s and 1990s, great changes occurred in employment services and opportunities for individuals with developmental disabilities. Prior to this time, the only employment option available to most adults and transition-age students with developmental disabilities was work in a sheltered workshop. In fact, many individuals did not have the opportunity to work at all and spent their days at an activity center. During the 1980s, a number of university research projects introduced the supported employment model and demonstrated the capacity of individuals with developmental disabilities to be employed successfully in community jobs (McDonnell, Hardman, & Hightower, 1989; Rusch & Mithaug, 1980; Sowers, Thompson, & Connis, 1979; Wehman, 1981). Between 1985 and 1993, the Office of Special Education and Rehabilitation Services (OSERS) awarded grants to states to enable them to shift from facility-based employment and day activity programs to community-based, supported employment services for individuals

The preparation of this chapter was supported in part by Administration on Developmental Disabilities Grant No. 900DN0014; U.S. Department of Education, Rehabilitation Services Administration Grant No. H128A4010; and U.S. Department of Education, Office of Special Education Programs Grant No. H158Q40054. The opinions expressed herein do not necessarily reflect the views of these agencies.

with developmental disabilities (Bellamy & Melia, 1991; U.S. Department of Education, 1985).

The supported employment initiative was advanced with the hope and promise that if implemented, most individuals with developmental disabilities would have the opportunity to gain access to community employment. In fact, great progress has been made toward this goal. In 1992, it was estimated that more than 200,000 individuals with developmental disabilities were working in community businesses (West, Revell, & Wehman, 1992). In addition, the number of programs offering supported employment assistance has greatly expanded (McGaughey, Kiernan, McNally, Gilmore, & Keith, 1995). It has been widely acknowledged, however, that the hope and promise of supported employment remains unfulfilled (Mank, 1994; Wehman & Kregel, 1995). Mank summarized the concerns of supported employment advocates: 1) the continuing unemployment of the vast majority of individuals with disabilities, 2) the poor quality of jobs obtained by many supported employees, 3) the low level of social interaction between supported employees and their co-workers, 4) the small number of individuals with severe disabilities who have obtained employment, 5) an increase in the number of segregated programs, and 6) lengthening wait lists for employment services.

Supported employment advocates maintain their commitment to community employment for all individuals who experience disabilities, including those with very significant disabilities. The challenge is to identify the factors that have served as barriers to more widespread implementation of community employment and to make the changes needed to achieve the original hope and promise of supported employment. There is wide agreement that the federal, state, and local policies that encourage segregated programs to exist and even grow must change (Agosta, Brown, & Melda, 1993; Murphy & Rogan, 1995; Wehman & Kregel, 1995). Advocates also agree that federal and state governments need to increase their investment in creating systemic changes through training and technical assistance grants. Although the initial investment was substantial, these governments underestimated the complexity and difficulty of changing a well-entrenched system of segregated services (Mank, 1994).

Some supported employment advocates have proposed that limitations of the job coach model itself might be hindering greater access to employment for individuals with severe disabilities (Nisbet & Hagner, 1988; Powers & Sowers, 1994). For example, it has been suggested that by assuming all or most of the responsibility for training supported employees, job coaches may make supported employees dependent on them. This dependency may contribute to the high levels of ongoing support required by many supported employees and supported employees' relatively high rates of job loss.

Other advocates have pointed to the job coach model's emphasis on the existing skills and experiences of individuals in determining the type of jobs that are sought for them as a factor hindering quality employment outcomes. The result of this practice has been that the majority of supported employees have been placed into low-quality "food and filth" jobs. These jobs have few of the characteristics associated with worker job satisfaction (e.g., good wages and benefits, perceived status, opportunity for advancement) and, thus, may contribute to high levels of ongoing support and job turnover of supported employees (Moseley, 1988; Sowers, Cotton, & Malloy, 1994). That supported employees and their families have little or no opportunity to choose or control how service funds are utilized has also been identified as contributing to the fact that few individuals with developmental disabilities are working in quality jobs in their communities (Cotton & Sowers, 1996; Mank, 1994; Wehman & Kregel, 1995).

Some supported employment advocates have identified approaches that they hope will offer individuals with developmental disabilities improved career and job opportunities and outcomes. These approaches have been collectively called *natural supports* (Curl, McConaughy, Pawley, & Salzberg, 1987; Fabian, Luecking, & Tilson, 1994; Hagner & Dileo, 1993; Murphy & Rogan, 1994; Nisbet & Hagner, 1988). Table 8.1 summarizes the key differences between a job coach approach and natural supports approach.

In 1991 the U.S. Administration on Developmental Disabilities (ADD) funded projects in six states, the goals of which were to identify natural support approaches to assist individuals with significant disabilities in making the transition from school to community-based employment; to evaluate the extent

Table 8.1. Job coach approach versus natural supports approach

Job coach approach	Natural supports approach
Focus is on supported employee's skills when deciding the type of job to seek.	Focus is on supported employee's unique interests, gifts, and talents.
During job placement, programs are promoted.	During job placement, the supported employee is promoted.
Match is made between supported employee's skills and job requirements.	Match is made between supported employee's training and support needs and the company's capacity to provide this training and support.
Program staff member (job coach) provides all or most of the training to the supported employee.	Program staff member (employment consultant) provides input to co-workers to enable them to train and help the supported employee.
Program decides how funds will be used to assist supported employee in becoming employed.	Supported employee and family takes lead in deciding how to use funds to become employed.

to which these approaches resulted in quality work outcomes for these individuals; and to serve as an impetus for local, state, and national systems change. The Institute on Disability (IOD) at the University of New Hampshire received one of these grants. In 1993 the IOD also received two additional grants to expand its efforts in the area of natural supports. The Office of Special Education Programs funded a grant to replicate the natural supports approaches in school districts in New Hampshire and Maine. The Rehabilitation Services Administration funded a project to implement natural supports with adults who received services through supported employment and day habilitation programs. Collectively, the activities of these three grants were called the New Hampshire Natural Supports Project (NHNSP).

During the 1990s, the NHNSP undertook three types of systems change activities. Initially, the NHNSP focused on researching and demonstrating natural supports approaches. After validating the effectiveness of natural supports, the NHNSP shifted the focus to providing training and technical assistance to stakeholders to enable them to implement natural supports approaches. Finally, NHNSP staff worked with state agencies to assist them in revising policies and regulations to enhance the use of natural supports. The tasks that were carried out for each of the three phases of systems change activities are described along with the lessons learned and outcomes achieved through the activities of each phase (see Table 8.2).

PHASE 1: RESEARCH AND DEMONSTRATION

The NHNSP conducted three research and demonstration activities. First, qualitative and quantitative data were collected to determine the effectiveness and feasibility of natural supports approaches and to identify the specific

Table 8.2. Systems change phases and purposes of the New Hampshire Natural Supports Project (NHNSP)

Phase	Purpose
Research and demonstration	To determine the impact of natural supports on individuals and systems
Training and technical assistance	To provide training and technical assistance about natural supports to key stakeholders
	To develop the capacity for this training and assistance to continue after the end of the project
Policy and regulation change	To identify and recommend policy and regulation changes to enhance the use of natural supports

strategies that result in optimal co-worker supports and quality employment outcomes for individuals with developmental disabilities. Through the second activity, the NHNSP demonstrated and field-tested innovative approaches for optimizing the choices and control that individuals and their families have related to employment goals, services, supports, and funding. The third activity of Phase 1 was to develop innovative organizational, staffing, and funding approaches for supported employment agencies aimed at enhancing the control and choices available to service recipients and the extent to which public employment service funds are effectively and efficiently utilized.

Activity 1: Natural Supports Strategies Were Evaluated

Using natural supports approaches, the NHNSP assisted 106 individuals in obtaining paid employment. Figure 8.1 shows the distribution of disabilities experienced by these individuals; Figure 8.2 shows the distribution of their ages. Data were collected on staff training time, job retention, co-worker training and support strategies, and supported employee training preferences.

Activity 2: Service Planning Approaches to Enhance
Individuals' Choice and Control Were Developed and Demonstrated

The Choice Through Knowledge demonstration project was developed as a collaboration with Region IV Developmental Services Agency in Concord,

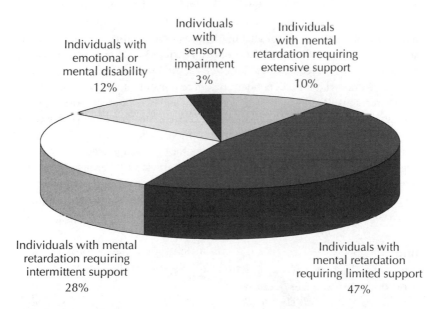

Figure 8.1.   Individuals participating in the New Hampshire Natural Supports Project (NHNSP).

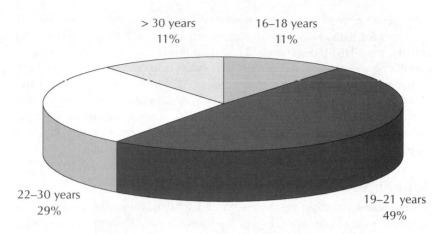

Figure 8.2.   Ages of participants in the New Hampshire Natural Supports Project (NHNSP).

New Hampshire. A detailed description of this project is available in a guide called *Choice Through Knowledge: Knowledge = Power, A Model for Empowerment Through Education* (Cotton & Sowers, 1996). The specific purpose of this demonstration project was to explore ways to promote the opportunity for people with disabilities to make informed choices among the full array of employment goals and support options available to all citizens, to control the quality of these supports, and to direct the manner in which funds are used to purchase these supports. Through this demonstration effort, a resource consultant organization (RCO) was developed. The RCO does not fund services, nor does it provide direct services. Through the RCO, the individual and his or her family works with an independent resource consultant and service broker. The resource consultant provides the individual and his or her support network with education, facilitation, and counseling to enable them to choose from among the full array of career and support options. The service broker assists individuals to advocate with funding agencies for the money needed to pay for the support and services they have chosen. The service broker also helps the individual to negotiate with service agencies and other support resources for the type and quality of services he or she wants, as well as for the cost of these services.

Annie

Annie wanted a career working with animals or in child care. She felt like no one was listening because she continued to be placed in cleaning jobs, each of which she disliked and lost after several months. The $12,000 allocated for her employment services went to the programs to *which she was assigned. Annie was unaware of the amount of money paid to the program or how the money was being used. Annie also felt that she had no control over her living situation.*

Annie remembers when her living situation changed as a result of her participation in the Choice Through Knowledge project. "I was living in enhanced family care. I had no control over what I was doing. Region IV was doing a new project [service brokering]. [My resource consultant] talked with me about what I wanted to do for work, where I wanted to live, how everything would come together. It came to where I interviewed places to get apartments and roommates. I picked this one where I am living now. I wrote an ad, put it in the paper for a roommate, found one. We looked for an apartment ourselves, not the program. I finally have control over where my money goes, how it is spent, what I do with it, how much I have in the account."

In planning for her career, Annie decided that she first wanted to try pet grooming. Annie also decided that she wanted to use most of her funds to pay a professional pet groomer to train her and the remainder to pay a supported employment agency to consult with the employer. The resource consultant assisted Annie in interviewing employment providers. Together, they developed questions and interviewed staff from four programs. Annie hired an employment consultant through a supported employment agency, who helped Annie develop an on-the-job training (OJT) arrangement with a dog groomer. Annie also decided that she wanted to hire a personal trainer to develop the strength and stamina needed to work in the pet grooming or child care fields. The resource consultant wrote a Social Security Administration Plan for Achieving Self-Support (PASS) so that Annie could pay for her gym membership and personal trainer fees.

Activity 3: Innovative Supported Employment Program Organizational Structure Was Demonstrated

Even if most supported employment and day programs begin using natural supports approaches, a significant gap will continue to exist between the number of people who want and need assistance and the resources available to provide this assistance. At present, many of these programs are organized hierarchically with several layers of directors, managers, and administrators. A significant portion of funds allocated for employment services are used for the salaries of these administrative staff, leaving little for those staff who actually assist individuals in obtaining employment. Using New Hampshire as an illustration, the typical hourly pay of supported employment specialists is between $7.00 and $12.00 per hour (an additional $1.00–$2.00 per hour is paid for benefits). The remainder of the $35.00–$40.00 per hour paid to agencies by VR covers the salaries of staff who are not delivering direct services, as well as program costs (e.g., rent, insurance). Thus, only about one third of employment assistance funds pay for direct services.

Day and employment service Medicaid funding provides another example of the discrepancy between funds allocated for services and the amount actually used for direct services. The typical rate of funding to programs from the New Hampshire Division of Mental Health and Developmental Services is between $8,000 and $24,000 per person, per year for individuals in supported employment and day programs. A person whose program is given $24,000 may receive one-to-one support from a staff person who makes $6.00–$8.00 an hour. Thus, a staff person who works with one person and earns $8.00 an hour for 6 hours (the typical number of hours provided for a person's day habilitation) will cost the program annually about $12,000 in salary, another $2,500 in benefits, and perhaps $1,500 in travel expenses, for a total of $16,000. The remaining $8,000 goes to salaries for staff not providing direct services and to general program costs. Many individuals funded in day habilitation programs, however, do not receive individual assistance but are supervised in groups (in a facility or in community-based enclaves or crews).

Many highly dedicated and competent staff work as employment specialists. There is widespread agreement, however, that gaining and maintaining competent staff is a major challenge faced by supported employment programs (Agosta et al., 1993; Buckley, Albin, & Mank, 1988; Everson, 1991; LeRoy & Hartley-Malivuk, 1991; Sowers & Powers, 1994). One of the major barriers to overcoming this challenge is the low wages paid to employment specialists (Everson, 1991). To attract and keep the best and brightest supported employment specialists, these specialists must be able to earn professional-level salaries. Offering higher wages has not been feasible within traditional hierarchical program organizations. Perhaps a fresh look is needed at how supported employment agencies are structured and how the public funds allocated for services are used.

The NHNSP developed a supported employment agency, New Hampshire Diversity Concepts (NHDC), to demonstrate innovative organizational and staffing strategies. NHDC was organized based on the following principles:

1. Individual service recipients should control to the greatest extent possible the services they receive, including the staff person from whom they receive assistance, the specific goals established for them (e.g., the type of job they will be assisted to obtain), and the specific nature of the supports they will receive to reach these goals (e.g., taking a class to help prepare for a job).

2. Most of the funds that are paid to agencies for services should be paid to the staff members who provide these services, whereas minimal amounts of service funds should be used for administrative and supervisory staff salaries.

3. Individuals should be able to use their service funds to pay for nonagency services and assistance (e.g., tuition for a college class, reimbursement to a business for OJT and high levels of ongoing support).

4. Funding agencies should be billed only for actual services provided rather than for a standard "slot" amount.

5. Natural supports should be facilitated, both to enhance the extent to which individuals are integrated with and connected to their co-workers and to reduce high-cost staff services.

NHDC was certified by VR as a community rehabilitation provider and by the state developmental disabilities agency as a day service provider. NHDC functioned as an employment service provider agency for approximately 3 years and incorporated these principles as much as possible. The following provides the vision on which NHDC was founded and developed:

- NHDC was conceived to function as an organizational umbrella under which independent employment consultants would work, which would be collectively managed by these staff and in which staff would support and encourage high quality work among themselves. Although there may be a managing partner or a part-time administrative staff person, this person's role is not to supervise the employment consultants. During the 3 years in which NHDC operated, the first author of this chapter provided administrative oversight to the agency for about 10 hours per week. In addition, a private business was paid for about 4 hours of bookkeeping assistance per month. Two staff members functioned as independent employment consultants, and they took on some of the roles that are characteristic of collective managing. The employment consultants were paid $15.00 per hour, which was possible because of the small amount of funds that were allocated for administrative salaries.

- Individuals who wanted employment assistance were encouraged to identify the employment consultants with whom they wanted to work. They identified one of the employment consultants based on positive information from other individuals with whom the employment consultant had worked or by interviewing each of the employment consultants to select the one from whom he or she wished to gain assistance. Thus, in contrast to traditional agencies, individuals were not referred to an agency and then assigned to a staff person.

- In contrast to typical service providers, NHDC billed only for the actual hours of services provided by an employment consultant. For example, if a consumer worked or was involved in some other billable Medicaid activity for 30 hours but the employment consultant only provided 5 hours of consultation activities, the developmental disabilities funding agency was only billed for the 5 hours. In addition, NHDC did not require or encourage individuals to work and to be involved in activity for the maximum number of slot hours merely to maximize billing. Thus, many individuals chose to work and to participate in other community activities for 10–15 hours per week rather than the allocated 30 hours. Through these approaches and the use of natural supports, NHDC charged less than 75% of the Medicaid and state slot amounts budgeted by the developmental disabilities funding agency. The remainder of the funds were thus available for other individuals' services.

Many individuals used their funds to pay for supports, services, and activities from sources other than NHDC. A number of individuals' funds reimbursed businesses for training and supporting them on their jobs. Funds were also used by individuals to pay for college classes or community workshops (e.g., ceramics) and for membership fees (e.g., to a health club).

Amanda

Amanda had a one-to-one assistant throughout her high school years to provide her with physical, personal care, and learning supports. When Amanda was no longer eligible for school services, her transition team planned for her to make the transition to a facility-based day activity program. Because of her perceived high support needs, $24,000 was allocated for her day services.

Amanda and her mother decided that she did not want to go to a facility-based day program and instead chose to work with an employment consultant from NHDC. By spending time with Amanda and her mother rather than reading Amanda's school assessments and records, the employment consultant learned about her unique talents, likes and dislikes, and the types of supports she might need. Amanda's mother revealed that Amanda loved arts and crafts, and the employment consultant began looking for jobs in which Amanda might be able to use her talents and express her interest in this area. The employment consultant partnered with the owner of a small company that makes wool throws to create a job for Amanda. Amanda and a co-worker worked as a team doing a variety of product quality-checking and packaging tasks. Amanda's funding was used to reimburse the company for the supports that the co-worker provided. Approximately $4,500 per year was spent for these supports. The employment consultant worked closely with Amanda's co-worker, providing her with advice and feedback related to training and supporting Amanda. The consultant billed only for the actual number of hours that she provided this consultation assistance, averaging about 10 hours per month (at a cost of $1,800 per year). Amanda lives in a rural community and commutes about 25 miles each *way to work. Because Amanda's mother works, the mother of another individual who received assistance through NHDC drove Amanda to and from work at an expense of about $6,000 per year. NHDC charged about $650 per year for administrative fees. Thus, the total cost of Amanda's employment supports for 1 year was about $11,000—a savings of $13,000 to the state's Medicaid Waiver Program. Plans were being made for Amanda to move into the town where she works, which would significantly reduce the transportation costs.*

Lessons Learned and Implications

This section identifies 10 key "lessons learned" during Phase 1 of the NHNSP. The qualitative information from which these lessons were derived is presented. In addition, the implications of the lessons are discussed. Shawn's story illustrates many of the lessons.

Shawn

Shawn was 17 years old when he began participating in the NHNSP. Prior to participation in the project, he was part of an unpaid work experience enclave at a nursing home where, under the supervision of the special education job coach, he worked in the laundry room and cleaned rooms. Shawn's interest in reading and books had never been perceived by school staff as a potential career for him. In fact, it more often had been perceived as distracting him from learning "functional skills." Through his career planning meetings, though, Shawn and his family identified reading and books as the area in which he would most like to pursue a career. In his senior year of high school, Shawn obtained an internship at a university library, where Bill, the assistant director, served as his mentor. On the advice of Bill, Shawn took three college-level computer classes. Like other students in need of financial assistance, his work in the library covered part of his tuition.

These experiences led Shawn to where he is today, working as a Senior Page (library assistant) at Hills Memorial Library in Hudson, New Hampshire. When asked whether Shawn was any more challenging to train than other employees, one of his co-workers said, "Not any harder, just different. We had to learn to be consistent." This co-worker also said that "having to think through the process of how to train Shawn has allowed us to be more thoughtful about how we train and support all employees."

Shawn's employment consultant had carefully analyzed the capacity of Hills Memorial Library and its staff to train and support Shawn prior to recommending that he be hired. The employment con-

sultant described his learning, performance, and personality styles to his co-workers, and provided them with suggestions about strategies that they could use to teach and support him. The employment consultant remained at the library throughout Shawn's first several workdays, providing input and support to his co-workers. In addition, the employment consultant continued to observe, meet with, and share ideas with Shawn and his co-workers on a frequent basis for the first 9 months of employment. During the 4 years that Shawn has been employed at Hills Memorial Library, his hours have increased from 4 to 20 hours per week and he has been promoted from Junior Page to Senior Page. His responsibilities include shelving, cataloguing, and checking in books.

The library received funding through the local branch of The Arc for his initial training. After the initial training period, Shawn paid the library for several hours of ongoing support each week through a PASS plan. Today, the library supports him without any financial reimbursement.

Lesson 1: Focus on the Individual   Focusing on individuals' interests and capacities appears to open a wider array of career opportunities compared with focusing on these individuals' skills and past experiences when identifying the type of careers or jobs they will pursue. A career planning process was used with project participants that was derived from processes known variously as "lifestyle planning" (O'Brien, 1987), "personal futures planning" (Mount, 1997), and "whole life planning" (Butterworth et al., 1993). The NHNSP's process began with the belief that each participant should have the opportunity to consider the full array of career options available to individuals without disabilities. The process was also based on the understanding that the extent to which individuals are satisfied with their jobs and motivated to maintain them is greatly influenced by how much their jobs reflect their personal interests and unique talents (Bolles, 1994).

As Table 8.3 illustrates, project participants were assisted to obtain a wide array of occupations. This result contrasts with the limited range of jobs typically reported for supported employees (Kregel, Hill, & Banks, 1988; Shafer, Banks, & Kregel, 1991; Sowers et al., 1994). In fact, a survey of supported employment programs in New Hampshire found that approximately 52% of the jobs in which supported employees worked were cleaning jobs (New Hampshire Division of Mental Health and Developmental Services, 1997). In contrast, only about 27% of the jobs in which project participants worked were cleaning and food service jobs.

Lesson 2: Supported and Typical Employees Require Similar Time and Strategies for Training and Support   The time and strategies used to train and support many participants was similar to those used to train and support typical employees. The job coach approach is based on the assumption that

Table 8.3. Number of job types in which New Hampshire Natural Supports Project (NHNSP) participants were employed

Type of job	n
Cleaner/dishwasher/janitor/food preparer	32
Assembler/packager	18
Clerical/office work	16
Stocker	14
Child care/personal care assistant	6
Animal grooming/care assistant	5
Greenhouse assistant	5
Delivery person	4
Customer assistant	5
Cashier	3
Mechanics assistant	3
Laundry worker	2
Wig design assistant	1
Construction worker	1
Graphics artist assistant	1
Newspaper columnist	1
Artist	1
Self-employed	3
Total	**121**

supported employees require much more time and very different strategies to learn a job than typical employees require. In addition, it has been assumed that job coaching is needed because businesses are neither willing to devote this amount of time nor do they have knowledge of these training strategies.

Project staff interviewed supervisors and co-workers regarding their experiences hiring, training, and supporting the project participant who was employed at their company. Co-workers were asked to compare the amount of time it took to train and support the supported employee with the amount it took to train and support other employees without disabilities in the same position. Approximately 67% of the co-workers indicated that it took about the same amount (31%) or a little more (36%) time to train the supported employee, whereas 33% indicated that it took a lot more time to do so. Approximately 62% felt that they needed to devote about the same amount (18%) or a little more (44%) time to providing ongoing supervision to the supported employee, whereas 38% felt that they needed to devote a lot more time doing so. Co-workers were also asked to compare the type of strategies they used to train and support the supported employee with those used with typical employees. Approximately 51% of the co-workers perceived that the strategies were exactly the same (10%) or about the same (41%), whereas 39% and 10% perceived that they used somewhat different and very different strategies, respectively.

These results suggest that the key assumptions on which the job coach approach is based may not be valid. It appears that advocates may have over-estimated the amount of time for systematic instruction needed by many supported employees and underestimated the amount of time and effort businesses are willing to provide.

Lesson 3: Employees Prefer to Be Trained and Supported by Co-workers The project's participants appeared to prefer being trained and supported by co-workers. Another assumption on which supported employment approaches have been based is that supported employees want a job coach to train them. It is assumed that by having the job coach present, the supported employee feels less insecure and anxious about social situations and about learning new tasks and skills.

Project staff interviewed participants and asked, "Are you glad that (name of co-worker) trained you, or would you have liked (name of employment consultant) to have done more of the training?" All of the participants were interviewed with the exception of five individuals who experienced very significant cognitive disabilities and were unable to respond to the question. The wording of the question was tailored to each individual to optimize his or her understanding of the question's meaning. In response to this question, 96% of the participants indicated that they preferred being trained by their co-worker(s). The behavioral responses of the participants as reported by their employment consultants also provided some corroborating evidence that the participants did in fact prefer being trained and supported by their co-workers as compared with receiving such aid from an agency job coach. A number of the consultants suggested that the supported employees seemed to feel that the jobsite was their territory (different from home, a residential program, school, or other "special" program where staff or family directed them), where they had established their own relationships and were perceived on an equal basis with others there. These employees seemed to perceive the consultants as intruders into this territory and these relationships.

Some professionals and families have voiced concern about the potential for physical and/or emotional abuse when co-workers take the primary responsibility for training and supporting a supported employee, especially those with the most significant disabilities. No participant, family member, or staff person reported or suggested any occurrence of physical or verbal abuse.

Lesson 4: Match Employee Support Needs with the Support Capacity of Worksites Careful analysis and matching of employee support needs and worksite support capacity is critical. Making a good job match has long been recognized as a critical supported employment practice (Rusch & Mithaug, 1980; Trach, 1990; Wehman & Moon, 1988). The NHNSP found that careful job matching is especially important when an employee is trained and supported by co-workers. In a natural supports framework, the assessment of the employee includes those factors that enhance his or her ability to learn new skills (e.g., which teaching strategies are most effective when a person is learning a new skill), the time it will probably take the person to learn different types of new skills, the type of supervisory strategies that are most effective, the specific types of supports that he or she will probably need, and work environment characteristics that foster success. This information is critical not only to make the best match but also to enable the employment consultant to most effectively give input and advice to the co-workers who will train and support the employee.

In addition, when using a natural supports approach, it is critical to carefully analyze a business's capacity to provide the type and amounts of supports that a supported employee will need to succeed. Questions that should be considered include 1) "How much time can a co-worker(s) devote to training the supported employee on a daily basis?" 2) "What specific strategies does the company use to train a new employee in this position or similar positions, and how does this match the needs of the supported employee?" 3) "How much and what type of ongoing supervision is provided and to what extent will this meet the needs of the supported employee?" and 4) "On the basis of answers to these and similar questions, what type of accommodations and consultation will be needed?"

Lesson 5: Natural Supports May Help More People Benefit from Supported Employment   A natural supports approach may result in increased numbers of individuals gaining access to supported employment services. One of the hoped-for outcomes of natural supports is that if co-workers take on more of the responsibility for training supported employees, the amount of staff time needed for this purpose will be less than is required by the job coach approach. In addition, it is hoped that supported employees trained by their co-workers will develop less dependency on agency staff, thus easing the fading process and decreasing the need for high levels of ongoing support. If these two outcomes are realized, increased numbers of individuals may be able to access employment assistance.

To evaluate the amount of time that staff using a natural supports approach actually devoted to supported employees during their first 12 months on the job, two project staff members and six staff members from five supported employment agencies and one high school recorded the amount of time (in 15 minute increments) that they spent assisting 35 participants. The mean age of these participants was 22 years. The percentage of types of disabilities experienced by the participants in this study were as follows: mental retardation requiring intermittent support (27%), mental retardation requiring limited support (45%), mental retardation requiring extensive support (13%), emotional and mental illness (12%), and other disabilities (3%).

Figure 8.3 shows the average percentage of project and worksite staff time devoted to the 35 supported employees. This time includes direct training of the employee at the worksite, observation of the employee at the worksite, consultation with the employee's supervisor or a co-worker, and off-site activities (e.g., off-site training, meetings, transportation). The percentages were computed by dividing staff time spent on the supported employee by the minutes worked by the employee. Also shown are data obtained via a nationwide survey of supported employment agencies who used a job coach approach conducted by the Rehabilitation Research and Training Center at Virginia Commonwealth University (1994).

The comparison of the data from the NHNSP in which staff used a natural supports approach and from the nationwide survey of supported employment agencies that used a job coach approach suggests a substantial difference in staff time allocation during the first 2 months of employment. Percentage of

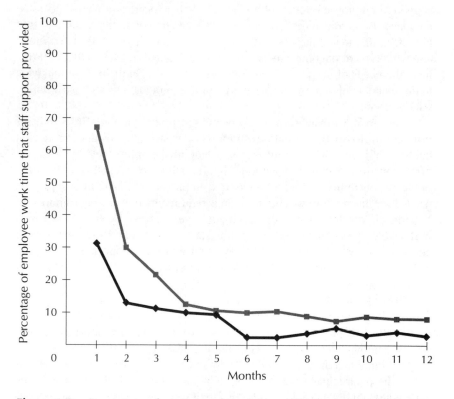

Figure 8.3.   Percentage of project and worksite staff time spent supporting 35 employees. (Key: black diamonds = natural supports approach used in the New Hampshire Natural Supports Project; gray squares = job coach approach used in supported employment agencies across the nation)

staff time devoted to employee support in the NHNSP was about 31% for Month 1, 13% for Month 2, and 10% for Month 3 compared with 65% for Month 1, 29% for Month 2, and 22% for Month 3 found in the national job coach survey. These findings have obvious implications in terms of utilization of public funds. Take the example of a supported employee who works 20 hours per week. In New Hampshire, the Division of Vocational Rehabilitation (VR) pays supported employment agencies at least $30.00 per hour (most receive between $35.00 and $40.00 per hour) for job coaching or employment consultation. At $30.00 per hour, the cost to VR for the first 3 months of services to an employee participating in NHNSP would be approximately $1,349, whereas the comparable cost for the supported employees in the national survey would be $3,981.

By Month 6, the staff time percentage differences decreased: agency staff who participated in the NHNSP spent less than 5% of their time assisting supported employees compared with about 8% for those using a job coach approach. These percentages remained about the same in Month 9 and Month 12.

Lesson 6: Natural Supports May Facilitate Quality Work Training for Students   Providing students with quality community work training experiences may be more feasible through natural supports. Certo, Pumpian, Fisher, Storey, and Smalley (1997) pointed out that it is not unusual for a moderate-sized school to assign an employment specialist and possibly an assistant to help as many as 30 students to obtain work experiences and employment. Thus, it is not surprising that a high school work experience program may be able to offer students with significant disabilities the opportunity to "work" for only a few hours per week, often as part of an enclave or crew with other students with disabilities in cleaning occupations at volunteer sites. These students leave high school with few marketable skills.

The high student-to-staff ratios described by Pumpian, Fisher, Certo, and Smalley (1997) make providing quality work experiences to students a challenge, regardless of the approach used. The results of the project, however, suggest that using a natural supports approach may make doing so more feasible compared with the job coach approach that has been adopted by many school programs.

Lesson 7: Employment Specialists Are Critical to a Natural Supports Approach   The role of employment specialists is still critical when using a natural supports approach. Many supported employment staff have expressed the concern that advocating a natural supports approach implies that the assistance of employment specialists is no longer needed or is needed to a much lesser degree. Many supported employment agencies fear that the natural supports approach threatens the viability of their agencies and many employment specialists have feared that it threatens their jobs. In truth, these fears are not unfounded. Some funding agency staff (e.g., VR counselors, developmental disabilities service coordinators) have used natural supports as a rationale for not funding training or services for individuals, which reflects their misunderstanding of natural supports. These staff members need to understand that *natural supports* does not mean that no or minimal assistance from employment specialists is required for individuals to be successfully employed but that this assistance is primarily devoted to consulting with co-workers rather than to directly training the supported employee.

Lesson 8: Greater Funds Should Be Allocated for When the "Honeymoon" Is Over   Supported employment funding agencies should consider allocating less funding for initial training and more when the "honeymoon" is over. Supported employment funding resources typically are concentrated on the initial training period. In New Hampshire, VR typically reimburses agencies several thousands of dollars to train a supported employee to perform his or her job. After a supported employee has learned to perform the job and has been employed for at least 60 days, his or her case can be and is usually closed and funding is terminated. In part, this concentration of funding during the initial training phase reflects VR's policy of time-limited service. The funding pattern also reflects the underlying assumptions of the job coach model that supported employees require much more time and different strategies than do typical employees to learn a job and that businesses cannot provide this training. Again, project results suggested that with input and advice from an employment consultant, co-workers do not find it difficult to train most supported employees.

Project results, however, also suggested that co-workers began to experience some difficulties and increased need for consultation after many of the participants had been on the job for several months. Most job coaches will recognize this pattern. A job coach completes the initial training, fades his or her presence, and then conducts follow-ups a few times per month for several months. All goes well for a few months, and then problems begin to surface. As many job coaches have described it, the "honeymoon" is over. These difficulties usually do not arise because the supported employee forgot how to perform his or her job but rather because of work-related issues— for example, the employee is now comfortable enough with his or her co-workers to reveal the less flattering side of his or her personality, and the employee's initial high motivation to perform to the best of his or her ability begins to wane (of course, these phenomena are common for employees with or without disabilities). This finding is supported by much of the research literature that has shown that employees with disabilities lose their jobs more frequently because of work-related behavior and issues than because of an inability to learn or to perform job duties (Foss & Peterson, 1981; Greenspan & Shoultz, 1981).

Thus, it is important that employment consultants are prepared for and available to provide co-workers with support after the initial honeymoon period is over. State funding agencies should consider decreasing funding for the initial 2 or 3 months of training, allocating the savings over a 6- to 12-month period, and extending the months of employment required for closure.

Lesson 9: Job Retention Levels for Natural Supports and Job Coach Approach Are Comparable Participant job retention in the natural supports approach was comparable to that reported for employees who were job coached. Supported employment advocates have expressed the concern that supported employees who are not provided job coaching may not be able to retain their jobs. There is irony in this concern, given the relatively high turnover of supported employees trained by job coaches (Shafer et al., 1991). Of the many reports of supported employment outcomes, rarely have more than 60% of supported employees retained their jobs beyond 1 year. In fact, the retention percentages reported are most frequently between 40% and 50% (Ellis, Rusch, Tu, & McCaughrin, 1990; Ford, Dineen, & Hall, 1984; Kregel, Wehman, Revell, & Hill, 1990; Shafer et al., 1991).

The NHNSP found that 55% of participants remained on the same job for 1 year or longer. Consequently, fears that not providing job coaching will result in increased job loss appear to be unfounded. The results, though, do not suggest that using a natural supports approach results in significantly improved job retention. It should be noted, however, that the average age of project participants was significantly younger than those typically represented in reports of supported employee job retention rates. More than 65% of project participants were in high school or had left school within 1 year of the beginning of their job. Thus, the reported job retention percentages include many after-school and temporary positions.

Lesson 10: Individuals Should Decide How Their Funds Will Be Used Allowing individuals to determine how their funds will be used enhances the use of natural supports and career path alternatives. Typically, a person with a significant disability who wishes to become employed is referred to a program that offers supported employment services. These programs offer a defined package of services—a staff person assesses the individual, identifies the type of job that will be sought for him or her, searches for this job, and coaches him or her. The service program and funding agencies negotiate the amount of money that will be paid for these services, and all or most of the funds go directly to the program. This system provides little opportunity for individuals to choose other paths, such as college, technical training schools, apprenticeships, or a self-run business. In addition, the funding arrangement limits individuals' opportunity to choose the types of assistance or the sources of assistance that they will use to achieve their career goal. For example, individuals usually are not offered the option of using supported employment funds to pay a classmate at college for tutoring, to gain career planning assistance from a community member who has expertise in a particular career area, to invest the funds in purchasing a business, or to reimburse a business for their expenses in providing OJT or ongoing supports.

NHNSP participants, their families, and professionals involved with them were encouraged to think outside traditional service and program boxes. They were assisted in considering the full array of options available to typical students and adults for pursuing careers and the many sources of assistance and support available for achieving their career goals. Rather than allow funding categories to drive and determine options and services, the project has assisted participants and their networks to determine what they wanted and to use the funds to support these choices. Matt's story illustrates what can be achieved when an individual and his or her family are supported to use funds flexibly and creatively.

Matt

Matt was 19 years old and had 2 years of school service eligibility remaining at his neighborhood high school when he began participating in the project. Matt was living with his family in a rural town in New Hampshire. Cathy, Matt's mother, has always been committed to Matt's participating fully in their community. She understands how important it is to Matt to be active, to feel productive, and to have social connections. She was determined that after Matt completed school, he would work in a job that he would find rewarding, that would give maximal opportunity to interact and connect with others, and that would allow him to make a real contribution to the community. Given the small number of businesses and employment opportunities in the community and Matt's need for high supports, she understood that making this dream a reality was going to be a real challenge.

Cathy took the lead in bringing people together to plan for Matt's future. She met with a number of his teachers, the special education director, a VR counselor, and a developmental disabilities services coordinator. She described her dream for Matt and asked for help in making it a reality. After several brainstorming meetings and research on local job opportunities, Matt and Cathy decided that they wanted to start their own delivery business. Matt loved riding in cars, staying on the go, visiting different places for short period of time, and meeting and socializing with people. Cathy and the group had also found out from local businesses and organizations that there was a real need for a delivery service—none of the local restaurants offered deliveries, there was a fairly large number of older adults who had difficulty getting to the grocery store and drugstore, and it took several days for local auto repair shops to get needed parts.

Matt and Cathy decided to start with delivering lunch for area restaurants. Cathy and an assistant at Matt's school worked together to talk with the restaurants and to identify businesses where he would deliver lunch. In addition to paying the assistant, the school paid for the assistant's mileage and her car insurance and assumed the liability risks of the operation. Cathy took the lunch orders and kept the books. During the summer, VR paid Cathy to support Matt in his daily deliveries and to continue to develop the business, including Cathy's tuition for a small business start-up course. After Matt completed high school, he and Cathy wanted to continue and expand the business. VR purchased a radio system for Matt and Cathy's truck to ease communication with the restaurants and businesses and containers to maintain correct food temperature. The developmental disabilities services agency permitted Matt and Cathy to use Matt's day habilitation funds to hire a driver and another assistant for Matt and to defray the costs of mileage and insurance. Matt's Delivery Service has now been in operation for more than 2 years. Matt or Cathy are not getting rich through their small business, but it has provided the chance to fulfill their original dream. Matt spends his days traveling around his community, he has gotten to know many of his customers well, and the service he provides is highly valued by the many who use it.

PHASE 2: TRAINING AND TECHNICAL ASSISTANCE

The focus of Phase 2 of the NHNSP was to disseminate the lessons learned through Phase 1 to stakeholders throughout New Hampshire through training and technical assistance.

Activity 1: Staff and Family Training Was Conducted

Project staff used the experiences and lessons learned via research and demonstration activities to create the Naturally Supported Employment Training Series. The training series was first offered to high school transition staff, adult services provider staff, VR counselors, and developmental disabilities services coordinators in one community. The sessions' topics were introduction to naturally supported employment, career planning, job search, employment consultation strategies, and creative funding strategies. Approximately 20 staff members from two high schools and four adult services programs, along with counselors and service coordinators, attended the series.

After this first six-session training series, the VR director arranged for funding for the training series to be conducted throughout the state. He required that all VR counselors attend the series and that each community rehabilitation provider organization send at least one staff member to the series to retain its supported employment certification and, thus, retain its funding for providing these services. The training series was conducted in five locations and was attended by approximately 150 staff members.

The VR natural supports training initiative also included families. The division's family liaison (also a mother of an adult with a disability) and a mother of a student who had participated in the project led these training sessions in 12 regions in the state. The training sessions provided an introduction to natural supports and transition and were held in the evening to enable as many families to attend as possible. The regional developmental disabilities services coordination agencies collaborated in organizing these meetings. They sent notices, made personal invitations to families, and assisted with respite care and transportation. Approximately 70 parents attended the meetings.

The original natural supports training series was revised and expanded for staff who were interested in achieving advanced competency as an employment consultant. Ten staff members who had demonstrated particular motivation and skill in employment consulting were invited to take the Advanced Employment Consultation Course. Staff attended 1 full day of training per month for 9 months. Each of the agencies for whom the staff members worked gave their commitment to support their staff member's class attendance, homework completion (including reading and written assignments), and practicum activities (including the implementation of natural support strategies with at least two individuals served by the agency).

Project staff served as mentors to course participants. Mentoring activities included on-site technical assistance 1 day each month and telephone discussions on an as-needed basis. The mentor rated the extent to which the participant implemented each of the Naturally Supported Employment Quality Practices and Indicators (Sowers, Cotton, & Nisbet, 1997). These ratings, along with class attendance, and homework completion, determined whether a participant received a Certificate of Employment Consultation. Six of the students received this Certificate.

The Advanced Employment Consultation class was taught for a second year. This second class had 35 participants from 14 adult services programs and four high schools. In addition, two participants were parents of individuals with disabilities. The six staff members who had received their certification through the prior class served as mentors to class participants. The mentors provided monthly on-site technical assistance to the students and were paid $15 per hour for their consultation time. Thirty-one participants received their Certificate of Employment Consultation.

Activity 2: Business Training Was Conducted

Businesses are key stakeholders in the effort to increase the number of individuals with significant disabilities who gain access to employment. Project staff did not want to make the usual "hire the disabled" presentations at lunch meetings. Instead, the desire was to identify avenues that reinforced the concept that businesses should value and adopt training and supervision approaches that promote the job satisfaction and productivity of all employees, including those with diverse learning styles and backgrounds. A training series for business managers and supervisors was conducted in collaboration with the University of New Hampshire's Business and Technology Center. Ten managers representing a diversity of industries and company sizes attended this training series. In addition, employment consultants from six supported employment agencies attended the series. Business and management trainers and consultants taught these classes, which focused on employee management strategies. The last class reinforced the fact that most of the strategies the managers had learned in the prior classes were applicable to employees with disabilities. In addition, the issues and approaches that are unique to hiring, training, and supervising employees with disabilities were covered in this last session.

Lessons Learned and Implications

Lesson 1: Employment Consulting Requires More Sophisticated Staff Skills As mentioned previously, one of the primary barriers experienced in supported employment is attracting and keeping quality staff. We have suggested that one solution to this dilemma will be the reorganization of agencies to permit a greater share of the current funding to be allocated to staff salaries. The necessity of attracting and keeping the best and the brightest is particularly important if programs and staff are going to shift from a job coaching to a natural supports approach. Much more sophisticated skills are needed to help a person with a significant disability to identify a career path from the full range of career options than are required to conduct a skills assessment. More sophisticated skills are required to partner with a business to make the necessary accommodations to enable an individual to be employed in his or her career of interest than are needed to place a person into the jobs with high turnover in which supported employees typically work. In addition, consulting with co-workers requires staff to not only have a thorough knowledge of training strategies but also to have the ability to describe these strategies so that co-workers can and are willing to use them.

Lesson 2: Greater Resources Should Be Devoted to Educating Individuals and Families About Directing Supported Employment The greatest successes occurred when participants and/or their families had an understanding of naturally supported employment strategies, were facilitated to advocate for their use, and took an active role in directing the process. The stories of Annie and Matt are good illustrations of this lesson. The lack of resources devoted to training individuals with disabilities and their families and the fact that training has typically provided only a cursory overview of approaches and strategies reflects the existing professionally driven and specialized paradigm. This paradigm assumes that individuals with disabilities and their families do not have the capacity to understand or direct their services and supports. To truly move toward a new self-directed and natural supports paradigm, much more of the training resources must be shifted to individuals, families, and community members.

Lesson 3: Greater Resources Should Be Devoted to Enhancing Businesses' Capacity to Direct Supported Employment   There has been a long-held and widely voiced belief that the business community must be engaged more actively in the goal of increasing access to employment for individuals with disabilities. The typical and repeated means for engaging businesses are public relations campaigns aimed at encouraging them to "hire the disabled"; providing information about the American with Disabilities Act (ADA) of 1990 (PL 101-336); and inviting businesses to become a member of a board, task force, or advisory committee. Few attempts have been made to actually provide business managers with the information and tools that will allow them to take the lead in hiring, training, and supporting individuals with disabilities (Fabian et al., 1994). The results of the NHNSP suggest that businesses are interested in learning these skills and are able to apply them successfully. The experiences gained through the NHNSP's business manager training series was particularly enlightening. These managers were eager to participate in the training when they understood that the information contributed to their ability to manage all of their employees better. The key to the success of the series was partnering with business consultants and trainers who had both knowledge of management strategies and credibility in this arena.

Lesson 4: Schools Need to Redefine Their Roles and Those of Their Teachers and Staff   Teachers and other school staff continue to define their role and responsibilities within the confines of the school building, classroom environment, and school day. In addition, students with significant disabilities continue to be educated primarily by a separate "special education" program. They receive all or most of their assistance from special education staff, and few have the opportunity to take advantage of the vocational and occupational programs available to typical students at their high schools.

The School-to-Work Opportunities Act (SWOA) of 1994 (PL 103-239) reflects an understanding that schools and teachers must begin to move outside of the confines of the classroom and school building and into their communities and businesses. SWOA clearly emphasizes that schools should provide students with the skills and experiences they will need to pursue professional and technical careers and that these efforts should include all students, including those with significant disabilities. Thus, the act provides the opportunity for general education and special education programs and staff to truly merge for the first time. Unfortunately, as of 2000, students with disabilities, especially those with severe disabilities are not being included in most school-to-work initiatives. Without question, the improvement of employment outcomes for students with disabilities is inextricably linked to school-to-work transition, educational reform, and school restructuring for all students. This linkage will require that special educators become actively engaged in these efforts and advocate for the inclusion of students with severe disabilities.

PHASE 3: POLICY AND REGULATION CHANGE

In the early stages of systems change, stakeholders who are open and motivated to view and do things differently will adopt and implement new approaches. These stakeholders have both the creative capacity and the strong commitment to use new approaches in spite of policies and regulations that may serve as disincentives. They are able and willing to figure out how to get around these policies, to operate outside the letter of the regulations, to risk possible censure, and to forego financial gain or possibly incur financial loss in their commitment to see and do things differently. For widespread systems change, however, it is necessary for policies and regulations to be changed.

Activity 1: Facilitated Division of Vocational Rehabilitation Policy that Employment Consultation Is a Billable Service

The New Hampshire VR funds two types of supported employment services. Through Individual Job Assessment (IJA) funds, providers are primarily paid for job search activities, and through Transitional Employment Program (TEP) funds, providers are paid during a supported employee's initial training phase. When the NHNSP began, the TEP funding description emphasized job coaching. Providers and counselors believed that TEP policies required that employment specialists take the primary responsibility for directly training supported employees. Not surprisingly, providers were concerned that they would not be paid if they began to shift their role to providing consultation to co-workers. To assuage this concern, VR's director communicated to providers and counselors VR's commitment to natural supports and that employment consultation was a billable TEP service.

Activity 2: Willingness to Fund Both On-the-Job Training (OJT) and Employment Consultation Was Facilitated

Through the OJT funding program, businesses are reimbursed for their expenses incurred in training an employee with a disability. The OJT program recognizes the advantages of having co-workers involved in employee training who are experienced and skilled in an occupation as well as knowledgeable of the specific work performed at a company. OJT, however, was rarely used as a service or funding option for supported employees in part because VR permitted the funding of only one service at a time for an individual. Thus, if OJT funds were given to a business to train an employee, the provider would not be able to receive funding for providing consultation to the business. The NHNSP emphasized that even if a business is reimbursed for training a supported employee, most businesses need consultation in order to be able to do so successfully.

On the basis of the results of the project, the VR office revised its policies to permit the simultaneous reimbursement of businesses for training costs through the OJT program and the funding of supported employment agencies to provide consultation. VR stipulated that the amount of funds allocated for both of these services should not exceed the amount that would have been paid for either service for the individual.

Activity 3: A Natural Supports Funding Package Was Devised and Field-Tested

One of the most important lessons learned through the NHNSP was how critical the career planning and job search phases were to the success of supported employees trained by their co-workers. Providers in New Hampshire are typically limited to billing for 32 hours for IJA. Through IJA a provider both assists a supported employee in identifing the type of career or job he or she would like to pursue and in locating a job in that career area at a business that is willing to hire, train, and support him or her. Because of this limited funding, providers often must simply place individuals into jobs with high numbers of openings (e.g., cleaning). VR is more liberal in its reimbursement to providers for training activities after the supported employee is placed in a job. This funding policy, in combination with the limited career planning and job search funding, further functions to encourage providers to make quick placements into whatever job happens to be available.

The NHNSP assisted VR in developing a new supported employment funding package designed to encourage providers to do the careful planning and job search needed to increase supported employees' access to quality careers and co-worker training and support. All of the components of the package were aimed at encouraging staff to devote more time and effort to career planning and job search activities, in order to decrease the need for job coaching and ongoing support and, as a result, increase the likelihood of long-term job retention. The Natural Supports Service Package increased the number of hours that providers could be paid for career planning and job searches and decreased the number for job coaching or employment consulting. Specific guidelines were established that required providers to use a career planning process that focused not just on existing skills but also on an individual's interest, talents, and capacities. In addition, the new guidelines did not permit job searches outside of the career goal identified by the supported employee, and it required providers to analyze the willingness and capacity of a business to train and support the potential employee. Finally, the guidelines required providers to gain prior approval from counselors for placing a person at businesses at which provider staff would be expected to take primary responsibility for training the supported employee.

Activity 4: Medicaid Rules Were Revised to Encourage Natural Supports

New Hampshire's supported employment Medicaid waiver program had emphasized skill assessment and job coaching. A staff member at the Division of Mental Health and Developmental Services took the lead in guiding a stakeholder task force in rewriting supported employment rules to emphasize natural supports. The division has also revised New Hampshire's Medicaid waiver day habilitation rules to deemphasize therapeutic services and to emphasize community integration, including work in community businesses.

FACTORS THAT ENHANCE
SYSTEMS CHANGE OR SERVE AS BARRIERS

The NHNSP used a multielement approach to contribute to the evolution of New Hampshire's employment service system from one that was professionally determined and specialized to one that is more customer determined and natural. Hopefully, this approach and specific activities undertaken by the project will be useful to other states and locales interested in devising plans to evolve their employment service systems. Advocates experienced in systems change efforts, however, understand that many factors influence the outcome of a particular effort and the effectiveness of specific strategies. A strategy that may be effective in one state or locale may be less so in a different state or locale. In this section, characteristics and factors that appear to have facilitated to change in New Hampshire's employment service system as well as those that served as barriers to this change are identified and discussed.

Factors that Enhanced Change

New Hampshire has a number of characteristics that positioned it well to evolve its system of employment of services for individuals with developmental disabilities. Key among these are a wide network of stakeholders who have a long history of commitment to community inclusion; leaders in key state agencies who are willing to try innovative approaches to achieving this outcome; and the small size of the state, which makes it relatively easy to widely disseminate training and technical assistance.

Local Stakeholders with a Long-Held Commitment to Community Inclusion   New Hampshire has led the nation in developing community services for individuals with disabilities. Through past efforts, there exists widespread commitment to community inclusion for individuals with disabilities. New Hampshire has had the good fortune to have state agency leaders with a clear vision of full community inclusion for all individuals with disabilities. In the state, families have taken the lead in advocating and being actively involved in community inclusion policy reform and service development. New Hampshire's employment service providers formed one of the first state chapters of the Association for Persons in Supported Employment. Each day provider and employment provider in the state offers supported employment services; few continue to maintain facility-based programs. The vast majority of school districts have active community-based employment training and experience programs for their high school students with severe disabilities, and some have made great strides toward including these students in general education classes and vocational programs. Finally, because of the fairly widespread implementation of supported employment in the state, many businesses have had the opportunity to employ individuals with significant disabilities. Thus, the project had a strong baseline of acceptance and inclusion on which to build. The task was not to convince most stakeholders that they needed to include individuals with disabilities in their communities but that the extent and quality of this inclusion should be expanded and that the means to achieve this outcome would require a different paradigm and different approach.

Through past systems change efforts, stakeholders have gained not only a commitment to community inclusion but also an understanding of the process of change and a degree of comfort with change. Change is not something that comes naturally to most people. Change is a behavior, and like other behaviors, the more experience you have doing it, the more comfortable it becomes to you and the more fluent you become at making change. Furthermore, when positive outcomes result from these change efforts, the more likely a person will be to engage in change again. New Hampshire's stakeholders have experienced the rewards of past change efforts, through both the improved quality of lives experienced by individuals with disabilities and the recognition of having created a system that is among the best in the nation.

Willingness of System Leaders to Innovate   The most important factor that determines how much a system (or organization) changes is perhaps the extent to which individuals in leadership positions have a clear vision of where the system should be headed, are willing to take risks, and encourage innovation by others. The proactive leadership of key staff members at VR was particularly important to the project's efforts. They partnered with the project and used its information and resources to influence VR policies and regulations as well as the practices of both counselors and providers. A staff member at the Division of Mental Health and Developmental Services took a leadership role in support of the natural supports paradigm and approaches. In addition to leading the revision of the supported employment and day habilitation program regulations, she has implemented a statewide tracking system that includes measures key to natural supports (e.g., quality of job, co-worker supports, social integration) and initiated a demonstration project aimed at increasing individual's access to ongoing employment consultation.

In addition to individuals who by nature of their positions are designated leaders, the emergence of others who were willing to take a leadership position was important to systems change efforts. It is critical that people involved in creating systems change attempt to identify, use, and reinforce similarly inclined individuals. Two VR counselors made particularly important contributions to our efforts. Both were willing to creatively and flexibly fund supports for project participants. Through these efforts and their many presentations at project training sessions and conferences, these two individuals encouraged other counselors to ask providers to use natural supports and to fund them to do so.

Size of State   Without question, the small size of New Hampshire eased the ability to influence systems change. Because of the relatively small geographical size, it was relatively easy for staff from around the state to attend training sessions held in a central locale and for project staff to routinely travel to communities to provide on-site training and technical assistance. It was also feasible for project staff to have frequent contact with providers because of the small number of high schools and employment programs in New Hampshire (reflecting the small state population, including those with significant disabilities).

Factors that Served as Barriers

New Hampshire faces many of the same challenges that other states face in attempting to continue to evolve its employment services for individuals with developmental disabilities. These challenges include overcoming a tendency to become complacent after an initial period of innovation, especially as the changes that may be needed become less dramatic and more subtle.

Complacency   We have suggested that New Hampshire's history of service system innovation served to facilitate efforts to continue to evolve employment services that are self-determined and natural. At the same time, this history may also serve as a barrier to systems change. "Resting on one's laurels" is a phenomenon common for organizations and systems that have had a vision, have put much effort into achieving the vision, and have been successful in doing so. This phenomenon may result for a number of reasons. First, individuals who expended much emotional and physical energy on making change may simply need to rest and reenergize before feeling prepared to make additional changes. Second, systems or organizations that have achieved a status of "one of the best" may have little motivation to try to become even better. Finally, stakeholders may recognize that significant time and effort need to continue to be devoted to change to achieve the desired outcomes, and they may implicitly or explicitly wonder, "Is the effort really worth the return?" During the early years of supported employment, there existed the expectation that once the model was accepted and implemented by agencies, most individuals with severe disabilities would be employed. The reality is that reaching this vision is much more difficult and complicated than once hoped. Motivating and enabling agencies to close their facilities is a greater challenge than originally presumed. In addition, at a very practical level, assisting many individuals with significant disabilities to obtain and maintain jobs will always be a challenge. During the initial years of supported employment, most individuals targeted for assistance experienced mild disabilities. Much success was experienced with relative ease. As more efforts have been made to assist individuals with more significant disabilities, the challenge has greatly increased. One reaction that is not surprising is to begin to question the feasibility of the original vision of community employment for all individuals and the value of it, given the effort required.

The challenge of complacency is not unique to New Hampshire and, in fact, may be generalized to the national supported employment movement. Many supported employment advocates have devoted a great deal of effort to achieving significant changes in a relatively short span of time. Hopefully, the late 1990s have provided the opportunity for advocates to fully enjoy what has been achieved and to reenergize. Ideally, this time has also allowed them to recommit to the original vision and to commit to a new vision based on a new paradigm that recognizes the real willingness and capacity of businesses to hire, train, and support individuals with disabilities.

Subtlety of Changes   Systems change is always challenging. Change, however, is easier to achieve when there is a fairly clear difference between what is and what should be than when that difference is more subtle—although not less important. The differences between living in an institution and living in the community are easily understood. The differences between spending one's days in a sheltered program and working in a typical business and the differences between the relative benefits of each are also clear to most people. The differences between a job coach method and a natural supports approach are more subtle. It is a challenge to help staff and others to understand these differences and how they contribute to the outcomes achieved (e.g., quality of employment, success of an individual on the job, cost of services).

CONCLUSIONS

Employment services (as well as other services) are at a critical juncture. The voices of those who doubted that it was possible or appropriate for most individuals with severe disabilities to work in community environments are once again beginning to be heard. In addition, some individuals who have been strong advocates of supported employment are now beginning to waiver and question whether community-based employment is feasible for all individuals, especially those with the most severe disabilities. There also exist individuals who have not been a part of the evolution of services and who are suggesting "new" approaches such as forming businesses that will employ groups of individuals with disabilities (i.e., sheltered workshops). Finally, the trend toward managed care presents the possibility that individuals with disabilities will once again be grouped together and "warehoused" as a means to reduce costs.

On the positive side, the growing recognition that supported employment approaches have fallen short of their original goals provides the opportunity for stakeholders to continue to evolve these approaches to achieve the original hope and promise of supported employment. Some advocates have suggested that natural supports is simply another set of supported employment strategies that can be used along with the existing approaches (Kregel, 1994). In fact, many providers and funding agency staff seem to view natural supports as another model on the continuum of employment services. In 1988, however, Taylor provided a powerful description of the pitfalls of conceptualizing services as a continuum. As suggested previously, natural supports is not simply another set of supported employment tools but rather is a new paradigm of services and supports. This paradigm derives from a moral and philosophical belief that services (including service funds) should be controlled by supported employees and their personal networks. It also reflects an understanding that access to the full range of supports and to quality services will only occur when supported employees and their personal networks are in control. In addition, the new paradigm is based on an understanding that full community and workplace inclusion of individuals with severe disabilities cannot be achieved as long as services and supports are viewed as programs. In essence, through supported employment individuals have moved out of the workshop into community environments, and the program, staff, and training strategies have simply moved with them. Natural supports implies that stakeholders must start with the community and workplace and the supports that are there. The role of supported employment staff is to support the managers and co-workers in these workplaces so that they may most successfully fulfill their natural role.

The new support paradigm implies a need for significant changes in the structure and organization of adult services employment and school-to-work systems, including policies; regulations; funding mechanisms; and the roles of service coordinators, vocational rehabilitation counselors, and supported employment and school programs staff. The 21st century holds the potential for great strides in significantly increasing the number of individuals with severe disabilities who are employed and earn a wage that enables them to move out of poverty. This original supported employment promise will only be fulfilled if advocates are willing to fully embrace this new paradigm.

REFERENCES

Agosta, J., Brown, L., & Melda, K. (1993, April). *Job coaching in supported employment: Present conditions and emerging direction. National survey results: Data summaries.* Salem, OR: Human Services Research Institute.

Americans with Disabilities Act (ADA) of 1990, PL 101-336, 42 U.S.C. §§ 12101 *et seq.*

Bellamy, T., & Melia, R. (1991). Investing in people: Launching supported employment on a crowded public agenda (Part 2). *Journal of Disability Policy Studies, 2*(1), 19–38.

Bolles, R. (1994). *A practical manual for job hunters and career changers: The 1994 what color is your parachute?* Berkeley, CA: Ten Speed Press.

Buckley, J., Albin, J.M., & Mank, D.M. (1988). Competency-based staff training for supported employment. In G.T. Bellamy, L.E. Rhodes, D.M. Mank, & J.M. Albin (Eds.), *Supported employment: A community implementation guide* (pp. 229–245). Baltimore: Paul H. Brookes Publishing Co.

Butterworth, J., Hagner, D., Heikkinen, Ferris, S., Demello, S., & McDonough, K. (1995). *Whole-life planning: A guide for organizers and facilitators.* Boston: Children's Hospital.

Certo, N., Pumpian, I., Fisher, D., Storey, K., & Smalley, K. (1997). Focusing on the point of transition. *Education and Treatment of Children, 20*(1), 68–84.

Cotton, P., & Sowers, J. (1996). *Choice through knowledge: Knowledge = power. A model for empowerment through education.* Durham: University of New Hampshire, Institute on Disability.

Curl, R., McConaughy, E., Pawley, J., & Salzberg, C. (1987). *Put that person to work! A co-worker training manual for the co-worker transition model.* Logan: Utah State University, Developmental Center for Handicapped Persons.

Ellis, W., Rusch, F., Tu, J., & McCaughrin, W. (1990). Supported employment in Illinois. In F. Rusch (Ed.), *Supported employment: Models, methods, and issues* (pp. 31–44). Sycamore, IL: Sycamore Publishing Company.

Everson, J. (1991). Supported employment personnel: An assessment of their self-reported training needs, educational backgrounds, and previous employment experiences. *Journal of The Association for Persons with Severe Handicaps, 16*(3), 140–145.

Fabian, E.S., Luecking, R.G., & Tilson, G.P.J. (1994). *A working relationship: The job development specialist's guide to successful partnerships with business.* Baltimore: Paul H. Brookes Publishing Co.

Ford, L., Dineen, J., & Hall, I. (1984). Is there life after placement? *Education and Training of the Mentally Retarded, 19,* 291–296.

Foss, G., & Peterson, S. (1981). Social-interpersonal skills relevant to job tenure for mentally retarded adults. *Mental Retardation, 19,* 103–106.

Greenspan, S., & Shoultz, B. (1981). Why mentally retarded adults lose their jobs: Social competence as a factor in work adjustment. *Applied Research in Mental Retardation, 2,* 23–48.

Hagner, D., & Dileo, D. (1993). *Workplace culture, supported employment and people with disabilities.* Cambridge, MA: Brookline.

Kregel, J. (1994, Fall). Natural supports and the job coach: An unnecessary dichotomy. *RRTC Newsletter,* 1–6.

Kregel, J., Hill, M., & Banks, P. (1988). An analysis of employment specialist intervention time in supported competitive employment. *American Journal on Mental Retardation, 93,* 200–208.

Kregel, J., Wehman, P., Revell, G., & Hill, M. (1990). Supported employment in Virginia. In F. Rusch (Ed.), *Supported employment: Models, methods, and issues* (pp. 15–30). Sycamore, IL: Sycamore Publishing Company.

LeRoy, B., & Hartley-Malivuk, T. (1991, April–June). Supported employment staff training model. *Journal of Rehabilitation,* 51–54.

Mank, D. (1994). The underachievement of supported employment: A call for reinvestment. *Journal of Disability Policy Studies, 5*(2), 1–24.

McDonnell, J., Hardman, M., & Hightower, J. (1989). Employment preparation of high school students with severe handicaps. *Mental Retardation, 27,* 395–405.

McGaughey, M., Kiernan, W., McNally, L., Gilmore, D., & Keith, G. (1995). Beyond the workshop: National trends in integrated and segregated day and employment services. *Journal of The Association for Persons with Severe Handicaps, 20*(4), 270–285.

Moseley, C.R. (1988). Job satisfaction research: Implications for supported employment. *Journal of The Association for Persons with Severe Handicaps, 13,* 211–219.

Mount, B. (1997). *Finding directions for change using personal futures planning: A sourcebook of values, ideas, and methods.* New York: Graphic Futures, Inc.

Murphy, S., & Rogan, P. (1994). *Developing natural supports in the workplace: A practitioner's guide.* St. Augustine, FL: Training Resource Network, Inc.

Murphy, S.T., & Rogan, P.M. (1995). *Closing the shop: Conversion from sheltered to integrated work.* Baltimore: Paul H. Brookes Publishing Co.

New Hampshire Division of Mental Health and Developmental Services. (1997). *Results of supported employment survey.* Concord: Author.

Nisbet, J., & Hagner, D. (1988). Natural supports in the workplace: A reexamination of supported employment. *Journal of The Association for Persons with Severe Handicaps, 13*(4), 260–267.

O'Brien, J. (1987). A guide to life-style planning: Using *The Activities Catalog* to integrate services and natural support systems. In B. Wilcox & G.T. Bellamy (Eds.), *A comprehensive guide to* The Activities Catalog (pp. 175–189). Baltimore: Paul H. Brookes Publishing Co.

Powers, L., & Sowers, J. (1994). Evolving perspectives on transition to adult living: Promoting self-determination and natural supports. In S. Calculator & C. Jorgensen (Eds.), *Providing communication supports to students with severe disabilities in regular classrooms* (pp. 214–258). San Diego: Singular Press.

Pumpian, I., Fisher, D., Certo, N., & Smalley, K. (1997). Changing jobs: An essential part of career development. *Mental Retardation, 35,* 39–48.

Rusch, F., & Mithaug, D. (1980). *Vocational training for mentally retarded adults: A behavior analytic approach.* Champaign, IL: Research Press.

School-to-Work Opportunities Act (SWOA) of 1994, PL 103-239, 20 U.S.C.§§ 6101 *et seq.*

Shafer, M., Banks, D., & Kregel, J. (1991). Employment retention and career movement among individuals with mental retardation. *Mental Retardation, 29,* 103–110.

Sowers, J., Cotton, P., & Malloy, J. (1994). Expanding the job and career options for people with significant disabilities. *Developmental Disabilities Bulletin, 22,* 53–62.

Sowers, J., Cotton, P., & Nisbet, J. (1997). *Naturally supported employment: Quality practices and indicators.* Durham: University of New Hampshire, Institute on Disability.

Sowers, J., & Powers, L. (1994). *Access and barriers to supported employment for people with severe physical disabilities.* Durham: University of New Hampshire, Institute on Disability.

Sowers, J., Thompson, L., & Connis, R. (1979). The food service vocational training program. In T. Bellamy, G. O'Connor, & O. Karan (Eds.), *Vocational rehabilitation of severely handicapped persons: Contemporary service strategies* (pp. 181–206). Baltimore: University Park Press.

Taylor, S.J. (1988). Caught in the continuum: A critical analysis of the principle of the least restrictive environment. *The Journal of The Association for Persons with Severe Handicaps, 13*(1), 41–53.

Trach, J. (1990). Supported employment program characteristics. In F. Rusch (Ed.), *Supported employment: Models, methods, and issues* (pp. 65–86). Sycamore, IL: Sycamore Publishing Company.

U.S. Department of Education. (1985). *Special projects and demonstrations for providing supported employment services to individuals with the most severe disabilities and technical assistance project* (CFDA #84.128). Washington, DC: Author.

Virginia Commonwealth University, Rehabilitation Research and Training Center. (1994). [National supported employment longitudinal survey data]. Unpublished raw data.

Wehman, P. (1981). *Competitive employment: New horizons for severely disabled individuals.* Baltimore: Paul H. Brookes Publishing Co.

Wehman, P., & Kregel, J. (1995). At the crossroads: Supported employment a decade later. *Journal of The Association for Persons with Severe Handicaps, 20*(4), 286–299.

Wehman, P., & Moon, S. (1988). *Vocational rehabilitation and supported employment.* Baltimore: Paul H. Brookes Publishing Co.

West, M., Revell, G., & Wehman, P. (1992). Achievement and challenges (Part I): A five-year report on consumer and systems outcomes from the supported employment initiative. *Journal of The Association for Persons with Severe Handicaps, 17*(24), 227–235.

9

Consumer and Family Leadership

The Power to Create Positive Futures

Mary Schuh and Beth Dixon

With each new birth, families begin to dream and hope for the future of their child as well as for the future of the world. A child born with a disability has the potential to suspend those hopes and dreams in the hustle and bustle of the practical decision making of everyday life. But do those dreams disappear forever? Does the child's impact on the world go unnoticed? How are families and individuals with disabilities capturing their hopes and dreams and moving toward positive futures? Through leadership-building experiences and the discovery of a vision of disability rooted in high expectations and positive dreams of making a lasting impact on the culture in which we live, families and individuals with disabilities are taking their rightful places as contributing citizens in a global society. As political activists, community organizers, and leaders in general and human services organizations, individuals with disabilities and their families are beginning to equalize the attitudes and perceptions of society to a competency-based definition of disability—one tied to expectations and contributions rather than to human impairment and pity.

Lessons learned from suffragists demanding women's right to vote, leaders of the civil rights movement demanding equality among the races, and the workers of the labor union movement demanding fair pay and working conditions are being applied by today's disability rights activists. Individuals who share the same struggles and are provided with the necessary support and information to dream of a positive future for themselves and their counterparts are the most effective change agents in local and national political systems. There is no truer evidence of this than stories behind the New Hampshire Leadership Series.

Beginnings—Beth Dixon

In 1988, I was invited to participate in the Institute on Disability's (IOD) first Leadership Series. At that time, I had never heard of the IOD and couldn't imagine why I had been nominated to participate. My qualifications, I assumed, were my four children—including my 5-year-old son who had disabilities. At that time, life was hectic. I was very busy trying to be everywhere I needed to be—doctors' offices; therapy visits; four different schools in Concord; my own business; and, yes, even occasionally home. After my husband convinced me that the world could go on without me for a few days, I made a commitment to attend the sessions at the University of New Hampshire. Those days dramatically changed my life.

As I entered the conference room on that first day of the Leadership Series, I was nervous and not at all sure what I was doing there. The session began with introductions, and I felt that many of the participants were a lot more knowledgeable about the issues than I was. I remember introducing myself as "just a parent," but before long, I learned there is no such thing as "just" anything.

I quickly discovered that the parents in this room shared many of my fears. We had faced similar struggles, and we shared a common desire to make the lives of our children the best that they could be. Unfortunately, we had no idea what the best was or how to make it happen. We hadn't yet learned that it was okay to create visions for our children that were more typical than special. At the same time, most of us felt that what our children were getting was not good enough. We felt as if we were just settling for what professionals told us was possible. We hadn't yet dared to dream.

That was the beginning of the very first New Hampshire Leadership Series. The goal of that series, as for all subsequent series, was to empower families and individuals with disabilities with knowledge and skills, create camaraderie, and change systems that support individuals with disabilities. Thirty-three parents were selected to attend that first series—nominated by representatives from their regions of the state for their leadership potential. Throughout the series we heard from professionals, adults with disabilities, and other parents who had achieved positive outcomes for their sons and daughters. We received the latest and best information in the areas of education, positive behavioral

approaches, family support, employment, housing, community organiz-
ing, negotiation skills, and the legislative process. My head began to
swirl with all of this new information.

The presenters were inspirational, but what was most valuable to
me—and to most of us—was what we learned from each other. We lis-
tened to each others' stories and cried each others' tears. A bond formed
that is impossible to describe. To this day, we all know that when sup-
port is needed—in a small way, such as brainstorming ideas on the tele-
phone, or on a larger scale, such as organizing a letter-writing cam-
paign, attending a legislative hearing, or testifying at a school board
meeting—we can count on each other to be there.

The Leadership Series helped me rediscover the ability to dream
and provided me with the strategies to make those dreams come true.
My dream—to have my son's life be both typical and extraordinary—has
come true. Andrew now attends a general education fifth-grade class,
goes to the local Boys and Girls Club after school and during the sum-
mer, has friends, goes to parties, and loves life. This is in direct contrast
to the future that had been predicted for him. For too long I had heard
about all of the things that Andrew couldn't, wouldn't, and shouldn't
ever do. Leadership helped me to focus on all of the things he would,
could, and probably wanted to do. It taught me to look for the positives
instead of the negatives, for his strengths and not his weaknesses. It
taught me the meaning of the word typical *and to believe in the phrase*
"only as special as necessary." It helped me change my son's life.

The Leadership Series also changed my life. I now work with the
IOD and have coordinated all of the Leadership Series since 1990. Each
year I am impressed with the new group's determination and creativity
to make the world a better place for their children and for themselves. I
have learned that change doesn't ever happen quickly or without strug-
gle, but it is well worth the energy and time it takes. I have also learned
that bringing people together makes any struggle much easier. Most
important, I have learned that having a vision is the first step to chang-
ing the world.

LEADERSHIP DEVELOPMENT AND THE DISABILITY MOVEMENT

During the 1990s, leadership training has gained increasing popularity in many
states as an innovative and successful approach to creating positive futures for
people with disabilities and their families. This approach assumes that family
members and individuals with disabilities, when given vital information about
exemplary practices in disability issues, can gain the power necessary to create
important, sustainable change. Through leadership training, family members
and individuals with disabilities are recognized as key change agents and supported to assume these roles. This support includes the following: information

delivered from leaders in the field of disability and community inclusion, child care, respite care, personal care attendants, overnight accommodations, meals, and travel expenses throughout the leadership training event.

Modeled after Minnesota's Partners in Policymaking leadership training, the New Hampshire Leadership Series was developed in 1988 to assist individuals with disabilities and family members to create a vision for themselves and to achieve positive futures. Since 1988, the IOD, in collaboration with the Developmental Disabilities Council, People First, the New Hampshire Division of Mental Health and Developmental Services, the state's Department of Education, and other organizations, has sponsored 10 Leadership Series for individuals with disabilities and their families. The series continues to undergo revisions and expansions to reflect the everchanging issues faced by individuals with disabilities and their families. But certain themes of the series have remained constant: the importance of belonging in fully inclusive communities; providing resources to families; supporting family choices, such as community-based child care and early education; full-time participation in neighborhood schools and typical classes; naturally supported employment; and homeownership. This chapter, based on our experiences and conversations with Leadership Series graduates, provides a comprehensive understanding of the New Hampshire Leadership Series as well as the steps necessary for replication.

LEADERSHIP SERIES IN NEW HAMPSHIRE

"Leadership gave me a vision of a positive future for my child; it gave me the self-confidence to dream and design my own vision and the...skills to make my dreams a reality!"

*—1989 Leadership Series
graduate and parent of a young
child with significant disabilities*

New Hampshire has achieved national recognition in the 1990s for its innovative approaches to supporting people with disabilities and their families within their communities. Opportunities such as attendance in general education classes in neighborhood schools, homeownership, employment, family support, and access to quality health care and assistive technology are becoming increasingly typical experiences for individuals with disabilities and their family members.

New Hampshire, however, was not always able to boast of such accomplishments. Substantial change has taken place during the late 1990s. Many of these changes are a direct result of the work of the more than 300 parents and adults with disabilities who have graduated from the New Hampshire Leadership Series.

These leaders have a clear vision for themselves and their family members with disabilities and knowledge of state-of-the-art supports for individuals with disabilities. They are skilled in advocating with service providers, using the legislative process to achieve change, and organizing communities to support inclusion. Families and individuals with disabilities are using their combined strength and determination to change laws, persuade schools and businesses to include individuals with disabilities, and educate all people in the community about the importance of welcoming and including every member. Many of them serve on school boards, on family support teams and councils, in local and state governments, on community boards, and so forth. When asked about their entrance into these leadership positions, many graduates have pointed to attending a New Hampshire Leadership Series as a pivotal moment in their lives. As one 1994 Leadership Series graduate put it, "To make a change and a difference, you have to put your expectations very high and work toward them. [The Leadership Series] taught us that nothing is impossible!"

OUTCOMES OF THE LEADERSHIP SERIES

The effectiveness of the Leadership Series in New Hampshire and of similar efforts in other states has confirmed what many had known all along—that the best way to create positive change is to educate those individuals most directly affected by laws, policies, supports, and services for people with disabilities. By bringing together individuals who share the same struggles and providing information on exemplary practices and strategies to organize for change, family members and individuals with disabilities gain the necessary advocacy skills and confidence to influence policies and change systems. Who better to advocate for quality inclusive lives for people with disabilities than these people themselves? Which voices have more credibility to policy makers and service providers than the voices of those who are affected by the policies and individuals who use the services? A 1992 Leadership Series graduate with a disability noted, "Parents and people with disabilities have all the power. Unless they make their wishes known, the system will not change."

Leadership Series graduates have affected change at many different public and private levels. At the state level, two bills were passed into law by the New Hampshire legislature in 1989 with full funding support: a family support bill and a bill to reduce the waiting list for adult services. To affect this change, graduates from the first Leadership Series organized telephone networks, invited legislators into their homes, and testified in large numbers at public hearings. Following passage of the family support legislation, which created family support councils throughout the state, 80% of Leadership Series participants have served on their local councils. Several parent groups led by Leadership Series graduates have sprung up around the state and many participants have become involved in parent and support organizations at the local and state level. Undoubtedly, the Leadership Series has been a catalyst for change in tangible and profound ways. As one graduate of the first series remarked, "To me, the most important thought I am leaving Leadership with is that I'm allowed to dream of a great life for my son. So many times I've been told to be realistic, be practical, get real. I almost cheated [him] out of the kind of life he deserves. My child is not broken. He doesn't need to be fixed."

CREATING A CAPACITY FOR LEADERSHIP

The concept behind leadership development is straightforward. By removing individuals from their daily responsibilities and immersing them in state-of-the-art information about recommended practices and strategies to achieve those practices in a relaxed and comfortable environment, individuals are able to return to their daily lives with a commitment to affect change in minor and magnificent ways. In New Hampshire, parents and individuals with disabilities leave their daily routines behind for a total of 14 days, seven 2-day sessions over the course of 8 months. To help establish the right context and to free participants from the worries of everyday life, participants are provided with good food, fine accommodations, and all necessary travel and child care expenses. Hotel facilities are selected for the series based on their accessibility to individuals with disabilities, their ability to accommodate a large group, the quality of their food, and the courtesy of service. Because a portion of the series involves meeting with state legislators, a location that is within easy driving distance to the state capital communicates to participants a greater accessibility to their state leaders.

During each session, national, international, and state leaders as well as local policy makers share with participants the latest information about achieving the vision of quality lives for individuals with disabilities and their families. Participants receive empty binders organized by sessions and topics into which they can insert the reading material distributed during each session. At the end of the first session, everyone receives a T-shirt with the leadership logo and an inspirational quote. Photograph collages of individuals, families, and significant events are displayed throughout the facility. Fieldwork assignments are distributed during each session to provide a focus within families and local communities. During each session, time is scheduled for participant updates. Sharing in one another's struggles and successes creates interest, commitment, and a strong bond among participants. As a 1994 graduate stated, "The most valuable aspect of Leadership for me was the chance to meet, talk, and share experiences with others at the conference, from parents, to people with disabilities, to presenters."

Selection of Participants

Leadership Series participants are selected through a rigorous process of nomination and application. The process begins with a nomination in writing.

Nominations come from self-advocacy organizations; developmental service agencies (called *area agencies* in New Hampshire); parent groups, family members, independent living centers, friends, acquaintances, teachers, principals, or other people, such as neighbors.

Nominees receive a letter of introduction and an application form. The form asks questions about the applicant's family, experiences, community involvement, and special interests. Taking time out of a hectic schedule to complete and return the application form is often a difficult first step for the applicant. Individuals who need assistance in completing the application are provided with whatever support is necessary (e.g., telephone assistance, personal interview) to apply.

To promote cohesion among the group, space is limited to 30–40 participants. Usually more applications are received than can be accepted. A committee of approximately seven people reviews the applications and makes the difficult decisions of acceptance or denial. The committee consists of past Leadership Series graduates, policy makers, representatives from parent organizations, and members of disability advocacy organizations. Decisions are based on the applicants' commitment to attend all of the sessions; demonstrated leadership potential; and diversity of background, geographical location, age of family member with a disability, and disabilities represented. The Leadership Series works best when participants represent a diverse cross-section of the state. The application process is deliberately selective to reinforce the notion that participants represent a select group of individuals with an important mission.

Individuals who are not selected receive information about other upcoming training events and are encouraged to apply again the following year. Applicants who are selected return a signed confirmation form and contract and receive information about the financial reimbursement process. Participants are expected to make arrangements for travel, vacation time, child care, personal care attendants, and overnight lodging at the conference site. All of these expenses are reimbursed by the Leadership Series. Participants who reside in the same geographical region are given each other's names and addresses in case they wish to travel together.

Education by Current Leaders

"The most valuable aspect of Leadership for me was meeting people who were distinguished by their decency [and] meeting people with disabilities—something that just isn't part of the rest of my life."

—1993 Leadership Series
graduate and parent of a young child

Presenters for the Leadership Series represent a blend of leaders from the fields of self-advocacy, education, employment, community living, assistive technology, family support, negotiation skills, the legislative process, and community organizing. Presenters use a variety of interactive strategies such as role playing, cooperative learning, and small-group discussion to involve participants in the learning process.

Leaders selected to present and facilitate groups during each session of the Leadership Series come from a variety of backgrounds with a common thread woven among them. This common thread is the belief that all people, regardless of their differences, belong in all aspects of local communities. Expectations of presenters include the following: the delivery of current information through a variety of interactive formats, the use of person-first language, and the ability to set an example of high expectations and achievement of dreams for individuals with disabilities and their families. Often, presenters are selected based on recommendations from other people involved in leadership development for individuals with disabilities and their families.

The Leadership Series Begins

> *"The enthusiasm and energy of the presenters was infectious. The variety of approaches to communication and strategies to effect change were valuable tools. I leave Leadership with a big bag of tricks to improve the quality of life for me and my family."*
>
> *—1995 Leadership Series graduate and parent of a young adult with disabilities*

Leadership Series participants travel many roads to arrive for the first day of each session. As they walk in the door, they are welcomed with coffee, pastries, fruit, and warm smiles from the organizers. After a state policy maker gives a welcome address, the coordinator opens the day and asks the participants to introduce themselves briefly. Everyone wears a name tag and nervous smile. A sense of anticipation fills the room. Each participant brings different expectations, different backgrounds and experiences, and different needs to the series. Yet all share an as-yet unspoken desire to develop the most positive futures for themselves and their children. Following these brief introductions, participants are asked to talk about their vision for themselves, their children, and their families and their recent experiences. Each session begins with these family updates.

As the series progresses, the atmosphere quickly changes from the nervousness of the first gathering to one of camaraderie. Warm greetings are exchanged. Everyone is on a first-name basis. The room is alive with conversation. Eventually, participants settle in, and the family updates begin. Unlike the brief introductions of the first day, a stopwatch is needed to keep updates to the 3-minute time limit. Some participants find that in just a short period of time, many changes have taken place in their lives. Some stories leave the audience laughing. Others bring tears. The room is charged with an electrifying energy as each story unfolds—a child's accomplishments, a stressful meeting to advocate a move from a segregated to an inclusive environment, a connection made with other people in a community.

Following personal updates, participants listen to a panel of Leadership Series graduates who share how Leadership has made a difference in their own lives. For many participants this is the highlight of the Leadership Series. Participants lean forward in their chairs and question the speakers closely as they relate their stories. Three representative stories are presented here.

Leigh, a mother of three young children, attended Leadership shortly after her son Peter was born, and she had developed a strong commitment never to allow him to be segregated from his peers or society. From the beginning, Peter participated in family and community events. He entered child care at age 2 and began in a typical preschool at age 3. The message Leigh gives the participants is clear—go for inclusion right from the start!

Kathy and Tom share amusing stories of their large, blended family and discuss how their daughter, Heather, had been educated in a segregated environment. These two parents move the participants with the story of how they succeeded in getting Heather enrolled in her neighborhood school. They read the letter they wrote to the superintendent, principal, and school board members that described why Heather deserved to be a part of the same school system as her brothers and sisters. This powerful testimony and the support from family and educators allowed Heather to be welcomed as a full-time student in her local school.

Joseph Bauer never fails to inspire the participants of the Leadership Series. While other stories bring laughter, cheers, and hope, Joseph's story is one of segregation and disillusionment as he talks about his son, Joe Jr., who spent his school years in institutions and segregated classes ("18 years of kindergarten," as Joseph put it). Joseph's story clearly illustrates the need to remember the history of people with disabilities and helps listeners vow to never let outdated ideas return. Joseph closes with this admonition: "If we as parents can't see capacity, gifts, strengths, talents and abilities, *no one else will!*"

Developing the Dream

"Between the knowledge and the friendship, it's a great experience. The information learned, the friendships made, and the feeling of power is amazing!"
—A Leadership Series participant

A large portion of the series consists of workshops conducted by state, national, and international leaders. Nationally known speakers such as Tom Powell or Jeff Strully, both parents of children with disabilities, and Patrick Worth or Norman Kunc, self-advocates, lead participants through exercises to set the vision for their children and themselves. Discussion centers around people's involvement with friends and family in ordinary places doing every-day things. What are your dreams for your child? What are your dreams for yourself? What are your dreams for the future? Jeff Strully recommended that participants "dream about unlimited possibilities. If you can reach it and touch it quickly, it's not big enough!"

At some Leadership Series sessions, Jeff Strully relates the story of two teenagers. The first teenager is a young woman with many gifts and talents whose life is filled with joy and friendship and whose future is filled with hope and excitement. A very different story emerges as he speaks of the second teenager. He talks about the many labels this woman has been given. He men-tions all she cannot and will never do. He paints a picture of a young woman with a dreary future. When the story ends, an audible gasp escapes from the audience. Jeff, in fact, is describing the same person. There is only one young woman, his daughter Shawntell. Who she is depends on how he—and others—see her. Jeff's message is clear. If participants view themselves or their chil-dren in light of their limitations, the rest of the world will view them in the same way. Participants must see their gifts or their children's gifts and make certain that others do too. Participants keep this story in mind throughout the series as they describe themselves or their children as people with abilities and gifts to share.

Patrick Worth's personal story of segregation and abandonment teaches participants that belonging is important to each person and that the differences among us must be celebrated as integral components of a complete commu-nity. Patrick shares from his firsthand experience that the most serious dis-ability is loneliness and ostracism from a society that values perfection. Patrick explains the strategies he has found effective for gaining power and control over his life to achieve his dream of belonging.

The American Dream is a name we give to the ideal all of us want to achieve. Tom Powell, a Leadership Series presenter, reminds participants that this dream—a good job, a happy and healthy family, a nice place to live—is part of our American culture. Why, he asks, is it denied to his son Nick and to so many other Americans simply because they have a disability? To drive home his point, Tom tells the story of his son's "career" in a sheltered workshop and of the struggle to find Nick a decent job and place to live. With anecdotes and humor, he puts into words the thoughts and feelings many participants share: that each person deserves the right to achieve the American Dream. He gives participants strategies to achieve this dream for themselves and their families. One by one, participants come forward with their visions, and together the group discusses how these visions can become a reality.

Combining personal experience with professional expertise, Norman Kunc expresses his views on disability, belonging, and diversity in a powerful and dynamic way. He challenges participants to think about the messages that are received by children and adults with disabilities. What message does segregation give to people about their worth in society? Does therapy and remedial education teach people to value their gifts and abilities? Isn't it natural that people who are taught to dislike their differences wind up disliking themselves? These difficult questions spark earnest discussion among participants. Norman's paraphrase of the old axiom, "Actions speak louder than words," assists the participants in committing themselves to take concrete action to reach the goals they have set. At one Leadership series session, he explained, "by including everyone without regard to ability or disability, students can learn through experience that belonging is a right, not a privilege that must be earned."

At the end of each day, participants enjoy a casual dinner. The environment is informal, and participants linger over coffee and exchange stories. Most participants stay overnight at the conference site—some staying away from their children or family for the first time. Getting away from the everyday hassles and commitments of family life gives participants time to take a breath and mull over what they are hearing and how it relates to their own lives.

Occasionally a presenter will hold an evening session, and work continues far into the night. Homework is assigned at the end of the second day of each session. For the first homework assignment, participants are asked to develop a vision for their child, their family, or themselves. Each assignment following the first session builds on that vision and the steps necessary for achievement.

Recommended Practices and Participant Fieldwork

"The 'Home of Your Own' session really changed my mindset for my daughter. I realized that she could have a home if she desires and that she doesn't have to be part of the group home experience."

—1989 Leadership Series
graduate and parent of a young adult

With more sessions, formalities among participants disappear. The room is no longer a room of strangers but a gathering of colleagues drawn together by a sense of purpose. Throughout the weeks and months ahead, telephone calls are exchanged, information is read and reread, letters are written, and changes are begun.

The major focus of the final few sessions of the series is on giving participants up-to-date information on practices and ideas that have an impact on the lives of individuals with disabilities. Presenters from across the state and

country address the Leadership Series participants and provide the most current information on recommended practices and the how-to's for making
participants' dreams into realities. Topics include education, friendships,
recreation, assistive technology and communication, positive behavioral
approaches, employment, living/homeownership options, and family support.
Some presenters are from the IOD, and it is fortunate to have several IOD staff
members who are actively working on training, demonstration, and other projects in these areas. Other speakers are brought in based on their expertise in a
particular area. The three-ring binders begin to fill with resource materials and
handouts on each subject area.

Fieldwork assignments continue to be a focus for participants between
each session of the Leadership Series. Participants use these assignments as an
opportunity to work to achieve their vision and develop supportive connections throughout the state and in local communities.

Advocacy and Policy Change

An important aspect of leadership development is understanding how laws and
policies are formulated and influenced. This process is a major focus of one of
the final sessions, titled "Changing Laws to Create a Positive Future for All."
Allan Bergman of the United Cerebral Palsy Association brings his experience
with the legislative process and communicating with policy makers to the
Leadership Series. He explains how a bill is introduced and the path it travels
to become a law. Participants receive information on testifying before a legislative committee, developing a telephone tree, establishing letter-writing
campaigns, and influencing legislators. One series graduate, an adult with a
disability, mentioned the need for this knowledge: "More people should be
educated about the accessibility of our legislators and that affecting change at
the state level is not out of our hands."

New Hampshire legislators are invited to the New Hampshire State House
for a round-table discussion sponsored by the Leadership Series. Small groups
of four to five participants give presentations on topics of interest to them, such
as inclusion in schools, health care reform, and fair housing. Legislators circu-
late among the groups giving feedback on presentation content and style.
Participants learn by seeing issues from the legislators' point of view and get
answers to questions such as "What do legislators need to hear from constituents?" "What are the next steps?" and "How do constituents best educate
their legislators?" More important, legislators receive information and opinions
from their constituents on a variety of "hot" topics, including the greatest areas
of need for people with disabilities, priorities, how the stumbling blocks toward
positive change can be removed, and what statewide supports can be provided
to create positive futures for all New Hampshire citizens. After the round-table
discussions, one series participant said, "Having attended the legislative ses-

sion, I am absolutely sure my actions will change. I intend to be a truly informed person—not only for personal concerns but also for community education. My intention is to be known as a contact—one who knows!"

For the final topic of the series, called "With a Vision and a Voice," several national speakers present on community organizing strategies and negotiation skills. Greg Galluzzo from the Gamaliel Foundation, Rich Male and Dan Lopp from the Community Resource Center of Colorado, or members from the national organization American Disabled for Attendant Programs Today share their expertise. Through small-group exercises and role playing, participants gain skills in conflict resolution, practice negotiation tactics, and learn to handle adversity. The session ends on an exhilarating note with participants prepared to go back to their communities with new insights, a final homework assignment, and a sense of what can be accomplished with a vision and a voice. One series participant said, "The information regarding negotiations and community organizing was very valuable, not only applicable to negotiating with schools but to all facets of life."

Life After the Leadership Series

"Leadership lit my soul on fire. The laughter is back where it belongs—in my home with my family!"

*—1994 Leadership Series
graduate and parent of a young child*

Participants depart from the series exhausted, overloaded, and exhilarated. Strengthened by the stories and ideas they have heard and the support they feel from the group, each participant leaves the series with a shared commitment to live his or her dream. Addresses and telephone numbers are exchanged, and promises to stay in touch are made. A reunion is planned for all participants.

EVOLUTION OF THE NEW HAMPSHIRE LEADERSHIP SERIES

The Leadership Series is constantly evolving to meet new challenges. The curriculum is continually updated to meet the changing needs of individuals with disabilities and their family members. As more information is added, the series agenda has expanded, and the number of sessions have increased. Additions to the list of topic areas include the history of self-advocacy and the parent movement, skills to facilitate a meeting, issues of independent living, and the impact of assistive technology. Some of these additions reflect an increasing emphasis on the participation of adults with disabilities in the series, whereas the earlier series participants were primarily parents. People with disabilities as well as their family members now are strongly encouraged to submit applications for the series. In addition, people with disabilities are featured speakers, core leaders and session facilitators.

> *"I have seen people blossom here. I have watched anger turn into action and people learn about ways to affect change in a constructive way. If the people that go through Leadership can't have an effect on New Hampshire policies and practices than I'm not sure what group can."*
>
> —*A Leadership Series graduate*

> *"Before Leadership I had all the pieces, but I didn't have the overall structure. I felt like the pawn [in chess]. Someone else was controlling all the action. Now, I'm the queen of the board!"*
>
> —*A Leadership Series graduate*

LEADERS TELL THEIR STORIES

The stories of people whose lives have dramatically changed as a result of their participation in the Leadership Series provide the inspiration to the series planners to continue and improve on the series. Such stories are the heart and soul of the Leadership Series and inspire and motivate new participants each year so that new stories of leadership continue to unfold.

The stories that follow are based on interviews with Leadership Series graduates. The stories illustrate the impact of vision and education first on families—on how parents see their children and on how different decisions result from different beliefs. The stories also illustrate the impact the graduates of the Leadership Series have had on the systems, policies, and practices of the state—on how students with disabilities are educated, how adults with disabilities are living and working in communities, and how families are supported. These stories and the information presented in this chapter can be a source of inspiration and motivation for others to create positive change through leadership development.

Dare to Dream

Toni Sweedler was the first to admit that she had no expectations of what she would learn from the Leadership Series. "At that point in my life, I was drained of all energy—physically and emotionally. The system had me baffled, bitter, and empty. My self-esteem was in the basement, and I had lost all sight of what I wanted for my son. When I got accepted to Leadership I thought that maybe I would learn some small thing that would help me feel more in control," she said.

Toni said that what happened to her at the Leadership Series was "just short of miraculous." She said that she discovered "new-found dreams, ideas, and challenges" and explained, "I no longer viewed my son as a burden or someone to apologize for. I learned that it was okay to love him for all of the wonderful things he has to offer—wonderful things I had lost sight of because I had been so busy trying to fix all of the broken parts."

Toni's son Caleb is now 15. Toni quipped that she is now in the "enviable" position of being the mother of three adolescents. "With two sisters in the house, life can be quite overwhelming if you're a boy and you want to get into the bathroom," Toni laughed. "But Caleb approaches it like any boy his age—he yells and bangs on the door! His sisters treat him very much like they would treat anyone—they yell back, get mad, and slam doors!"

Toni wasn't always so calm and accepting in dealing with her family. "For a long time, I had the feeling that things were just not right. I had so many questions about so many hard issues like inclusion, socialization, emerging adolescence, and the future," Toni recounted. "Before I attended the Leadership Series, I didn't know which way to go. I was at the point of reassessing my life—I was asking myself some tough questions about my son, my attitudes regarding my son, and other people's attitudes toward Caleb. I had a lot of questions, but I just couldn't seem to find the answers."

Toni attended the Leadership Series in 1990, and she stated, quite emphatically, that it changed her life. She went with burning questions and left with a clearer understanding of how to find answers. She reflected, "I think the biggest thing I learned was that I did know what I wanted for Caleb—it was exactly the same thing that I wanted for all of my children. And once I realized that I knew what was best, I became confident that I could make things happen." For too long Toni had assumed that professionals "knew best" and that she had to go along with whatever they recommended. After the Leadership Series, Toni said, "I became more sure of myself. I stopped apologizing and began to speak my mind. And to my surprise, as I spoke, the school district began to listen!"

Today, Caleb is a full-time student at his neighborhood school. He has lots of friends, has played on the football and basketball teams, and has challenged and changed everyone's ideas and expectations of him. "He is definitely a typical teenage boy," Toni said. "The only things he talks about are wanting to date and wanting to drive. He also spends a lot of time in front of the mirror fussing and primping to look his best, and that drives his sisters crazy. As you can imagine, there is never a dull moment in our house!" Toni laughed.

Now that things are going well for Caleb, Toni has turned her attention to her community and the state. "Leadership gave me a unique perspective of the larger picture," said Toni. "I have found that getting Caleb included has paved the way for other children in our district to return to their neighborhood schools." Toni stated that the school's principal has embraced the philosophy of inclusion and is always encouraging her to include Caleb in activities that she hadn't even thought about.

Toni is extremely community minded and has incorporated her philosophy of inclusion into all facets of her community involvement. She served for 3 years on the local school board and was able to influence the board to make major policy and educational changes. "It's now a given that kids go into regular education classes. Teachers and staff are beginning to see that there really isn't that much difference between education for kids with and without disabilities," said Toni. As a director of the local fair, Toni saw to it that all fair buildings were accessible and that there were parking spots and restrooms adapted for people with disabilities. In addition, she writes a column in a weekly newspaper and is committed to making sure that issues regarding people with developmental disabilities are always written about respectfully.

Her involvement does not stop at the community level. Toni participated in New Hampshire's Medicaid waiver study by interviewing a number of people in the state. She purchased a computer and has become an avid letter writer—expressing her strong opinions to state legislators and policy makers. Toni is making her voice heard around the state.

Toni continues to make her mark in her community and the state, but she is proudest of her ability to "make things happen" for her son. Toni said, "Leadership taught me that it's okay for parents to advocate for their children." Throughout Leadership Series sessions, Toni listened and spoke to many parents who had achieved positive outcomes for their families. Many of these parents "spoke of the balance of knowing when to push and when to pull back—but never backing down on what you know is right," Toni remembered. "After Leadership, I went home and timidly tried out my new skills on my special education director. I told her what I wanted, and to my surprise she said 'yes.' Leadership taught me that I'm important, and I count—and my kid is okay, too!

"The Leadership Series," Toni continued, "was one of the most exciting and important things that has happened for me. I think Leadership should be renamed 'Dare to Dream' because that is what it made me do—I had forgotten how."

Proving Them Wrong

Shana Greely's story is best told in her own words. "My name is Shana Greely. I used to live at Laconia State School. I went there when I was 4 years old. I left when I was 27.

"They called that place a school, but they didn't teach me much. I went to school there for 23½ years. Conditions were bad. It was a terrible place to live and grow up. The first place I lived was called Keyes Two. There were 125 beds on that ward. It was very noisy at night. I can remember being very scared. All of the residents were bigger than me. I was only 4 years old. Residents didn't always keep their clothes on, and sometimes they messed on the floor. It smelled bad, and I was embarrassed. People hit me while I lived there. People were always getting hurt at the state school.

"At Laconia I didn't learn to read. They said I couldn't do it. They didn't want to show me how to tell time. They said I wasn't smart enough. They didn't want to teach me anything. What kind of school doesn't teach you anything?

"When I left Laconia 16 years ago, I had never mailed a letter. I couldn't make change from a dollar. I never had a checking account or paid bills. I couldn't cook or do laundry.

"Most of what I know today I have learned since I left the state school. When I first left Laconia, I went to live in a group home. It was better than the state school, but it was still like a prison. The difference was you could stay up past 9 o'clock. You had to stay in your room but you didn't have to go to bed. How many 27-year-olds have to go to their room at 9 o'clock? They did have classes at the group home. I learned to read and make change.

"Then I went to a shared home. I lived with very nice people, but I didn't learn all that much. After that I went to a supervised apartment. Everywhere I lived there were too many rules to follow. Rules that most people don't have to follow.

"Now I have my own apartment. Last summer I planted my very first vegetable garden. I wrote a letter to my landlord to get permission. I bought the seeds I needed to grow vegetable with my own money. I have a job as an office receptionist. I attend adult education classes. I have a clothesline and a gas grill. I have a checking account and pay my own bills. I take organ lessons. I do photography as a hobby. I have my own friends. I am learning how to be a good home cook. I learn new recipes all the time. I stay up past 9 o'clock.

"New Hampshire Leadership helped me to advocate for my own rights and help other people feel they belong in the community like everyone else. But there is still more to be done. I still want to be able to choose my own services. I don't want some agency choosing for me. I made a lot of progress in my life. Most of the progress I've made was on my own.

"Here is what people need: They need control over their services. They need transportation. They need to go to regular schools. They need more opportunities and less agencies. The agencies are growing, not people with disabilities. The money should go to the people. Let people decide how to spend the money. All my life I heard people tell me I can't do things. All of my life I have been proving them wrong."

It's a Whole New World

Janet Williamson has three sons. Her eldest, Jeff, is 22 and is one of the first students with severe disabilities to graduate from high school in New Hampshire. Jeff graduated from West High School in 1992 and now works at a health care center. Jeff enjoys his job, takes aerobics classes at the YMCA, and successfully manages the people who provide assistance to him at home and on the job. Janet Williamson is a strong, determined, and loving mother who takes none of Jeff's accomplishments for granted. She now plays an active part in seeing that her son (and the sons and daughters of all parents) get what they need and what they deserve.

Beginning in 1989, the Williamsons went through 3 years of due process hearings (involving three appeals by the school district) to get Jeff included in his neighborhood school. This lengthy, painful, and frustrating process was unfortunately necessary for Jeff to achieve his rightful place in society. "I never wanted a fight," said Janet, "but once I knew what I wanted for Jeff, I wasn't going to stop trying until I got it." Deciding what she wanted for Jeff was a direct result of her participation in the very first Leadership Series in 1988. "Before Leadership, I knew Jeff needed and deserved more, but I just wasn't sure what was best. I went to the Leadership Series hoping it would give me some ideas on what Jeff's education should be like. I thought maybe I'd get a few suggestions and maybe be able to make a few changes," said Janet. What she soon discovered was that her participation in the Leadership Series would change her life.

Janet, who now works for the IOD's Technology Partnership Project, is an extremely strong advocate of parental involvement in education. Janet said that as a result of attending the Leadership Series, "I have learned that when children are young, parents must be in charge of the way services are provided for their children—the professionals should not be calling the shots. Of course as your son or daughter grows older, he or she then needs to be in control." Janet tells parents to "have a vision for your child and to work with the school system to achieve that vision." Now that her son is an adult, she noted that "Jeff and I work together to get a clear picture of what he wants and how he'll get there."

Janet said that Jeff's life has changed as a result of her participation in the Leadership Series. "Jeff has grown and blossomed in the last few years. He used to be an angry and self-abusive teenager, and now people describe him as loving, sociable, and friendly. Jeff talks more, looks taller, and is hard-working and eager to learn. He has a great deal of pride in himself and in what he does.

Janet doesn't dwell on the difficulty she had in coming to an agreement with the school district about Jeff's education. She was quick to point out that because of Jeff, "our school district is no longer totally segregated. Slowly, they are including more and more children in their neighborhood schools." Janet is proud of her family's efforts to have Jeff attend high school and hopes that they have made it easier for other parents to achieve full inclusion for their children.

Janet's advocating change does not stop with Jeff. Janet has taken part in a number of panel presentations—addressing professionals and parents about her experiences about how she supports Jeff to reach his goals. Although still nervous about speaking in front of a group, Janet knows that her family's story can inspire others to create positive change for all people with disabilities. "During Leadership I learned from other parents how important inclusion is for all people," she said. Now, Janet feels that it is her turn to teach others.

Janet believes that parent education is essential to help parents achieve positive outcomes for their children. "Leadership has been critical to Jeff's success, and I believe this training should be available to all families," Janet said emphatically. Carefully choosing her words, she added, "Every professional in our life has some type of degree and access to ongoing training, yet parents, who live with the outcomes of every decision, often remain in the dark." Janet said that thanks to the New Hampshire Leadership Series, she now understands the system. "I believe that the more parents know, the less time and money is wasted on decisions made by people who do not know the family or the child."

Janet describes the series' impact as profound. "It gave me confidence and strength in my beliefs," she said, smiling, "and I've begun dreaming again. The effect of Leadership is very difficult to put into words, but all of the graduates I know have made dramatic changes in their children's lives and in the way professionals treat parents. It's a whole new world for the young children in New Hampshire, and a lot of it has to do with the Leadership Series."

The Sky Is the Limit

If ever there was an example of a popular teenager, it is Jocelyn Curtin. She has many friends and is involved in countless school and after-school activities. Included in general education for the past 5 years ("And every year gets better," said her mother, Marlyn), Jocelyn is now in ninth grade. Marlyn credited the New Hampshire Leadership Series with "allowing me to dare to dream and plan for my daughter's future. Now I know the possibilities for Jocelyn just don't stop!"

Marlyn reeled off a list of Jocelyn's interests and activities: "She's joined the Girl Scouts, has gone to the Boys and Girls Club, spent a week at an environmental camp with her class, spends the summer doing fun things with her friends, takes horseback riding lessons, goes on the city Park and Recreation trips." At this point, Marlyn interrupted herself to emphasize that Jocelyn goes on these trips with her friends, not with a paid assistant. Then, she proudly continued the list: "This year, at the request of a friend, she joined CCD class at the local church and was able to make her First Communion. Early next year she's going to be a junior bridesmaid in a wedding—the bride is her friend first, a family friend second."

All of this began after Marlyn attended the New Hampshire Leadership Series in 1988. "The series and its participants energized me. Immediately after the first session, I contacted the school to begin the process of fully including

Jocelyn," said Marlyn. Up to that point, Jocelyn, who has Rett syndrome, had attended a self-contained classroom for children with disabilities, and Marlyn had believed that was all Jocelyn could do. As Marlyn reflects on that time, she grew more pensive and said, "Before Leadership, I had incredibly low expectations for Jocelyn. I believed all of the professionals who told me that Jocelyn would never succeed in the real world." Marlyn continued, "At that time, my biggest hope for Jocelyn was that someday she might be able to live in a group home! That was as high as I dared to dream. Now, I know that the sky is the limit! Jocelyn can do and be anything she wants. Recently, her friends were talking about where they would live in the future, and they thought that Jocelyn would want to live in her own apartment with her friends. I agree!"

Marlyn's life is just as busy as Jocelyn's, and she says that Leadership was the "giant stepping stone" to her involvement in local and state politics. Marlyn keeps up-to-date on all school and legislative issues and has testified at numerous public hearings on issues of family support and education. She has served on the local family support council and is currently working with the New Hampshire Parent-to-Parent network, offering support and information to parents in the Concord area. To keep the flow of current information going, Marlyn started a statewide Rett syndrome support network. She is passionate about inclusive summer experiences for children and works with the local school district and area agency to ensure that everyone can have these opportunities. Marlyn has become one of the strongest forces in the state on the issue of friendships between people with and without disabilities and is frequently asked to speak on this topic. Marlyn is certainly no stranger to struggle but views life in a very positive fashion. "Everything takes effort," she said, "but I look at problems as challenges instead of obstacles."

In recounting the high expectations she now has for Jocelyn, Marlyn remembered a conference many years ago. "I can remember listening to parents describe how their kids with disabilities attended regular classes. I thought, this is great for other kids, but it would never work for Jocelyn. I thought that Jocelyn was 'much too disabled' to have the kind of life these parents were talking about." The Leadership Series, she said, "showed me a picture of a positive future for my daughter, and gave me permission to dream." Most important, Marlyn said, "it gave me the self-confidence, resources, and support to make my dreams come true."

The Tapestry of Life

Sandy Whipple is the mother of two talented daughters, Erin and Amanda. As a college student in the late 1970s, Sandy worked at a state institution, and she said she "witnessed, firsthand, man's inhumanity toward man." She said she knows deep in her heart that "we must never allow even one human being to return from where we have come."

Sandy attended Leadership Series sessions in 1990. It was part of her quest for the best possible life for her daughter. Sandy said, "Thanks to what I learned from the speakers and participants at Leadership, Erin is now a full-time student at her neighborhood middle school and is well established in the academic and social realms of her life." Sandy said she views the experiences and contacts she made at the Leadership Series as "a kind of bank account or insurance policy to be tapped when and if necessary. On more than one occasion, the contacts I made at Leadership provided me with the information and support necessary to get through the day a little easier."

When asked to speak of the impact that the Leadership Series had on her family's life, Sandy mentioned Erin's remarkable achievements. These are possible, she said, thanks to the Leadership Series, which "gave me the knowledge and the skills to do what I always knew was right." Here is, in her own words, what Sandy said about her daughter and the New Hampshire Leadership Series:

"Erin recently played hostess to seven friends at her birthday party. She takes saxophone lessons, has participated in three school plays, and loves animals. Her dream is to become a veterinarian's assistant and live on a huge farm. She will be going to her first boy–girl dance this fall. She is very confident and self-assured and has a very sophisticated sense of humor. She also happens to have a label of mental retardation, with attention-deficit/hyperactivity disorder, speech-language impairment, fine and gross motor delays, and visual/perceptual problems.

"Erin spent 4 years in a segregated, out-of-district placement. I knew in my heart that this wasn't right and that she needed to be with lots of different kids. When she was younger she had been in a typical play group, and she loved it. So, I slowly began to get myself educated. I attended Leadership and heard about this 'novel' idea of kids with disabilities going to school in regular classrooms with their peers. Immediately, I knew I could make this happen for Erin. After gathering as much information as I could to support myself, I approached the principal of our neighborhood school, requesting that Erin be enrolled in this school. Much to my surprise, the principal agreed wholeheartedly. The rest, so they say, is history.

"Erin is a pioneer of sorts, as she is the first student with severe disabilities who has been 'returned' to our neighborhood school." Her success has paved the way for others to return to regular classrooms with their peers. Her courage, strength, determination and spirit are inspirational to many.

"There is so much to say about Erin. She is living proof that once the imposed barriers, limitations, and lowered expectations are removed, the human spirit knows no bounds. I have no doubt that she will accomplish much in her life. Perhaps her greatest gift has already been realized—she has helped many to see more clearly the intricately woven tapestry of life."

Just as Erin is a pioneer, so too is Sandy, who is an outspoken and busy advocate for inclusion. Last year, she spoke at the New Hampshire Family Support Conference. Feeling that "words don't always do justice to some situations," Sandy made a videotape to tell the story about inclusion at Erin's school. The videotape was very well received, and she has since shown it to her school board, other school districts, and the board of a local private preschool. Most important, Sandy's videotape is shown to all parents and children entering Erin's school.

Sandy is the newly elected co-president of the school's parent–teacher association (PTA). High on the group's list of priorities this year is updating the school's playground—and Sandy will make sure that it will be "safe, fun, and accessible." Sandy admitted that though she exposes Erin to many different things, she is like most other parents when it comes to letting go. She takes special pride in knowing that both of her daughters are compassionate and caring people and hopes that they will grow to appreciate differences in everyone. Sandy says, "I know that Leadership made a difference in my life, and every time I look at Erin, I can see the difference it made in her life."

From Disillusionment to Determination

Hearing Joseph Bauer tell his story is at once overwhelming and inspiring. Joseph and his wife, Gloryann, exhausted the services in two states before moving to New Hampshire and finding what they wanted for their son, Joe Jr.

The Bauers raised their two daughters and one son in a neighboring state. Joseph explained, "We had become disillusioned with the resources that were available for Joe there. Joe's early experiences preceded the federal 'right to education' laws and he spent his educational career in segregated classes in church basements and other hidden-away places. When he was 18, we said, 'enough of crayons and coloring books,' and...pulled him out of school. For all intents and purposes, Joe went from what amounted to kindergarten to a sheltered workshop."

Joseph said, "We found out quickly that the term *sheltered workshop* glosses over the reality of what it is—total segregation and the daily death of the soul." He goes on with his family's story about selling their home and most of their possessions and moving out west, where, through a close family friend, they had located what they thought would be "a marvelous, empathetic service" for Joe. After 5 years there, he was still participating in a totally segregated day program. The Bauers acknowledged, "We became sadly disillusioned when we realized there was no future in this for Joe and had to face the fact that we had made a serious error." The Bauers' oldest daughter, Lizbeth, was living in New Hampshire and encouraged her parents to move near her. It was a move they initially regretted—until the Leadership Series came into their lives.

In New Hampshire, Joe enrolled in a day program and was later, as his father recalled, "promoted to a sheltered workshop." Joseph, ever an activist, knew something had to be done to improve the quality of what was being offered to his son. He became involved with local parents of adult sons and daughters with developmental disabilities and eventually formed a chapter of the New Hampshire Arc. That involvement led to his nomination for the first Leadership Series.

"The Leadership Series," Joseph said, "made me realize that I had allowed myself—and Joe—to be browbeaten by professionals in three different states. I realized that we had passively accepted the crusts and crumbs that the so-called experts had handed to us throughout the years."

As a result of Joseph's experiences in the Leadership Series, everything began to change. He says, "I realized that I was the one who needed the help to identify, develop, and support our son's positive attributes." Joseph's commitment grew throughout the Leadership Series sessions. He vowed that "no professional would ever again take over the planning and decision making in our son's life. We—Joe and the family—could and would be the ones to call the shots." Meeting with other parents and hearing their stories of determination and success "was more than encouraging," Joseph said. "The speakers and presenters at the Leadership Series were positive, encouraging, and dynamic. As a result, I became more meaningfully involved with other parents, both locally and at the state level." Joseph began presenting to legislative committees and public hearings. He organized telephone networks, took part in numerous letter-writing campaigns, and encouraged other parents to take a more active role.

Joe's life has changed as a result of his dad's participation in the Leadership Series. "Joe got his first job in 1989, working in a small bakery," says his father. "He has learned to make use of typical community services, including riding the bus back and forth to work." Joseph proudly recounts one particular story, "To get to work, Joe had to cross an intersection filled with cars. After his first solo trip across the street, he confidently flashed a thumbs up victory signal. I can't help but think that the drivers of those cars were completely unaware that the universe had just expanded a little bit right before their eyes."

Joseph Bauer is now a highly sought speaker—especially by young parents. He shares the knowledge and beliefs that he learned through the Leadership Series with others throughout the state. "Contrary to what many believe, parents can exert a very special kind of influence. Don't underestimate the power of parents and families," Joseph said. "We have contributions to make that are unique. If we allow ourselves to feel helpless, that is what we will become." Leadership, he said, "is the road to the kinds of hope and vision we all need." For the Bauer family, those roads crisscrossed the United States and led them to New Hampshire, where, with energy and determination, they created a whole new life for each family member.

Leadership Turned Our Lives Around

Linda Steir and her beautiful daughter, Marika, once flew halfway around the globe to lecture about full inclusion in seven cities in Japan. Linda believes this is just the tip of the iceberg as she embarks on a very fulfilling career as the family support coordinator for one of New Hampshire's regional agencies.

How did this come about? "Leadership," Linda said, without hesitation. "The series taught me that it was okay to expect a better, more typical education for my daughter. It taught me to feel more positive about having a child with a disability instead of feeling isolated and at the mercy of systems and the professionals who run the systems."

Linda took part in the Leadership Series when Marika was 3. "In my heart, I knew that I had to find out what was out there before I could start making choices about what would work or wouldn't work for my daughter," she said. Linda was aware of the work being done in the state around inclusive education, family support, and leadership development and wanted to learn more. "I had met other parents who took the Leadership Series, and they were confident advocates—secure in their roles as parents of children with disabilities. I wanted to share in the enthusiasm I saw them applying to their child and family."

"High expectations for Marika" was Linda's immediate response when asked what her family gained from her participation in the 1990 Leadership Series. "We now know that she can do and be anything she wants," says Linda. As a family support coordinator, Linda is asked to run local, regional, state, and national workshops about family support systems. Linda's 3-week trip to Japan, accompanied by representatives from the Division of Mental Heath and Developmental Services, helped people from Japan "understand why full inclusion is so important and effective. The lectures were intended to motivate the Japanese to work toward deinstitutionalization and community integration." One year after the lecture tour, Linda and Marika still get letters of appreciation from people whom they met in Japan.

"The Leadership Series," said Linda, "taught me to advocate for full inclusion." She knows, too, that an important part of teaching others is self-learning. "I have become assertive and proud in my community. I have earned the respect of my peers who do not have children with disabilities. My daughter has been photographed on numerous occasions for local papers in very positive, inclusive situations. I feel equal to my peers in the community."

Linda and her family traveled a difficult route to get to where they are today. Before the Leadership Series, Marika attended a self-contained, segregated preschool program for children with various disabilities. It took almost 2 years to get Marika included in a typical kindergarten, a struggle that Linda called "incredibly difficult and draining for me and for my entire family. We nearly abandoned the process several times, but our strength to be persistent came from the professionals and parents we had met during Leadership. Much of our courage and perseverance came from knowing people who shared our vision and supported our struggle."

Linda said that the struggle was worth it and talked about Marika, who is now in second grade, goes skiing, and attends summer camp. "We've learned that nothing is impossible for our daughter." The entire family advocates for people with disabilities, Linda says, including Marika's 8-year-old brother, "who scolds people who illegally park in handicap spots and who advocates for elderly people in need of additional supports and understanding." The family's "changed attitudes," Linda added, "have carried over to our extended family, whom we have taught to use respectful language when talking about people with disabilities. They now expect a lot more from their communities in terms of accessibility and employment of people with disabilities." Linda credits the "high expectations and vision we have for Marika" as the motivating forces for her family and others in the community.

Linda pointed out four reasons that she encourages others to become involved in Leadership. "Become part of the Leadership Series," she says, "if you want to know where or how to begin to feel good about the future of your child and family, if you've ever felt rejected by friends or schools or society, if you've ever been at a loss for where to turn to get information or support, and if you've ever wondered what you can do as one small voice to make an entire system change." The Leadership Series "taught us that we will never be alone or lonely," Linda said. "After 3 years of fear and isolation, the Leadership Series turned our lives around."

LEADERSHIP DEVELOPMENT AND SYSTEMS CHANGE

A number of factors emerge as identifiable elements of the role of leadership development in creating positive change not only in the lives of individuals with disabilities but also in the systems that offer or provide support. During the 1990s, the following elements have been most powerful in facilitating systems change:

1. Supporting people who share similar struggles to come together to exchange information and strategies for change has been crucial in successful change efforts. Similarities should be related to the nature of the struggle—not to age, geographic location, or disability label.
2. Encouraging an atmosphere that is conducive to collaboration, dreaming of positive futures, and shared problem solving has fostered systems change.

3. Providing resources to assist individuals in maintaining their basic needs without worry (e.g., child care or respite care, accommodations, meals, travel expenses) helps them dedicate their attention to systems change efforts.

4. Delivering the "latest and the greatest" information on recommended practices in the field of disability is important. One can only begin to dream about a positive future if one has knowledge of all that can be possible.

5. Maintaining a level of accountability for participation in leadership-building events, such as fieldwork assignments with ongoing checkpoints and technical assistance from recognized leaders in the field, is necessary during systems change.

6. Providing assistance in the development of personal change goals as well as systems change goals for participants involved in leadership development is needed.

7. Using the legislative process and community organizing strategies to create change is key to leadership development. These strategies must be delivered with an emphasis on skills for negotiation.

8. Telling personal stories is of utmost importance during collaboration for systems change. Never underestimate the power of personal stories to change hearts and minds. All efforts of leadership development and systems change are rooted in the lives of individuals. These stories are the supporting structure of any change strategy and the base from which leaders emerge.

Conclusions—Beth Dixon

Five years ago, my life changed in a very dramatic way. For the first time since my son Andrew was born, I was surrounded by people who allowed—no, inspired—me to think positively about the future. Acknowledging my role as a leader gave me the strength and the commitment to change my family's life, and the lives of people all over the state and the country.

The stories in this chapter reflect the personal journeys of graduates of the New Hampshire Leadership Series. Although each situation is unique, all of these stories profoundly illustrate the common themes of the Leadership Series—a dedication to the ideals of inclusion, the power of new-found skills, the confidence that comes from knowledge, and the celebration of the abilities of all people. Each story expresses, in its own way, the metamorphosis from vulnerability, acceptance, and frustration to power, leadership, and hope. The families represented in this chapter are but a handful of the many families who have become leaders in the area of personal and systems change.

The effects of the Leadership Series do not stop with the people who attended the Series. Each graduate has extended his or her energy, insight, and enthusiasm to others, and the reverberations are felt in homes, schools, and communities throughout New Hampshire and the country and as far away as Japan.

The outcomes of leadership development are many. In response to the requests of parent and consumer leaders, many neighborhood schools and general education classrooms have opened their doors to students with disabilities. Community organizations and school boards have invited graduates to speak about the values of inclusion. At the state level, graduates have successfully lobbied for the passage of several state bills designed to increase family support in New Hampshire, improve health and dental care for people with disabilities, and reduce waiting lists for services. For some graduates, careers have changed as a result of new skills and abilities, and an ever-growing commitment to the belief that all families must have the opportunity to create positive futures for their children has emerged.

Being involved with the Leadership Series has inspired me and many other parents to become effective advocates for change. But, for me, the most important changes came from within. The Leadership Series taught me to look at my son's life in a different light. I learned that it is more important to support Andrew for who he is than to work to "fix" his disabilities. I learned that special isn't always better and, in fact, that typical can be quite extraordinary. As I advocated for Andrew to be a member of a general education classroom (in the same school that all of my other children had attended), I learned that someone who thinks of him- or herself as "just a parent" is actually capable of just about anything.

My participation in the Leadership Series changed me, but it also changed each and every member of my family. Both of my daughters have written essays for their college applications that described their feelings about inclusion, acceptance, and the power of families. My youngest daughter, Sarah, wrote in her 1993 essay,

> *Over the years I have watched Andrew become a respected member of his school by just being himself. Andrew has taught me that it is normal to be different, and it's those differences that make us great. He has taught me that no one is perfect, but everyone is O.K. I have learned from Andrew to respect all people and that everyone, no matter how they look or act, has a right to their own opinions and feelings. Andrew has opened up my mind immensely.*

And that's just what leadership development is all about—opening our minds widely enough to see the future in a new way and giving us courage and confidence to recognize our role in shaping it. I hope that each family will grow to have, as mine has, a most wonderful vision for the future and a most celebrated appreciation for today.

10

Witnessing the Possible for People with Disabilities

Thomas M. Reischl

Allow me to stand with you for a moment. I, like you, have just finished reading the previous chapters of this volume, and I am both impressed and puzzled. I am impressed with the ambition, the vision, the courage, the perseverance, and the success at the core of each account. I am puzzled at how these authors made it look so easy.

At various points while reading the chapters, I paused and mulled over my suspicions that I wasn't getting the whole story. I expected more details of the conflicts and the disappointments. I expected more stories about inflexible administrators and contrary social values. One of the lessons I learned in graduate school while making my first forays into alternative social services was that resistance is inevitable and often reveals the systemic barriers to change. So, I was expecting to read about failures, how things went awry, and how this revealed the flaws in the various service systems in which these projects occurred. I expected more accounts that blamed the system.

I now suspect that the way the authors chose to tell their stories reflects how they did their work and that this approach may be the chief reason for their victories. In all of the accounts, there is an *expectation of success* and an *expectation of creative problem solving* when resistance is encountered. These are the same expectations that each project is working to instill in the individuals who play key roles in providing services to individuals with disabilities.

Whether the work is in classrooms, in employment sites, or in mortgage company board rooms, the message is clear: *Expect success, and expect to be creative to make it happen.*

Success, of course, historically has not been the expected outcome for individuals with disabilities. The industrial revolution transformed human communities into larger, more specialized social systems. Life has become so complicated that now it is useful to think of human communities as multiple, overarching, overlapping, and reciprocating social systems. At the higher levels of analysis, there are political systems (states, nations, international alliances), economic systems (businesses, banks, markets), and cultural systems (language, beliefs). At lower levels of analysis, there are interpersonal systems (families, neighborhoods, schools, service environments, work environments, recreation environments)—the places of our daily lives. In this complex matrix of overlapping systems, little energy has been devoted to ensure that individuals with disabilities are successful participants. In fact, considerable effort has been given to building social systems that segregate and exclude people with disabilities.

Participating in these complex social systems requires ever greater resources and skills from each of us. And we all require support systems to negotiate these challenges, including information systems, transportation systems, water purification and distribution systems, food distribution systems, and energy distribution systems, just to name a few. We participate in an economic system that requires us to pay as we go to gain access to many of these support systems. For most of us to pay, we must work and earn wages, which requires us to play a contributing role in one or more of these and other systems. And to participate in work, we all must participate and succeed in education and training systems that promote our skill development for effective performance in specialized work roles.

All of us experience frustration (and alienation) as these systems undergo continual change. Even when I was a young boy in the 1960s, adults would ask me what I wanted to be when I grew up. This would start a conversation about how a young person might anticipate entering the world of work. Today, I would find it almost ridiculous to ask a child what type of job they think they might have as an adult. The conversation would inevitably end with me saying (or at least thinking), "Don't count on that job being around in 20 years." I suspect that many of us believe that our current jobs won't exist even a few years from now.

Other systems that touch our lives are changing as well. We now use grocery stores in which many of the products are marked with scanning bars rather than price tags—does everyone know how much a loaf of bread costs today? Our medical service system is more likely to be a corporation rather than an individual provider. For my banking, I spend more time in front of an automated teller machine than in front of a human teller. Most of my communications at work are now conducted on e-mail rather than on the telephone or by "snail" mail. I am writing this chapter without using paper!

To understand the importance of the work described in this volume, we should all think about how difficult it can be to participate in the changing and complex social systems of modern communities. Now think about how those difficulties are amplified if you need assistance to participate. I recently received a letter from my home mortgage company and noticed they had misspelled my last name (a common error in my case) and had also made a few errors in our home address. Even though the postal system had successfully delivered the mail, I was concerned that at some point these errors might create problems for me. I called the bank that had approved the mortgage (which had been based in Indianapolis but had recently moved to Phoenix and then had been sold to another company altogether). I had to make several calls to find the person who could correct the errors. The discussion was difficult because of communication barriers, but in the end, I thought the problem had been fixed. I was wrong. It took another telephone call for the company to eventually correct its database. I wondered about the viability of a mortgage company that had such trouble keeping track of those who owed them money and of the property they owned. This system was ineffective in handling a relatively simple special request from one of its customers—a request that would help their system be more effective! The upside of this experience is that I am better able to appreciate the work described in Chapter 7 by Klein, Wilson, and Nelson about guiding people through the confusing world of real estate and home mortgages.

The chapters in this volume remind me of how changing and complex social systems typically react to any transaction that deviates from a very prescribed and uniform mode of operation. Think about what happens when a classroom teacher requires children to be quiet and pay attention during a lesson and a single child begins to talk or becomes distracted. Imagine what happens when a health care worker provides medical treatment to someone who communicates with American Sign Language. Think about how an employer assists someone with short-term memory loss in successfully participating in profitable work. Deviations from what is typical are often viewed as bothersome problems. The chapters in this volume help us understand these transactions as opportunities to learn not only about assisting people with disabilities but also about the values and the limiting parameters of our social systems.

What follows are a set of thoughts and reactions about each chapter in this book. I chose to write about this book by first thinking about the specific project descriptions in Chapters 3–9. Next, I provide my thoughts about Hagner's historical perspective in Chapter 2 and his thoughts about paradigms and paradigms shifts. Finally, I reflect on the "lessons learned" in Chapter 1 by Nisbet.

WITNESSING THE POSSIBLE

Witnessing is a word with multiple meanings. It refers to the acts of *telling* and *paying attention*. It is an individual act and a communal act. These acts are also reciprocal because we want to tell what we have seen. A good story is worth paying attention to and is worth telling over and over again. This book is an opportunity for all of these acts. The authors provide testimony about the victories they have witnessed. Their stories also testify to the fact that success breeds further success. Small wins lead to larger systems change because success is hard to ignore. We are attracted to success. We pay attention to success. We want to be part of it. And we feel compelled to bear witness to others, because these stories convey hope and a sense of the possible. Finally, success stories provoke us to expect more success.

One of the victories of this volume is that the readers become more engaged in the type of thinking illustrated by these authors. We witness creative problem solving and its successful outcomes and find it invigorating to try it ourselves. I also believe that this act of witnessing in itself is one of the contributing factors in the systems change described in these chapters. When the authors describe how their work changed a social system, this description often involves a story in which the authors have shared their language of expectation and their problem-solving skills with someone in the system who is in search of a different vision of the possibilities for individuals with disabilities. The guiding principles of the Community Options in Early Care and Education project described by Nelson, Zoellick, and Dillon in Chapter 3 bear witness to the expectations of success and creative problem solving:

- All children and families belong in communities.
- Supports and services should be only as special as necessary.
- Children with disabilities and families must be supported with a family-centered approach and a "whatever it takes" attitude on the part of providers.
- Solutions to problems in a given community lie with the people who live and work in that community.

For example, the early intervention (EI) staff described in Chapter 3 supported and encouraged 2-year-old Lucy's parents to explore ways to keep their daughter involved at the early childhood center in their community rather than place her in a child care center for children with special needs. The EI staff also worked directly with the staff at the early childhood center. In these personal encounters, a vision and a language are conveyed to those most immediately involved with Lucy (her parents and the center staff), and their expectations were changed by these encounters.

The personal accounts conveyed in Chapter 4 by Shapiro-Barnard, Sgambati, Dixon, and Nelson remind us how change agents themselves are transformed by bearing witness to change in their work environments and through their involvement with individual children and adults. A disillusioned student encounters an oppressive institutional service system and becomes a disillusioned teacher in segregated and institutionalized schools before taking on a professional role to transform public school classrooms into effective and inclusive environments. A parent is changed by the belief that her son's disability does not need to be "fixed" in order for him to succeed in typical school classrooms. A special educator recognizes the limits of segregated schooling and works with other teachers to institute inclusive classrooms. Finally, a general education classroom teacher's view of inclusive classrooms is transformed by a personal encounter with a single student and by her faith that her students will find a way to build a classroom community that includes all students.

Lovett's stories in Chapter 5 emphasize the importance of creative problem solving to help children with emotional problems succeed in inclusive public schools. His stories also remind us that being successful may require creative ways of defining the terms for success. For instance, the exclusive use of the standard of performing at grade level may be too rigid for judging the developmental progress of children who bring a variety of resource and learning needs to a classroom. Similarly, it is more effective to employ a variety of responses and teaching strategies with children when they act inappropriately. Finally, Lovett's stories emphasize the importance of support, especially support from school administrators.

Jorgensen and Tashie also emphasize the importance of support systems in Chapter 6, but they venture into an important set of reflections on their own interventions to support more inclusive practices in high schools and colleges. More than any other chapter in this volume, they examine critically their own role in changing the systems in which they work. Although school staff may be less interested in these reflections, these accounts are vital for anyone desiring to effectively support change in a service system. These stories help us acknowledge our own abilities to attend to individual needs, to the need for creative thinking about systems, and to the role that change agents such as the Institute on Disability play in the change process.

Klein, Wilson, and Nelson's chapter on promoting homeownership for individuals with disabilities (see Chapter 7) is striking for two reasons. First, the chapter opens with the bold claim about the way people with disabilities are coming to be supported to own homes and control personal assistance: "This change is not merely a shift or a shuffle but is a true metamorphosis.... It is a change that requires the debunking of myths, the reengineering of bureaucracies, and the rethinking of priorities and values." Yet, as bold as this claim is, as I read the accounts of the home purchases and the delight of the homeowners and their loved ones, I started thinking that the claim might be understated. Before reading these accounts, I would have found it very surprising to think about people with disabilities with limited financial assistance as being able to secure home mortgages and purchase their own homes. My own stereotypes were exposed and debunked in less than 10 minutes.

The second striking feature of these accounts of working with mortgage companies is that problems of exclusion and dependency often need to be addressed by changing the existing systems that regulate resource allocation. This type of intervention may be more successful in accomplishing the goal of homeownership than would attempts to change the functional living skills or wage earning potential or some other attributes of individuals with disabilities.

Assisting individuals to succeed on the job and to strive for economic self-sufficiency, however, is obviously a worthy objective. The multielement approach to systems change described by Sowers, Milliken, Cotton, Sousa, Dwyer, and Kouwenhoven in Chapter 8 provides a detailed map for anyone interested in changing a state employment system. Perhaps more than in any other chapter in this book, I felt I was missing the story of system resistance throughout this chapter. In the end, I learned that the employment system may have demonstrated the highest level of openness to change. In hindsight, I probably should not be surprised by this openness. Assisting people to move from receiving public assistance and being unemployed to being gainfully employed in the private sector has been the one of most important public policy goals of the 1990s, and a tremendous amount of innovation has occurred in the name of this goal. To the credit of those involved in this work, the success described in the chapter was probably the result of a clear vision of the type of changes needed to support individuals with disabilities in work environments.

Finally, Schuh and Dixon's accounts of the New Hampshire Leadership Series in Chapter 9 illustrate how the potential of individuals with disabilities and their families can be nurtured and unleashed to create a sense of empowerment and increase political engagement. But this intervention was not just about teaching people how to be better advocates. This intervention created a community of more than 400 activists, which became a network of support and advocacy for and by people with disabilities who have a powerful voice in the highest levels of state government as well as in local school districts and regional service agencies.

Each chapter is full of stories of victories. Some of the victories may seem small, as they concern a single student or a single homeowner (although the positive impact for those individuals is certainly huge). It is important, however, to recognize the radiating impact of each victory as they change our expectations for what is possible for people with disabilities. Likewise, this entire body of work provides a broad vision for a new way for service providers to act on the behalf of individuals with disabilities. Hagner's discussion of paradigms in Chapter 2 sets us up to expect this vision, but to fully understand the importance of Hagner's chapter, the reader should probably reread and reconsider it after reading the other chapters. I did just this, and what follows are my reactions and thoughts about what it takes to truly pre-scribe or adopt a fundamentally new way of providing social services.

PARADIGMS AND PARADOXES

After rereading Chapter 2, I am still sorting out what it means to move from a programs paradigm to a supports paradigm. Hagner asserts that the work described in this volume embraces the ideology of the supports paradigm, including the principles of inclusion; self-determination; natural supports from an individual's peers, co-workers, and family members; individual life goals; and community membership. I am not altogether sure that I agree with Hagner's assessment, or perhaps I don't fully understand it because my mind-set is still stuck in a programs paradigm. After reading each chapter, I find myself attaching the word *program* to each body of work. They look like pro-grams to me, with paid, professionally trained staff. The staff worked in offices and had telephones, photocopying machines, and so forth. The programs had official names and used the IOD at the University of New Hampshire as an institutional base.

At the same time, the authors of the chapters in this book seem to make a conscious effort not to write about their work as programs. This effort has important symbolic meaning—that the people seeking to implement systems change do not want to position themselves at the heart of the service system. They prefer to position themselves within the system but to the side, where they can provide technical assistance or support services. It is interesting to note that these authors seem to be modeling how they hope existing service systems will act in relationship to the people who receive services: Stand to the side and provide assistance. This means that service providers must adopt a different role in relation the individuals whom they serve. In fact the words *provider* and *recipient* seem archaic under a supports paradigm. Ideally, under a supports paradigm, the target group will be empowered to direct their own support services.

I can't help but think, though, that there is a great public need for the type of work described in this volume. It seems to me that we need *programs* like the ones described in this volume, in which thoughtful individuals with pro-fessional experience in service systems take a critical perspective on these sys-tems and provide a vision for alternative approaches.

To think that a public policy based on the supports paradigm could exist only on its own ideals would be a mistake. In fact, at least some risk exists that promoting a supports paradigm approach to services will lead to policy deci-sions that reduce funding for services because the target group is thought to be autonomous and no longer in need of services. We have already seen this type of rhetoric in the wake of the deinstitutionalization movement because funds for community support services have been easy targets for budget reductions. For a supports paradigm to flourish, professionally trained and experienced

staff will still need to work with (and sometimes on the behalf of) individuals
with disabilities.

My puzzlement is very similar to the dilemma discussed by Rappaport
(1981) even as he invoked the word *empowerment* as an alternative public policy goal to the more prevalent goal of prevention in the field of community
psychology. Although he argued for a symbolic ideology grounded in the principle that professionals' work should enhance the possibilities for people to
control their own lives, he worried about people who

> Push for "freedoms" and "rights," including the right to be different to the
> point of missing the freedom to be the same as others, to obtain help, edu-
> cation, or services. Having rights but no resources and no services available
> is a cruel joke.... This position easily becomes one of "benign neglect."
> (1981, p. 13)

Rappaport placed himself in the rhetorically awkward position of *acknowledging the self-determination rights* of people who have historically been
excluded from the privileges of ordinary citizenship while at the same time
promoting a symbolic ideology so that professionals can more effectively
serve the needs of these same people. How can he have it both ways?

The interesting feature of Rappaport's (1981) argument is that he seemed
most comfortable teetering on the fulcrum of this rights versus needs dialec-
tic. He argued that most social/community problems (such as the unjust exclusion of some individuals) are paradoxical in nature. Acknowledging that both
policy goals—rights and needs—are valid in spite of their divergent implications, Rappaport claimed that the paradoxical perspective is the most authentic. The authentic professional role, then, is the following:

> Look for paradox.... Once discovered, we will often find that one side or the
> other has been ignored and its opposite emphasized.... That is the under-
> standing part. The action part of our job is then to confront the discovered
> paradoxes by pushing them in the ignored direction. To take this seriously
> means that those who are interested in social change must never allow them-
> selves the privilege of being in the majority, else they run the risk of losing
> their grasp of the paradox. That is one reason why social change is not an end
> product but rather a process. (p. 3)

Another implication of embracing paradox as an authentic activity for the
professional change agent is that it forces us to engage in divergent thinking
and to seek multiple, possibly contradictory solutions. If finding a single solution to social problems becomes the exclusive approach, this solution soon
becomes our next "problem."

Hagner's historical analysis in Chapter 2 suggests that the field of disability has undergone at least two major paradigm shifts in only a few decades.
I believe that Rappaport (1981) would approve of the critical stance of those
doing the paradigm shift work described in this volume because the prevailing

programs paradigm fails to adequately address the rights of individuals with disabilities to be valued and empowered participants in our communities. At the same time, Rappaport might worry that as the champions of this innovative work promote the promise of a new paradigm, these change agents may fail to recognize the need for multiple solutions. If the supports paradigm is ever fully embraced in the same way the facilities and the programs paradigm have been, we should expect to see problems. We only need to look at the ways we critique the prevailing paradigms to predict what problems might occur. One of the ways we critique the prevailing methods of doing business is to examine critically the assumptions at the core of these activities. Seidman (1983) provided a template for engaging in this type of critical thinking.

UNEXAMINED PREMISES OF SOCIAL PROBLEM SOLVING
Systemic reasons cause service systems to conform to a prevailing mode of operation. Most of these reasons are rarely exposed in the actual service provision or openly revealed to either the service providers or the service recipients. I believe that Seidman's (1983) thoughts on how the definitions of social problems are conceptualized and addressed help us better understand why service systems behave the way they do. By "unpacking" these often unexamined determinants of social problem-solving processes, we are in a better position to understand how prevailing service paradigms are shaped and transformed by broader systemic forces. These determinants can be grouped into four kinds: mindscapes, the spirit of the times, dominant societal values and traditions, and stakeholders.

Mindscapes
The term *mindscapes* refers to the broad ways in which individuals think—the ways they reason, plan, make decisions, and so forth. In the human services field, as in most human enterprises, participants think, talk, and write in prescribed ways. Paradigms are built on mindscapes. A paradigm is identified by the way its proponents define and talk about the problem of interest and the methods for solving the problem.

A paradigm also can be identified by virtue that it attracts and controls the allocation of resources for solving the problem. A paradigm is not just an approach to a social problem, it is also the discourse of power. For instance, when we have the opportunity to review grant proposals, we expect to see a particular way of thinking about the problem (a request for funding) and the approach to solving it (denying or allocating funds). These ways of thinking represent the prevailing mindscape. For instance, we expect to see valid deductive and inductive arguments. We expect to see the conventions of expository writing (sentences, paragraphs, spelling, grammar) and of language use (use of jargon common to the field). If we read proposals or reports that fail to follow these conventions, we conclude that the authors are unqualified or "don't get it." Even if we are open to different forms of thinking and discourse, we think that the ideas are doomed unless the authors either find someone to teach them to "do it right" or find someone to "do it for them"—either way, those "in the know" carve out a necessary niche for themselves. This is one way power structures are maintained. The disadvantage to delineating a "correct" way of thinking is that we risk losing truly innovative ways of approaching social problems.

To avoid rigidity and the loss of innovation, we must expose or deconstruct the prevailing paradigms, mindscapes, and discourse for what they are—not a set of irrefutable truths but rather attempts to make meaning from a confusing set of phenomena. We need to acknowledge that new ways of thinking will also be based on a particular mindscape and that this will determine how innovative we can be. To address a social problem, we must define it, and these definitions will be based in on a circumscribed worldview.

Acknowledging the limits of a mindscape, however, does not mean that we should avoid the political dogfights. There are times when a paradigm's policies are so harmful that we should put aside the niceties and make bold claims that the prevailing paradigm is based on assumptions that are categorically wrong. Of course, stepping up on that pulpit also makes us an easy target for other deconstructing hounds. To avoid becoming targets, we should claim or, better yet, celebrate that our language and our thinking is paradoxical and evolving rather than categorically true and final.

Spirit of the Times

The term *spirit of the times*—the *zeitgeist*—refers to the impact of historical precedents and current fads in the culture. How we define a social problem or implement a social change is greatly influenced by the particular social and historical trends of the day. During the economic depression of the 1930s, it was relatively easy for Franklin D. Roosevelt to garner support for the rhetoric and the systems changes called the New Deal. Unemployment was not viewed as a problem of human motivation but as a problem caused by the collapse of the uncontrolled economy of the 1920s. After the post–World War II economic boom, employment came to be defined by some as problem of human laziness or a lack of adequate job skills. Thus, the problem is now viewed as being "in the person" not in the economy. It is interesting to note that World War II also greatly influenced how we have thought about disability issues in the latter half of the 20th century. With so many soldiers returning to the United States with battered bodies and traumatized minds, we became acutely aware of the inadequacies and the inhumanity of institutionalized treatment policies and practices.

In the final years of the 20th century, the predominant theme of social policy has been the promotion of self-sufficiency and individual responsibility. Policy goals for individuals with disabilities, likewise, focus on promoting full and *autonomous* participation in community life. To propose a different direction today, such as in the Fairweather Lodge communal work programs (Fairweather, 1980) is to risk being viewed as "out of touch" or even "un-American."

The stated goals of the supports paradigm also are framed in terms that espouse the virtues of *self-sufficiency*. Although this wording may be strategic for mobilizing resources for a truly new way of delivering services, we should remain vigilant about how this philosophical alliance with the predominant social values might eventually shift the direction of these program efforts. I can imagine, for instance, that there will be increased pressure for these efforts to be evaluated in terms of service or caseload reductions, in the same way that the success of welfare reform policies is gauged. Achieving self-sufficiency under a supports paradigm, however, may be best judged by noting how much power a person yields in directing their support services, not by how quickly someone stops using these services.

Dominant Societal Values and Traditions

Every culture has a set of conventions that (although socially constructed) assume the status of collective knowledge or objective reality. Such values are so fundamental that unlike mindscapes and historical trends, we rarely recognize them or acknowledge their impact on our lives and thinking. Seidman (1983) cited several fundamental values that have this status in the United States (and in most cultures in the world) that influence how we deliver services.

Individualism is one of these values. This value holds that individual attributes such as motivation and skill levels determine one's lot in life. This value focuses our vision on individual circumstances rather than on the attributes and welfare of collectives such as families, clans, or communities. We rarely recognize how individualism influences our thinking and our social policies. Can we imagine thinking about issues around disabilities without thinking about individuals and their specific circumstances? It is probably safe to say that without this dominant value, the disability field would cease to exist. What we attend to and label as individual differences (like disabilities) would have little meaning to us. Because there is little chance that individualism will become devalued anytime soon, it is important that we attend to the implications of this dominant value.

The supports paradigm, for instance, calls attention to the paradox that all individuals are embedded in networks of natural social support and must have access to and participate in these support systems to thrive in community life. At the same time, the supports paradigm also embraces individualism by espousing the ideal that individuals with disabilities should have the opportunity to exercise their individual rights to privacy, autonomy, and self-determination. It is worth considering whether such ideals are uniformly embraced by people from all cultural traditions. It is also worth considering why we think that innovative practices that promote more autonomous lives for individuals represent a systems change. Perhaps we are reluctant to frame these issues in terms of higher-level systems changes, such as restructuring social institutions or redistributing wealth and other resources, because such system-level changes are less likely to garner the necessary political support. Or, perhaps we are just reluctant to really change these higher-level systems because they challenge our own standing as stakeholders in these transactions.

Another dominant value in the United States and many other cultures is that there ought to be *uniform solutions* to similar problems, lest we risk the perils of unequal treatment in a program or under a social policy. Many of the efforts described in this volume attend to the specific circumstances of an individual's life, meaning that different individuals will receive different services. Some may find this approach a violation of their principles of fairness.

For instance, although I greatly admire the work to assist individuals with disabilities in purchasing their own home (described in Chapter 7), I can readily imagine the rancor of others (with and without disabilities) who have not been able to purchase a home when they read about the use of tax dollars to help people achieve the "American dream."[1] If the idea of individualized treatment is central to the supports paradigm, it is likely that detractors will call for fairness and equal treatment. In the supports paradigm, individuals will receive different types of services, and this will be viewed as unfair. In our culture, calling a program unfair will attract attention.

There is no easy way out of the debate on fairness versus individualized approaches because this debate is one of those wonderful paradoxes in our social fabric. I believe we should embrace both values and find ways to promote more equitable outcomes using individualized approaches. This is easy to understand for parents with two or more children. Despite outcries from their offspring, most parents would agree that engaging with children in different ways based on the situation by itself does not constitute unfair treatment. We should think of individual adults and children as moving on different developmental trajectories and acknowledge that children's developmental needs will change at different rates. We should also avoid the temptation to think that uniform solutions will produce uniform outcomes.

The cultural value of uniform solutions also serves our pragmatic sensibilities. Uniform solutions are often easier to implement. So as innovative programs mature, there will be calls to pare down the program to its most

---

[1]Ironically, there is wide political support for the home mortgage interest deduction on U.S. federal income tax returns, which provides much greater amounts of public support dollars for home purchases. This benefit, however, is distributed to only those who earn enough income to take advantage of this deduction.

effective features or to cut administrative costs. This elimination will produce pressure to make the program more uniform and less individualized.

Stakeholders

The way a problem is defined and how it is addressed is largely a function of who is at the table when resource allocation decisions are made. One of the interesting aspects of the disability field at this point of history is the variety of stakeholders, including service recipients, who have a voice in allocating resources. For the purposes of keeping paradox at the forefront of social problem solving, the involvement of multiple stakeholders involved is very beneficial.

Seidman (1983) noted that often one group of stakeholders has the formal authority to make decisions about services and that this group is rarely the service recipients. Those with decision-making authority often are accountable to a network or a system of donors (e.g., voting taxpayers) who are not experts in the field of service delivery and who are creating pressure for decisions that are based on prominent mindscapes, social values, or recent historical events rather than on the firsthand experience of recipients. Such decision makers also rely on the recommendations of service system administrators and providers who hold a financial stake in maintaining the current system of service delivery. Seidman also noted that the recipients who are present at the decision-making table often have views very similar to the other stakeholders. Those with radically dissenting viewpoints are typically dismissed or are never invited to the table.

Finally, Seidman (1983) warned that social scientists are often at the table under the assumed but impossible posture of being unbiased sources of information. Social science, like other forms of human enterprise, is largely driven by the biases and demands of the larger culture. Social science activity, for instance, is largely funded by the same system of donors that funds social services and is susceptible to the same set of influences.

As a social scientist myself, I am a bit unnerved by Seidman's (1983) warnings. Not only do I feel exposed to the other stakeholders at the table, but I also feel ambivalent about what I have to contribute to the decision-making processes. I also realize that to take these revelations seriously, I must acknowledge that I am like the other stakeholders at the table. I hold a set of beliefs and a way of thinking about social problems that both enlightens and limits my vision. I may be able to offer certain technical skills that may produce valuable forms of information (research results), but I worry about the accessibility of these results and the temptation to promote this information as more valid or more valuable than other forms of knowledge.

Rick Price (1989) wrestled with a similar set of dilemmas after noticing a growing skepticism about the relevance of social science knowledge in government affairs. In the end, Price offered a tentative model connecting social knowledge and community well-being that is grounded in three "impulses to action." The first action was *taking sides:*

> Rather than avoid the issue, and fail to do the analysis that identifies the actors in the conflict, the beneficiaries, and the victims, we can begin by admitting that we must be partisans. To admit it is a liberating act, but we must each for ourselves find what we regard to be the most urgent cause. We must also make a candid admission of our role as advocates. To be candid requires some courage, but it is a major antidote to ambivalence. (1989, pp. 161–162)

The second action that Price described was *bearing witness:*

> We have available to us a wide range of arenas for action in addition to scholarly publication. We should not be afraid to use them. Their very use sometimes violates explicit or implicit professional norms about the proper way to communicate one's insights, but I believe an engaged social scientist can do nothing else. It might be argued that we are acting most responsibly when we communicate in ways most likely to be heard, even if it involves a "popular" magazine, whistle blowing, a radio program, a community forum, or the witness stand. We must be heard to make any difference. (1989, p. 162)

Price's third action was *telling the truth:*

> Truth-telling can come in many forms. Many theories of social life contain empirical propositions that yield to hard-headed social research and analysis. That is one kind of truth to tell. Telling the truth about what we do not know as well as what we do is another way of telling the truth. Hardest of all, we may have to tell the truth about those for whom we advocate. Even victims have secrets, and we must weigh the cost of telling the whole truth about those for whom we advocate. (pp. 162–163)

When social scientists are sitting at the stakeholders' table, it is unlikely (and perhaps unethical) that they will take a disinterested and unbiased stance in relation to the issues at hand. The authors of the chapters in this book provide terrific role models in this regard. They seem to convey little reluctance to sit at the stakeholder table. They take sides. They bear witness. And they tell the truth about the possibilities for people with disabilities.

BACKING INTO THE FUTURE

In the mid-1990s, I had the opportunity to teach in New Zealand while on sabbatical. Like most visitors to New Zealand, I was intrigued with the growing influence of the indigenous Maori culture on New Zealand's developing national identity. One of the gems of Maori wisdom that was becoming part of the cultural mainstream was an orientation that moving forward into the future should be done with a keen understanding of the past. This orientation was conveyed in the phrase "backing into the future." At first I didn't understand this idea, but it literally means one should turn around (face the past) and walk backwards (toward the future).

This orientation is strikingly different from the predominant mindscape in the United States, where we are so quick to dismiss the past. For instance, I have often heard the quote (attributed to Satchel Paige, the first African American elected to the Baseball Hall of Fame), "Don't look back. Someone might be gaining on you." Walking backwards into the future is a wonderful example of embracing paradox: looking to the past and looking to the future at the same time. This stance leaves us open to a greater variety of understandings and strategies to promote a greater variety of outcomes.

I believe Nisbet's opening chapter is an account of her thoughts as she backs into the future. She writes about the future of the IOD but focuses on the meaningful experiences of the past. Nisbet's chapter is also full of paradox, which invites a greater variety of ideas. Nisbet thinks about mistakes as "lessons, pointers, and clarifiers" rather than as failures. This attitude allows her to celebrate the lessons learned from mistakes. She acknowledges the paradoxical implications of working for systems change while also working within the system. This way of thinking allows her the flexibility to keep a vision but respond in multiple ways. This is illustrated by the account of promoting an innovation (facilitated communication) and then disbanding the effort (because of extreme public pressure) and finally supporting the innovation again from a different position in the system. Although abandoning a change strategy may appear to be a retreat from the goal of systems change, such a move may promote the possibility for more sustainable systems change in the future. Other paradoxical lessons are embedded in many of the section titles in Nisbet's chapter:

* Balance Systemic Reform with Individual Support
* Invest in Leadership, but Don't Rely on Leaders
* Remember that Systems Are Made Up of People
* Look Nationally, but Retain Local Ties

In the end, she reaffirms the vision of systems change but upholds that it takes a variety of solutions and strategies to get from here to there. This message echoes the themes of the other chapters: *expect success* and *expect to be creative* in getting there.

CONCLUSIONS

I lamented at the start of this chapter that I wished that this book had contained more accounts of the failures. I worry that without those stories we may fail to fully understand what it takes to achieve success. I agree with Nisbet: We learn from failure. Failure provokes reflection and is at the core of creative problem solving. I also worry that attending only to success can lead to arrogance and an inability to see when our solutions to the old problems evolve into a new set of problems or are no longer the best solutions.

Embracing paradox (Rappaport, 1981) is one antidote to arrogance. By acknowledging that human and social problems are filled with contradiction, we are better positioned to witness both the successes and the failures. We also are positioned better to understand what is required to address the next set of emerging social problems. Perhaps most important is that embracing paradox allows us to witness a greater variety of possibilities for individuals who are excluded from full participation in our communities.

REFERENCES

Fairweather, G.W. (1980). *The Fairweather Lodge: A twenty-five year retrospective.* San Francisco: Jossey-Bass.

Price, R.H. (1989). Bearing witness. *American Journal of Community Psychology, 17,* 151–170.

Rappaport, J. (1981). In praise of paradox: A social policy of empowerment over prevention. *American Journal of Community Psychology, 9,* 1–25.

Seidman, E. (1983). Unexamined premises of social problem solving. In E. Seidman (Ed.), *Handbook of social intervention* (pp. 48–67). Beverly Hills: Sage Publications.

Index

Page references followed by *f* or *t* indicate figures or tables, respectively.
References followed by *n* indicate footnotes.

Preferences
  for training and support, 216
  see also Choice and control
Preparation
  career, 145
  personnel, 7
  see also Training
Preschool
  enrollment in, 61
  options for, 61
  planning for, 57–58
  segregated programs, 69
  transition from early intervention to,
    65–67
Problem solving, 172
  creative, 265–266, 279
  social, 273–278
  solutions to complex school reform
    problems, 168–169
  uniform solutions, 276
Process consultation strategies, 36
Professional development and roles,
    33–34, 272
Profound disabilities, students with,
    132–133
Programs, 271
  early childhood
    availability of, 60–61
    benefits for children with
      disabilities, 60
    enrollment in, 69
    options for, 61–62, 69
    quality of, 60, 62–64
    vignette, 76–79
  early intervention (EI), 56–57
  funding, 210
  housing, 179–181
  versus places, 53–54
  reverse mainstream, 54
  segregated, 69, 166
  self-contained, 69
  shift to supports from, 21–25
  special, 55–57
  special education, 64
  teacher education, 159–161
  see also Community programs
Programs paradigm, 19
  shift to, 19–21
Progress, 47–48
Providers, 76–77, 271
Public education

in New Hampshire, 126
  see also Education; General education

Quality
  in early childhood programs, 64
  in education, 101

RCOs, *see* Resource consultant
    organizations
Readiness
  to belong, 59–60
  case against, 185–186
  criteria, 19
  for homeownership, 185–189
  for a job, 20–21
  vignette, 187–189
Recipients, 271
Reform
  education, 166–171
  general education, 174
  hasty, 169–170
  high school, 134–139
  personnel preparation, 7
  school, 168–169
  "School Reform and Inclusive
    Education: Equity and Excellence
    for All" conference, 159
  standards-based, 158–159
  superficial, 169–170
Region IV Developmental Services
    Agency, 207–208
Regulation
  Medicaid rules revision, 229
  New Hampshire Natural Supports
    Project (NHNSP) change phase,
    227–229
  service, 32–33
Rehabilitation Act of 1973 (PL 93-112),
    Section 504, 52
Rehabilitation Act Amendments of 1992
    (PL 102-569), 27
Rehabilitation Services Administration,
    206
Relationships, 5–6
  partnerships, 190–191, 197
  personal, 38–39, 197
Research, 206–223
Residential services
  history of, 179–185
  individuals receiving, 179